Translating the Poetry of the Holocaust

BLOOMSBURY ADVANCES IN TRANSLATION SERIES

Series Editor: Jeremy Munday, Centre for Translation Studies, University of Leeds, UK

Bloomsbury Advances in Translation Studies publishes cutting-edge research in the fields of translation studies. This field has grown in importance in the modern, globalized world, with international translation between languages a daily occurrence. Research into the practices, processes and theory of translation is essential and this series aims to showcase the best in international academic and professional output.

OTHER TITLES IN THE SERIES:

Translating the Poetry of the Holocaust

Translation, style and the reader

JEAN BOASE-BEIER

Bloomsbury Academic
An imprint of Bloomsbury Publishing Plc

B L O O M S B U R Y
LONDON • NEW DELHI • NEW YORK • SYDNEY

Bloomsbury Academic

An imprint of Bloomsbury Publishing Plc

50 Bedford Square
London
WC1B 3DP
UK

1385 Broadway
New York
NY 10018
USA

www.bloomsbury.com

BLOOMSBURY and the Diana logo are trademarks of Bloomsbury Publishing Plc

First published 2015

British Library Cataloguing-in-Publication Data
A catalogue record for this book is available from the British Library.

ISBN: PB: 978-1-4411-7865-7
HB: 978-1-4411-3952-8
ePDF: 978-1-4411-5588-7
ePub: 978-1-4411-8666-9

Library of Congress Cataloging-in-Publication Data
Boase-Beier, Jean.
Translating the poetry of the Holocaust: translation, style and the reader/Jean Boase-Beier.
pages cm. – (Bloomsbury advances in translation)
Includes bibliographical references and index.
ISBN 978-1-4411-7865-7 (paperback) – ISBN 978-1-4411-3952-8 (hardback) –
ISBN 978-1-4411-5588-7 (epdf) 1. Poetry–Translating. 2. Holocaust, Jewish (1939–1945),
in literature. 3. Poetry–Psychological aspects.
4. Poetics–History–20th century. I. Title.
PN1059.T7B63 2015
418'.041–dc23
2014037404

Series: Bloomsbury Advances in Translation

Typeset by Deanta Global Publishing Services, Chennai, India

Contents

Preface

I set out, in this book, as I did in the research that preceded it, to find answers to some pressing questions about the translation of Holocaust poetry. I wanted to know, first and foremost, what most writers on Holocaust literature and representation say about translation. The answer is simple: nothing. Of course, there are welcome exceptions, but they are few and far between. Yet, without the translators, English-speaking readers would have no access to the vast body of Holocaust writing. Holocaust poetry has a special role to play, because of poetry's whole reason for being: to convey what goes deep into the mind of the reader and forever changes the way he or she sees the world. How can we translate so that the translated poem also speaks to the reader in this way? I also wanted to find out what has been translated and what has not, what could be translated, how it could be translated, how readers read it. And I wanted to suggest that we must – in this case more than in any other – read translated Holocaust poetry as a translation, in full awareness of what that means.

The book is not an attempt to document and categorize existing translations, or the lack thereof. Instead, it uses the framework of cognitive poetics to try and get to the heart of the poetry and its cognitive effects, and think about ways to read it in translation, and to translate and present it so that it can be read for its full effects.

The book is aimed at all those readers with an interest in literary translation, in Holocaust writing, in questions of Holocaust representation, in stylistics or in cognitive poetics. I hope it will ask more questions than it gives answers, and so will encourage other thinkers, students and researchers, at any level, as well as translators and publishers, to explore new ideas and discover new texts.

A note on translations and references:

Where I refer to translated poetry, I generally do so under the name of the translator. Thus Hamburger (2007) is Michael Hamburger's translation of Celan, and Felstiner (2001) is John Felstiner's. Where I am referring to translated philosophical or critical works, I tend to do so under the original author's name. Thus Stephen Rendall's translation of Walter Benjamin is Benjamin (2012). This goes against the grain somewhat, but I am afraid anything else would be too confusing. I hope it is always clear in the context. And I apologize unreservedly to any translators I have thus made less visible.

Acknowledgements

The research for this book formed part of the project of the same name, for which I received funding from the Arts and Humanities Research Council (AHRC). I am extremely grateful to the AHRC, not only for helping me find time to do the research but also for providing the means to talk about my work at a number of public events. I would also like to thank the University of East Anglia (and especially the School of Literature, Drama and Creative Writing) for granting me additional study leave.

The number of individual people who have corresponded with me, discussed points with me and sent me references and even books is vast, and I know I shall forget someone here. I am afraid anyone in that position will not take comfort from the fact that I am sure to remember them the minute the book has gone to press. First of all, I would like to thank my Research Associate, Marian de Vooght, for her support at many of the project's events, as well as for the many interesting facts and references she has sent me. I am also very grateful to PhD students past and present, and especially Nozomi Abe, Antoinette Fawcett, Lina Fisher, Helen Gibson, Wanda Józwikowska, Robert Stock, Alex Valente and Philip Wilson, and to all my MA students, and especially Olivia Hanks, Cole Konopka and Valentina Konstantinidi for practical help, discussions and ideas. I would also like to thank colleagues at UEA and elsewhere for their helpful thoughts, especially John Collins, Peter Davies, Francis R. Jones, Cecilia Rossi and George Szirtes. And finally, many thanks to all those others who have sent me their ideas and suggestions, and their work, and provided me with so much inspiration, in particular Raficq Abdulla, Dror Abend-David, Marianne S. Bertsch-Junger, Marlen Gabriel, Iain Galbraith, George Gömöri, Atar Hadari, Paul Hartal, Angela Jarman, Solly Kaplinski, Thomas Ország-Land, Michael O'Siadhail, Martin Pigott, Keiron Pim, Kristine Pommert, Richard Sheppard, Gloria Tessler, Barbara Wind and Aldi Wolfson.

Particular thanks, as ever, to my husband, Dieter Beier, for his help in producing what I kept saying was the final version of the typescript.

Copyright acknowledgements

I am grateful to the copyright holders of the following material for permission to reprint extracts. Full details of all works can be found in the References:

Smokestack Books, Middlesborough, for 'Gustav!' by András Mezei, translated by Thomas Ország Land, reproduced from *Christmas in Auschwitz*, copyright ©2010.

Helmut Braun of the Rose Ausländer-Stiftung, Cologne, for poems by Rose Ausländer. The Rose Ausländer-Stiftung are the copyright holders.

Suhrkamp Verlag, Frankfurt am Main, for 'Einmal' and 'Weggebeizt' by Paul Celan, reproduced from *Atemwende*, copyright ©1982.

Verlag Klaus Wagenbach, Berlin, for 3 poems by Volker von Törne, reproduced from *Im Lande Vogelfrei*; copyright ©1981.

S. Fischer Verlage GmbH, Frankfurt am Main, for extracts from 'Bei Wein und Verlorenheit', by Paul Celan, reproduced from *Die Niemandsrose*, copyright ©1963; 'Bukowina I', by Rose Ausländer, reproduced from *Die Sichel mäht die Zeit zu Heu. Gedichte 1957–1965*, copyright ©1985; 'Als gäbe es' and 'Biographische Notiz', by Rose Ausländer, reproduced from *Im Aschenregen die Spur deines Namens. Gedichte und Prosa 1976*, copyright ©1984.

1

Holocaust poetry and Holocaust poetics

1.1 What is Holocaust poetry?

There have been several attempts to define Holocaust poetry as a specific category of writing, explicitly or implicitly. Rowland (2005: 3), for example, distinguishes between 'Holocaust poems written by those involved in the events unfolding in Europe from 1933 to 1945' and 'post-Holocaust poems' written by those not involved in these events. He refers to both as 'Holocaust poetry'. Rowland also addresses the question of whether, for example, a British poet such as Tony Harrison can thus be called a Holocaust poet (see also Rowland 2001), and argues that, even as a poet not immediately caught up in the events of the Holocaust or their aftermath, one is still faced with a choice: either to reflect or to ignore the effects of these events in one's writing (Rowland 2005: 3).

It would also be possible to argue that no one writing poetry, at least in Europe or America, in the aftermath of the Holocaust, could fail to reflect its effects, because they have become a part of the way we write, read and understand poetry (and all literary texts), irrespective of the extent of our awareness of these effects.

These are important questions, not least because of the feeling of unease that the use of Holocaust imagery in poetry Rowland discusses such as Sylvia Plath's 'Daddy' (Plath 1981: 222–4) can give rise to, especially in readers and critics who themselves, or whose families, were directly affected by the events of the Holocaust, and even in readers not thus affected. Rosenfeld, for example, argues that the problem with Holocaust imagery in Plath's poems is that there is too big a gap between 'self-inflicted wounds' and the catastrophic mass murder of the Holocaust (Rosenfeld 1980: 181). Franklin points out the dangers of possible 'overidentification', especially by children of survivors (Franklin 2011: 225). It is a danger to which no one is immune. Franklin concedes that it partly arises in response to views such as that expressed by Elie Wiesel (in numerous interviews) that those who were not there can have nothing to say (Franklin 2011: 83–4). Schiff, in the 'Introduction' to her anthology *Holocaust Poetry*, worries that some readers might feel Holocaust imagery is 'exploited' (Schiff 1995: xxiv) in the service of some other concern of the poet's; indeed, this is exactly Rosenfeld's point about Plath.

It is not the purpose of this book to try and define specific categories of Holocaust poetry or post-Holocaust poetry, or to pronounce on who has the right to write what. This is partly because I am not convinced that any such categorization would serve a useful purpose, especially given that, as Rothberg (2000: 12) suggests, it is often difficult to distinguish between events themselves and their aftermath, in psychological, social and cultural terms.

The questions that arise in the process of such attempts at categorization are more interesting than any definitive delineation of categories itself, and these questions will certainly play a role here. But another reason for avoiding strict categorization is that this book is about the *translation* of Holocaust poetry, however defined and delimited. I want to explore what issues arise because of the fact that it is the translation of poetry that both deals with Holocaust events and responds to them in its poetics. It deals with events that were real and terrible, and so questions about the truth of poetry, the purpose of poetry and the effects of poetry arise naturally and compellingly. Much of the poetry I discuss will make what could be considered fairly clear reference to the Holocaust, though even such reference is open to question: do we, for example, read Paul Celan's use of the word '*Schrunde*' ('deep wound'; e.g. Celan 1982: 27) as a Holocaust reference because we know that he lost both parents in the Holocaust, or because all poetry after the Holocaust suggests to its readers a sense of the wounds of history, as well as personal wounds? Or do we do so because there are other elements in this particular poem, and in his other works, that suggest to us that a reading of '*Schrunde*' in this way is appropriate?

This latter possibility is, at least for the purposes of this book, the most interesting. Poetry is Holocaust poetry (with its various sub-categories, including post-Holocaust poetry) because it makes possible, and likely, not merely historically, but also poetically, a reading that acknowledges the Holocaust as an important element in the context of its understanding. Where reference to the Holocaust is less explicit, the poetics of Holocaust poetry become more important. For those writing in the aftermath of the Holocaust, the difference these events had wrought was not merely about possible and appropriate subject matter but also about how to write. Rowland (2001, 2005) describes such poetics as 'awkward' (attributing the term to Kristeva 1987: 225; see Rowland 2001: 158), that is self-reflexively and ethically attempting to respond to questions of what literature after the Holocaust can do and how it should do it. Such poetry is engaging with earlier Holocaust poetry, which tended to describe events as they were unfolding, as much as with the Holocaust events themselves (Rowland 2005: 2). Its characteristics may include the undermining or subverting of traditional lyric poetry by irregular rhythms, linguistic compression, syntactic fragmentation, paradox, 'anti-rhetoric' and so on (Rowland 2005: 11–12). Taking these considerations into account, I shall therefore generally use the term 'Holocaust poetry' in this book to include poetry that uses more obvious Holocaust imagery as well as poetry that responds to the Holocaust in other ways in its poetics. In the next section, I will set out in more detail what I mean by Holocaust poetics.

For the study of translation, an understanding of Holocaust poetics is crucial. Translation of poetry, or of any literary text, is never solely or even mainly about the transfer of content or reference. The importance of poetic style to the translation of poetry has been emphasized many times (see e.g. Weissbort 1989; Boase-Beier 2006, 2011b; Jones 2011: 147–72) and, indeed, its importance cannot be overstated. If poetry, rather than merely documenting or describing, engages the mind, the thought-processes and the emotions of its readers, then the way this happens will be at the heart of the translator's concern with the original text.

Yet, to say that Holocaust poetry, and other poetry that deals with or is influenced by catastrophe, depends crucially upon its style, and that its translation is therefore, above all, the translation of its style, might appear to run counter to a particular strand of the debate: is an aesthetic response to the Holocaust, and other disastrous events, especially when they have been brought about by human evil, possible at all?

Intuitively, one might feel that to write poetry in the aftermath of such events is to take upon oneself a right to which, as a human being and therefore, by association, as part of the cause, one should not aspire. In the case of victims of the Holocaust, this is likely to be judged less of a problem than it is in the case of those who are several removes from the events. But there is still the question Adorno addressed so famously: is there a danger that we might aestheticize suffering? Adorno, writing in 1951, spoke of the barbarity of writing poetry 'after Auschwitz' (Adorno 2003: 30), a statement that has variously been interpreted as rejecting poetry in the aftermath of the Holocaust (e.g. Steiner 1985: 72), or accepting a necessary barbarity, a stylistic roughness, as a proper response (Rowland 2001: 13). It is easy to share Adorno's revulsion at what might seem, to use the words of one well-known Holocaust poet and translator, Michael Hamburger, 'a merely aesthetic game' (2007: 42; cf. also Hoffman 2004: 15). For this reason, and out of such feelings, poets have struggled to write appropriate poetry and critics and other writers have argued that literature must document with 'unpretentious objectivity' rather than aim for the 'construction of aesthetic or pseudo-aesthetic effects' (Sebald 1999, translation Bell 2003: 53). And the translator in turn must find a way to translate that will not falsify the particular poet's poetic response.

There has been much discussion, and many books have been written, about poetics and aesthetics after the Holocaust, and it is impossible to properly engage with all aspects of the argument here. It is particularly interesting, though, that Adorno later qualified his initial statement by saying that art after Auschwitz is as necessary as it is impossible (Adorno 2003: 452) and also suggesting that poetry may be more like a cry of pain (Adorno 1973: 355). The first statement is in line with the notion of 'negative dialectics', a way of thinking that is self-consciously aware of what it is not, that defines itself against what it is not, and that does not result in synthesis (Kiedaisch 1995: 15; Buck-Moss 1977: 63). But the notion that poetry that is like a cry of pain is acceptable suggests an opposition between aesthetics and response that cannot, I would argue, be maintained. It is as though the aesthetic cannot be a cry of pain; this is also implied by Sebald's coupling of 'aesthetic' with 'pseudo-aesthetic' effects, as though the aesthetic itself were not real. Yet, when I asked the Tamil poet Cheran, who was giving a reading at the University of East Anglia on 11 October 2013, why he wrote poems about the Sri Lankan civil war, he said simply 'Because that is what poets do'. That is, for the poet the aesthetic and the expression of pain are not separate. How, then, does poetry combine them? Rothberg (2000) argues convincingly that the distinction between, on the one hand, realism in representing the Holocaust, which is intimately tied up with the view that we can know and understand it, and, on the other, the impossibility of realistic depiction and the connected sense of the impossibility of understanding, is in fact hard to maintain. Rothberg accepts that there are two different views: he includes writers such as Arendt (see 2006), Goldhagen (1996) and Bauman (1989) among those who think we can explain the Holocaust, and Wiesel (see 1990) and Lanzmann, who made the film *Shoah* (see Lanzmann 1995), among those who think we cannot (Rothberg 2000: 3–7). And he develops the notion of 'traumatic realism' (Rothberg 2000: 14), a form of 'documentation and historical cognition attuned to the demands of extremity' (Rothberg 2000: 14), which, like Rowland's 'awkward poetics' (2005), describes the type of writing, in Rothberg's understanding both historical and aesthetic, that bridges the divide between the two views. Both 'traumatic realism' and 'awkward poetics' are useful terms in thinking about Holocaust poetry and its translation and I shall return to them several times.

Quite independently of the questions of Holocaust understanding and its concomitant, representation, raised by the scholars mentioned earlier, and many others (see e.g. Lang 1988: 1–15; Lang 2000; Semprun 1997; Leak and Paizis 2000), the question of specifically poetic representation and of the distinctions between aesthetics, on the one hand, and expressions of pain and suffering, on the other, have to do with how we understand the concept of poetics. In many recent studies of style, whether in poetry or other literature, a great deal of emphasis has been placed on the view that literature is not, or not merely, a separate, aesthetic form of human activity which we choose to produce or receive (see especially Turner 1996). According, in particular, to those views that roughly fall within an understanding of style known as 'cognitive poetics' (see e.g. Stockwell 2002; Semino and Culpeper 2002; Tsur 2008; Oatley 2011), the mind is essentially both embodied, that is, it is grounded in and in part determined by the physical body, and literary (Turner 1996: 3–25). We group experiences together as stories in order to understand them (Herman 2003: 17), we think in metaphor in order to think at all (Lakoff and Turner 1989), we process events as blends of other events (Fauconnier and Turner 2002), not because we are thinking in a specifically literary way, but because that is how we always think. In poetry the expression of emotion, or physical pain, can follow rhythmical and other patterns either because such patterns are part of the basic 'involuntary physiological processes' of our bodies or because such patterns echo 'conscious control and the exercise of will', or both (Tsur 2003: 179). These latter two observations indicate that the apparently aesthetic or stylistic features of poetry cannot be equated with aesthetic embellishment (cf. also Jakobson 1960: 377), nor can they be contrasted with cries of pain or other expressions of feeling, or with the ways our minds work to conceptualize the world. Neither metaphor nor poetic rhythm is in itself a sign that what the poem says has been transmuted into or overlaid with something aesthetic. In a view that equates the poetic with our most instinctive ways of thinking and feeling, a distinction between crying out in anguish and writing a poem cannot be maintained on such grounds. Intuitively, one feels this to be the case when reading Celan's 'Wolfsbohne' ('Wolf's-Bean'; Hamburger 2007: 398–403), for example, with its repeated despairing cries to the dead mother. But this is more than a matter of individual poems expressing highly specific and personal emotions. What is at stake here is the nature of poetry itself. If one takes cognitive poetics seriously, then poetry is in essence a communication between a state of mind (with all its bodily resonances) represented in a poem and the mind (with its bodily resonances) of the reader. Everything in the poem has its cognitive counterpart. In '*Wolfsbohne*', a number of connotations are suggested by the lines:

Mutter,   dir
mother   to-you

die   du   Wolfsbohne   sagtest,   nicht:
who   you   wolf's-bean   said   not

Lupine
lupin

(To you, mother, who said wolf's-bean, not lupin)

They include the connotations that the speaker's mother spoke a particular dialect of German, that she is no longer alive, that there is another word in German for the plant called '*Wolfsbohne*' and that this other word also suggests 'wolf-like'. But more than this, the reader will experience cognitive effects, including a sense of involvement and identification (Oatley 2011: 161–2; Stockwell 2009: 135). That is, the word 'Mother', repeated nineteen times in this poem, is not merely registered as though it were a designation of a relationship on an official document (though even here the word may not be devoid of cognitive weight and effect), but it is felt by the reader to be a direct address to the speaker's mother, and will, in many readers and hearers, be felt to express, or it may even give rise to, an overwhelming feeling of sympathy, sadness and helplessness. It is indeed a cry of pain, but it is more than a cry of pain: it is a cry of pain that evokes a deeper and more lasting response in the reader than an involuntary cry of pain, because it is contextualized within a pattern of poetic elements that carry the cry of pain beyond an involuntary response to a considered one. I shall take up this idea of response and consideration of response again later, when discussing empathy in Section 1.3. And we will see that such poetic contextualization goes beyond the single poem in question. But for the moment the important point here is that poems are not separate from either ways of thinking or ways of feeling: they are those ways of thinking and feeling poeticized.

It is the ability not only to express feelings but also to have cognitive effects on the reader that makes poetry so important and necessary a response to the Holocaust. And it is this very ability to have cognitive effects that is at the heart of the difficulty of translating it. Though there is a long tradition in translation studies of considering how effects can be kept (see Boase-Beier 2011a: 23), other studies (see e.g. Chesterman 1997: 35) have suggested the impossibility of judging effect because of the different contexts in which different readers read. However, stylistics and, especially, cognitive poetics, have generally taken a great interest in what Pilkington calls 'poetic effects'

(2000). While Pilkington is specifically arguing from a Relevance-Theory perspective, so that he sees such effects as the direct result of the mental construction of contexts during reading using inferential procedures that derive more complete forms than those actually expressed by the text, the idea that poetic effects are part of what stylistics explains is not limited to studies based on Relevance Theory. As the reader or hearer has taken on greater prominence in literary theory since the 1970s (see Iser 1971, 2006: 57–69) and linguistic theory has placed greater emphasis on pragmatics and context, so stylistics has incorporated ever more sophisticated notions of readers' contexts and structures of knowledge (see also Verdonk 2013: 113–22). These structures are generally expressed as 'schemata' (cf. Cook 1994: 191–206; Semino 1997: 119–59; Oatley 2011: 61). Schemata are partially fixed 'cognitive patterns' (Verdonk 2013: 117) that readers have built up over time, but which are also 'constantly reshaped and reorganized in the course of our cognitive activities' (Semino 1997: 149). It is often said (see e.g. Stockwell 2002: 8) that the essence of cognitive poetics lies in the interaction during reading between such structures and the stylistic detail of the text.

As schemata are called into play in the mind during reading, they can be augmented or disrupted by their interaction with what is read. These processes result in cognitive change. By 'cognitive change' I mean not only changes to what we know, but also changes to what we feel and believe (cf. also Palmer 2004: 19). Cognitive changes, then, whether radical disruptive changes in belief or reinforcements and additions to what we know, are all cognitive effects. Pilkington's 'poetic effects' (2000) are simply a type of cognitive effect. Consider, for example, how different readers might begin to interpret the poem '*Saisons à Buchenwald*' ('Seasons in Buchenwald'), written by Franz Hackel, an inmate of the concentration camp, in different ways, depending upon their schemata. The poem (Kirsten and Seeman 2012: 87) starts:

Nul	oiseau	ne	chante
no	bird	(neg)	sings
Dans	la	forêt	morte
in	the	forest	dead

This could be translated straightforwardly as:

No bird sings
In the dead forest.

When we read the first line (in French or English, or, indeed, in Kirsten and Seeman's German), we will probably start to imagine places where birds do not sing: city centres, deserts, or the world Rachel Carson described in 1966 in *Silent Spring* (see Rachel Carson 1999), where chemicals have killed the birds. The second line will cause us to revise such views, and we will try to interpret 'the dead forest' according to whatever schemata we have. Forests are usually living, so a dead forest may suggest a forest that existed in the past, a prehistoric forest or, indeed, a polluted forest as in Carson's book. If we are conscious of the title of the book in which the poem appears '*Der gefesselte Wald*' (*The Chained Forest*), and the fact that the poems were written in Buchenwald (literally 'beech forest') concentration camp, we might conjure up images of concentration camps or, indeed, of Buchenwald itself, especially if we have been there. We are likely to revise our idea of why a forest might be dead, again depending on what we know and what we believe, as well as what interests us. Readers who have read Semprun's book about life in Buchenwald will be aware that there were said to be no birds in the forest around the camp because they had been driven away by 'the smell of burning flesh' (Semprun 1997: 94), so for those readers crematoria in concentration camps will be part of their schema of a dead forest. For readers without this background knowledge, the existing schema for a forest that contains wildlife including birds will be revised to include the possibility that there is no life in the forest, though the reason will remain obscure. In this sense the notion of context is a dynamic, cognitive one: a cognitive context builds on existing schemata, changing and adapting as we read.

There is a sense in much Holocaust scholarship that the most important thing for those writing was to share suffering, and to have their suffering respected, because 'suffering that is misunderstood or dishonoured can turn on the self in unendurable pain' (Hoffman 2004: 49). Literature, as Franklin (2011: 13) says, does offer a way of communicating suffering, by allowing 'imaginitive access' to it, a point also made by Semprun (1997: 229), and thus keeping memory alive (cf. Gubar 2003: 11). Communication works in poetry because we identify with the suffering character portrayed and work to build up a context for reading the poem, so that that context becomes part of what we know. Box 1 gives a few background facts about the Holocaust that we may or may not know.

Though I shall make the assumption that we can define Holocaust poetry by its poetics, this does not mean that there are no distinctions to be made, for the poetry has different origins. There is, for example, a substantial body of work written by poets while they were in camps, such as the poem by Hackel just mentioned, and the others in that collection (Kirsten and Seeman 2012). The extent to which this was possible was determined by the nature of the camp: in Terezín and Buchenwald, for example, inmates were more able to write poetry, as well as to pursue other forms of artistic expression, than in Auschwitz (or at least Auschwitz-Birkenau), or Treblinka, because the first two camps were not specifically extermination camps. In Auschwitz some people were kept alive, but usually only for a very short time. Treblinka, on the other

Box 1 Background to the events of the Holocaust

1914–18	100,000 Jews served in the German army
August 1920	Hitler's beer hall speech 'Why we are against the Jews'
1920	*The Destruction of Life Unworthy of Life* by Binding and Hoche
30 January 1933	Hitler becomes Chancellor of Germany
Spring 1933	Start of systematic exclusion of Jews from cultural activity (including publishing) in Germany
10 May 1933	At least 20,000 books by Mann, Heine, Marx and others publically burned by Berlin university professors, students and Nazi officials
22 March 1933	Dachau concentration camp established
1 January 1934	Start of compulsory sterilization of those with 'hereditary diseases'
September 1935	The Nuremberg Laws: Jewish Germans become non-German; Sinti and Roma people become 'alien'; political opponents lose citizenship
March 1936	Jews, Roma and Sinti lose the right to vote
1936	Start of increased persecution, imprisonment and deportation of homosexual men
Late 1930s	Start of systematic killing of Sinti and Roma population in Germany
9 November 1938	'Kristallnacht': synagogues burned and Jews killed and incarcerated
1939	Hospital doctors authorized to kill all disabled children (and subsequently adults)
October 1941	Start of deportation of German Jews towards Eastern Europe; most are murdered

hand, existed only to exterminate people. In Terezín, artists such as Petr Kien were able to draw and paint, though they were often transported to death camps later: Kien died in Auschwitz. In Buchenwald, in spite of the vast numbers of inmates murdered there or after transportation to extermination camps – Winstone (2010: 109) gives a figure of 50,000 – a certain number survived; around 21,000 Buchenwald inmates were freed by the US army. The poet Wulf

Kirsten, who with translator Annette Seeman co-edited the French-German bilingual edition (Kirsten and Seeman 2012) of André Verdet's 1945 French Buchenwald anthology, in which the previously mentioned poem by Hackel appears, explains how the writing of poems, though strictly prohibited, often on pain of death, became an important aid to survival (Kirsten 2012), a point echoed by Hoffman (2004: 152). Boris Taslitsky, the French painter interned there at the same time, says in a film of interviews with former inmates, which can be seen in the permanent exhibition at Buchenwald, that poetry was the most important 'weapon' the inmates had. Even those who, like Taslitsky, were not poets read and recited the work of famous poets as a way of helping them survive. Other poets who wrote in concentration camps include Spanish poet Jorge Semprun, as I have just mentioned (also in Buchenwald), the Hungarian poet Miklós Radnóti (who was in Bor in Eastern Serbia) and the French poet Christian Pineau (in Buchenwald). Such poetry often deals with the details of camp life: the poems written in Buchenwald, for example, often describe the 'sound of hoe and spade' (in a Pineau poem, in Kirsten and Seeman 2012: 115) or the work in the quarry (a Hackel poem, 2012: 83). Not all of these poets survived. Radnóti, for example, was shot while taking part in a forced march back towards Germany, his poetry from this time only recovered when his body was exhumed from a mass grave after the war (see Jones 2000: 9).

Other poets wrote in ghettos, which were specific areas of towns and cities, mainly in Poland and Ukraine, established or taken over by the Nazis as places in which to isolate, confine and concentrate the Jewish members of urban communities, as well as, in the case of Polish cities, to take up and imprison Jews expelled from western areas of the German Reich. They were used by the Germans as centres of mass deportation to extermination camps from 1942 onwards (see Winstone 2010: 6–7; Fulbrook [2012] describes the various stages in the development of the Będzin ghetto). Perhaps the best-known ghetto is the one established in Warsaw in October 1940, which was sealed off one month later, effectively turning it into a large prison within the city (see Winstone 2010: 213–23; Poliakov 1956: 86–103). The Warsaw ghetto uprising of April and May 1943, which caused considerable losses among the oppressors, also resulted in many deaths among its population; most of the rest were deported for extermination, and the ghetto was completely destroyed. Yet before this mass destruction of the Jews of Warsaw, a very large amount of poetry and other writing was completed, some of which survives. Especially notable among poets of the Warsaw ghetto is Władysław Szlengel, whose poetry, written in Polish, describes day-to-day life in the ghetto, and is translated into English by Frieda Aaron (see Aaron 1990). Aaron also translates and discusses the Yiddish poetry of Abraham Sutzkever, who, like Hebrew poet Abba Kovner, lived in the ghetto in Vilna, Lithuania, from 1941 to 1942 (see Aaron 1990: 29). Whereas Szlengel was killed in the Warsaw uprising, both Sutzkever and Kovner survived the Holocaust, emigrating to Israel, and much of their early poetry is preserved. In spite of the ease with which Yiddish can be translated into German, translations of Yiddish poets have appeared only fairly slowly in Germany (cf. Comans 2009: 13–18). But with recent translations of Lajser Ajchenrand (Witt 2006) and Sutzkever (Comans 2009), and several others, that situation is now changing.

Other poets were able to write poetry only after liberation. Primo Levi, for example, who was in Buna-Monowitz (a subsidiary of Auschwitz) and Dan Pagis, who was in several camps in Transnistria, Ukraine, only wrote later about their experiences.

Those who were not themselves in concentration camps include some of the most famous Holocaust poets, such as German-Romanian poets Paul Celan and Rose Ausländer, and German poet Nelly Sachs. Celan was in a Romanian work camp and both his parents were murdered by the Nazis, in the camp at Michailovka, in what was then Ukraine. Ausländer was forced to live in the Czernowitz ghetto before escaping, and Sachs escaped just in time to Sweden. The poetry of all three poets is concerned with life in the camps as it was reported to them and, in Ausländer's case, with personal experiences of life in the ghetto, but especially with life after the Holocaust. In the case of these and many other poets, the trauma of the destruction of family members, friends, and the Jewish people is inscribed in their poetry.

When Rowland (2005: 3) spoke of those with no personal connection to the Holocaust, but who nevertheless responded to its events in their poetry, he was speaking of American and English poets such as Plath, or Geoffrey Hill, both included in Schiff's anthology (1995). But poets such as Ludwig Steinherr in Germany (e.g. Dove 2010: 112–13), Tadeusz Różewicz in Poland (e.g. Howard and Plebanek 2001: 32–47) and Yevgeny Yevtushenko in Russia (e.g. Milner-Gulland and Levi 2008: 82–4) have also written poetry about or in response to the Holocaust. The further we move in time from the events of the Holocaust, the more difficult it becomes to make distinctions of this sort, and there are other issues, too, that make distinctions difficult. For example, the Hungarian poet János Pilinszky, translated by Ted Hughes and Jan Csokits, among others (see Weissbort 1991: 225–38; Gömöri and Gömöri 2012), is often said to have spent several months in prisoner-of-war camps (Weissbort 1991: 226) or simply 'camps' (Schiff 1995: 214), but in fact he was 'enrolled, rather than interned, by the retreating Nazis' (Rowland 2005: 7). For this reason he could be said to have an 'ambiguous' position (Rowland 2005: 143) as a Holocaust poet.

Pilinszky was not alone; the position of many of those writing Holocaust poetry was ambiguous. And whether it was ambiguous or not depends on who is judging. Some might judge Pilinszky a collaborator, others say he had no choice. Some might say Volker von Törne, whose father was a Nazi, was the son of a perpetrator, so his poetry cannot be compared with that of the children of survivors. Poets such as Ernst Meister, who stayed in Germany during the war years, but did not speak out, opting instead for what is referred to as 'inner emigration', are also sometimes viewed with suspicion (see Donahue and Kirchner 2005). I should perhaps state here that I think such judgements are sometimes impossible to make, for example in Pilinszky's case, and so it is more honest not to pretend to make them. In von Törne's case, it is clear that he could not help being the child of a Nazi. It is to his credit that his poetry expresses guilt, but it is misplaced guilt. Whether Meister and other poets of 'inner emigration' should have spoken out is completely irrelevant. Everyone should have spoken out, but most people did not.

There is, perhaps not surprisingly, little poetry by people who were active or passive supporters of National Socialism. There are studies in German (e.g. Loewy 1966; Bodensohn 2014) of the work of such writers. As Loewy (1966: 11) observes, it is better to use the Nazis' own word '*Schrifttum*' (which perhaps one might translate, in Loewy's sense, as 'written stuff') to designate these writings. Such work is not considered in this book.

Those now writing Holocaust (including post-Holocaust) poetry, in the sense of poetry that engages, in its poetics, with the Holocaust and its aftermath, are sometimes survivors or, more often, the children of survivors. They are often referred to as the 'second generation', a term that became common from the early 1980s (Hoffman 2004: 26). An example is Barbara Wind in New Jersey, the daughter of German Holocaust survivors, who writes in English (see e.g. Wind 1996). Her poetry has been translated by Marlen Gabriel into German (Gabriel 2004). Many other second-generation poets, such as William Heyen or Elaine Feinstein, are well-known as poets who write in English (see e.g. Florsheim 1989; Lawson 2001), but there are also many, such as Wind, whose work is less well known.

But it is not only the place of writing or the degree of the poet's involvement that affects the nature of Holocaust poetry. Language of origin, as suggested earlier, is another factor: there is Holocaust poetry in Polish, Yiddish, Japanese, German, Hungarian, Norwegian, Spanish, Italian, and many other languages, and there are examples of poetry from all these languages available in English translation.

And there were also many different Nazi victims. Though the vast majority of Holocaust poetry was written by Jews, as both the largest category of Holocaust victims, around six million, and the main specific Nazi target for annihilation, poems were also written by political prisoners in the camps. Some of these appear in Verdet's Buchenwald anthology; they include Hackel (mentioned earlier) who was a member of the German Spartacus League, a Marxist group established in 1914, Marcel Baufrère, who was in the French Résistance, and José Fosty, who was in the Belgian Resistance (see Kirsten and Seeman 2012). There must also have been Romani poets, including Sinti writers (those living in

Germany and Austria), who wrote Holocaust poetry, though their oral traditions mean that not much is preserved; an exception is Papusza (Bronisława Wajs), whose Romani poetry was translated into Polish by Jerzy Ficowski (1956) and has since been translated into English by Yala Korwin (see *The Hypertexts* website, www.thehypertexts.com). There was some, though very little, poetry by homosexual victims of the Nazis; an example is the poem '*La Guenille*' ('The Rag'), by André Sarcq (1995), dedicated to Pierre Seel and his lover Jo; Seel later wrote one of the most important Holocaust memoirs by a homosexual victim (Seel 1995). In the category of poetry by religious victims, the best known is that of Dietrich Bonhoeffer, the resisting pastor executed in 1945 (e.g. Bonhoeffer and Bonhoeffer 1947). Not all poetry was written by victims of the Holocaust about their own situation: besides the later poetry of writers such as Plath, already mentioned, poets who were themselves directly or indirectly involved in the Holocaust might write about other groups of victims. Ficowski, whose work, translated by Keith Bosley and Krystyna Wandycz, is included in Schiff's 1995 anthology, not only translated Papusza, but also wrote poems about Roma and other victims (Bosley and Wandycz 1981), as did von Törne (1981) and András Mezei (see Ország-Land 2010).

Although there have been translations into English of poems written in so many different languages and circumstances, the vast majority of Holocaust and post-Holocaust poetry is not translated. This means that, for the English-speaking poetry reader, a picture of Holocaust poetry has arisen that is influenced by the few anthologies or collections that do exist: by Schiff's anthology or by collections of the translated works of well-known poets such as Celan (e.g. Hamburger 2007), Sachs (e.g. Hamburger et al. 2011), Levi (e.g. Feldman and Swann 1992) or Radnóti (e.g. Jones 2000).

That picture is rather distorted. For one thing, it is dominated by the major poets, such as those mentioned: there have been selected works of Celan by at least three well-known translators (Hamburger 2007; Felstiner 2001; Fairley 2001, 2007) and many by less well-known ones (e.g. Popov and McHugh 2000) as well as individual poems or groups of poems (e.g. in Kirkup 1995). Pagis (Mitchell 1981), Ausländer (Boase-Beier and Vivis 1995), Kovner (Kaufman et al. 1971) and Bonhoeffer (Robertson 2003) have, for example, all been translated. For another thing, it is largely made up of the poetry of particular countries and languages: German, Polish and Hungarian poetry has been translated more often than Italian or Dutch, for example. And it is also to a large extent Jewish poetry, as most of the examples given earlier testify: a majority of this has been Ashkenazi (Northern and Central European) rather than Sephardic (Southern European, North African and Near Eastern) poetry. The recent anthology of translated Sephardic poetry by Lévy (2000) is an important attempt to rectify this imbalance. Furthermore, the English reader's picture of Holocaust poetry is largely determined by poetry that describes the details of life in camps and ghettos, in imprisonment or on forced marches: Sachs' best-known poem, based on the number of times it appears in anthologies and collections, is 'O The Chimneys' (Hamburger et al. 2011: 20–3) and Celan's is 'Death Fugue' (Hamburger 2007: 70–3). It is, of course, inevitable that such biases will exist: great poets attract many translators, those countries most affected by the Holocaust have produced the most recognizable Holocaust poetry and the Jews were the largest group of Holocaust victims by far. Though Schiff's anthology includes the categories 'Afterwards', 'Second Generation' and 'Lessons', it is striking that the later poetry of a poet like Sachs is not represented. What this means is that readers might perceive a clearer division than really exists between poets who wrote at the time and those who came later and wrote about the aftermath. In fact, some of the most powerful Holocaust poetry was written by poets such as Sachs many years after the events, when their own poetic technique had developed in response to discussions about poetry going on at the time, or by later poets such as von Törne, whose poetics was infused with a sense of the Holocaust events and its lessons right from the start. One of the arguments I shall be making in this book is that it is possible to establish some common features of the poetics of Holocaust poetry, as well as individual characteristics, and that it is the poetics that is of particular importance when it comes to translation.

Some facts about which poetry is typically available in translation can be found in Box 2.

1.2 Holocaust poetics

The simplest and most useful understanding of the term 'poetics' is that it is a description of how texts (of any genre) are put together, how readers interpret them, and how such possible or likely interpretations result from the elements of the text itself (cf. Wales 2001: 305).

Poetics is not specific to poetry, as a 1971 study by Todorov made clear (Todorov 1977; see also Jakobson 1960: 359), but because the adjective 'poetic' usually does refer to a quality or attribute of poetry, there is some slippage in the use of the term: sometimes it is a theory of poetry (see e.g. Tsur 2008: 1) and sometimes it is a theory of literary texts more generally, as in the sense in which Todorov used it.

In this book I shall generally use the term 'poetics' to refer to a theory or view of poetry held by a poet, a reader, a critic, a scholar or a translator. In many, if not most, cases, then, it is a theory that we (as reader or scholar) reconstruct from a text. I limit it thus, not because I wish to argue that it cannot apply to other genres of writing but because I am not on the whole

Box 2 Translated Holocaust poetry

Only a small fraction of Holocaust poetry has been translated. That most readily available in English translation includes the following:

- Collections by well-known poets, for example Paul Celan, translated by Michael Hamburger, Ian Fairley, John Felstiner and others.

- Collections by Jewish poets, for example Dan Pagis, translated by Stephen Mitchell, or András Mezei, translated by Thomas Ország-Land.

- Collections or selected poetry translated from German, Polish, Hungarian.

- Poetry with recognizable Holocaust imagery (ashes, smoke, chimneys, stars), especially in Holocaust anthologies.

As yet untranslated Holocaust poetry

Holocaust poetry that has rarely been translated into English (though there are exceptions in each case) includes the following:

- Poetry by or about Roma and Sinti victims of the Holocaust

- Poetry by Sephardic rather than Ashkenazi Jews

- Poetry by those persecuted or murdered for political reasons

- Poetry from other countries, for example Greece, Norway and the former Yugoslavia

- Poetry by or about victims of the 'Euthanasia' programme

- Poetry written in Yiddish

concerned here with other genres of writing, although some of what I say about how we read texts or build contexts applies just as much to prose. What most uses of the term 'poetics' have in common (cf. Wales 2001: 305) is that they see it as not focused on evaluation or interpretation *per se*, though it may be very concerned with the different possibilities of evaluation and interpretation that the text gives rise to and with explanations for documented instances of evaluation and interpretation. The main focus of poetics as a scholarly undertaking, and of stylistics, often considered to be the same thing (see Stockwell 2002: 6–7), is to explain how and why we read (and, by extension, write) poetry in a particular way. Because stylistics and poetics also explain what drove the writing of the text, they encompass views of style that see it as choice (see Verdonk 2002: 5–6; Short 1996: 68–71). If stylistics and poetics differ at all, it is only a difference in tendency; 'stylistics' has in the past been seen as narrowly linguistic or as tied to structuralism (cf. Simpson 2004: 2). Of course, linguistics has moved far beyond structuralism, and stylistics, like linguistics, has become increasingly interested in context (cf. Verdonk 2002: 19–22). 'Poetics' might possibly appear more open to developments in cognitive poetics (also known as 'cognitive stylistics') because of its concern with the way texts are put together for particular effects, but there is no essential difference, I would maintain, between poetics and stylistics when used to describe processes of literary reading and how those processes are driven by the language of the text. However, in literary translation, the process of writing is also crucial, because we read and analyse a source text in order to explain how, in relation to this analysis, we write the target text. When talking of writing, it seems more natural to use the term 'poetics'; thus we speak of the poetics of a particular poet – the set of their beliefs (conscious or unconscious) about how to link textual features to what is read and its effects – rather than that poet's stylistics. Of course, the poetics of the poet are not directly accessible to the reader, critic, scholar of poetics, translation scholar or translator. Readers of any type reconstruct the poetics of the poet and, if reading a translated text in full awareness of the role of translation, the poetics of the translator. Such a reconstructed poetics is consciously based on textual and contextual evidence, and furthermore, the poet or translator is in any case not in full control of all possible meanings and effects. Poetics thus aims to 'show what might have been done by a poem, whether or not it was done by design' (Jones 2012: 10). Jones was talking here about the close study of literary texts. Poetics adds the link between language and the way we reconstruct authorial choice, on the one hand, and between language and the effects on the reader, on the other.

Cognitive poetics is poetics that particularly goes beyond textual detail to try and explain perceived phenomena of the text such as alliteration or assonance or metaphor not merely as textual figures but also as figures having a cognitive dimension in both these aspects. That is, such textual phenomena have a mental contextual dimension in their representation of ways of thinking (of the perceived or reconstructed author of the text, or of a narrator or character in the text) and they have effects on readers that can be documented in empirical studies (such as van Peer 1986), or abstracted from such studies carried out by other scholars. As regards the first aspect, we cannot, as readers, know the mind of the author, but we can and do reconstruct it from the text, in much the same way as we reconstruct what we assume to be fictional participants in the textual discourse – narrators and characters – from the details of the text. In the case of the second aspect, we can only speak with certainty of the effects on ourselves as readers, but we can and do reconstruct likely effects on others, as does the author in writing a text. As I suggested in the previous section, context in this view is always cognitive: it includes thoughts, beliefs, attitudes and knowledge. For a translator, it is exactly this reconstruction of the mind of the author that plays a central role in the reading of the source text, and a calculation of the effects on the reader that influences the writing of the target text. For the reader of the translated text, whether a translation scholar or a general reader, the reconstruction of the mind of the author is especially complex, because we know the author was a translator, who had in turn reconstructed the mind of the source text author in reading the original text. There has been much discussion in both literary criticism and stylistics about the role of the actual author, and the various reconstructions the reader makes (see Stockwell 2002: 42 for a concise and illuminating overview), but for translation, the question of the translator's identification with and loyalty to the author of the original text (see Boase-Beier 2011a: 47–58) means that views of the nature of authorship are not just theoretical; they carry practical consequences. Cognitive poetics is useful to translators and translation scholars because it provides helpful means of explaining and describing the interaction between author, text and reader.

Cognitive poetics is not a particularly new or clearly defined type of poetics or stylistics. It is simply a development that puts more emphasis on the mind, on cognitive context, on cognitive effects and on what we know about patterns of thought and feeling, than does traditional stylistics. But traditional stylistics was always concerned with the mental context: from its structuralist beginnings in the 1920s and 1930s in the work of scholars such as Mukařovský or Jakobson (see the collection by Garvin 1964 or Jakobson 1978) to the influence of proponents of the close reading of texts such as I. A. Richards (e.g. 1929) and including what Fowler, in 1975, called 'The New Stylistics', stylistics has been concerned with such cognitive matters as choice, feeling, understanding and effect. Indeed, Tsur (2008: 2) traces the concern with the cognitive processes shaping literary texts back to Aristotle (see Aristotle 1951: 30). Terms such as 'mind-style', first used by Fowler in 1977 for the 'distinctive linguistic presentation of an individual mental self' (Fowler 1977: 103; see also 1996: 9, 150), already underlined the importance of the cognitive aspect of stylistic analysis, because they indicated that a description of textual linguistic detail is not limited to the detail itself but takes in the attitude, state of mind, mental process, emotion or other cognitive entity that it could be seen to represent, and also, increasingly, and under the influence and development of reader theories such as that proposed by Jauss (e.g. 1982) and Iser (e.g. 1971), among others, to suggest to the reader.

It is also important, and especially important in the case of Holocaust poetry, not to see cognition and emotion as separate entities; 'cognitive' in cognitive poetics has never suggested its separateness from the emotional, but rather places emphasis on the fact that the mind and the body, and rational thought and emotional response, are interconnected: this interconnection is particularly clearly expressed in titles such as Johnson's *The Body in the Mind* (1987). The term has occasionally been misunderstood, for example by Iser (2004: 11–12). In fact, cognitive poetics argues for the centrality of the emotions to our writing and reading of literary texts (see e.g. Burke 2011 or Stockwell 2009), because emotion is 'that process in life by which events become meaningful to us' (Oatley 2011: 115). That includes events and actions in texts. In this book I am taking what has been called a 'cognitivist stance' (Toolan and Weber 2007: 107). That is, I use a framework of cognitive poetics, because I regard it as essential for the study of translation for the reasons just given. I try to avoid overly technical descriptions, because they might be less accessible (or simply boring) to those who work primarily in Holocaust Studies or other areas of literary study. Where particular cognitive descriptive tools are useful, I shall explain them with examples. Besides such notions as cognitive context, blending and knowledge schemata that have already been mentioned, and one or two others that will be introduced later, the main elements of a cognitivist stance are as follows:

(i) It focuses on the construction of meaning during reading, on reading as a process, rather than on the product of a particular interpretation.

(ii) As a result of the process of constructing meaning, it is assumed that the reader's cognitive context will change, grow, develop or be revised, not just in relation to the actual text in question but also with more far-reaching consequences for the way we think and see the world.

(iii) Because making meaning from texts is dynamic and individual, it is not fixed or pre-determined; this has particular consequences for the study of translation.

What these three points emphasize is that, besides representing, connoting, suggesting or embodying cognitive entities such as thought-processes and emotions, poems and other literary (as well as non-literary) texts give rise to them in the reader, as the example from Celan's '*Wolfsbohne*', 'Wolf's-Bean' (Hamburger 2007: 398–403) in the previous section suggests. In that particular case, I mentioned the feelings of sympathy, sadness and helplessness that a reader may experience upon hearing or reading this poem. Such effects have often been documented; West, tracing the development of cognitive stylistics, notes how I. A. Richards' concern was to 'explain the nature of literary experience' (West 2013: 3) after he himself, as a young teenager, had responded with tears to reading Swinburne (2013: 1). Richards' early study (1929) was in fact empirically based. Later, more sophisticated empirical studies by van Peer (1986), mentioned earlier, and others (e.g. Miall and Kuiken 1994; Emmott et al. 2006), set out to test such effects on readers.

Foregrounding, which van Peer (1986) tests, is a good example of a stylistic feature of texts that has long suggested the need for a concern with the mind. From its origins in the early years of the twentieth century in the work of Russian Formalists such as Shklovsky and Prague Structuralists such as Mukařovský (see Lemon and Reis 1965 for Shklovsky and Garvin 1964 for Mukařovský), in the translations in the 1960s of work in the above collections and especially in the stylistics of the 1970s and 1980s, the term 'foregrounding', the 'throwing into relief' (Wales 2001: 157) of elements of a text in relation to the rest of the text or to the background of normal language use, has always been seen as designating not only a textual feature but also 'the dynamic interaction between author, (literary) text and reader' (van Peer 1986: 20). As Iser says, it is 'bound to draw the perceiving subject into the object observed' (Iser 2004: 8).

We can see the effects on the reader if we consider the translation of 'Wolfsbohne'. Effects may be triggered by the use of a German word in an English poem, if the lines are translated like this:

> You, Mother
> you who said *Wolfsbohne*, not:
> lupin.

In Hamburger's translation (2007: 399), the lines read:

> You, Mother,
> who said *wolf's-bean*, not:
> lupin.

The italicized '*wolf's-bean*' here also suggests spoken language, but not the German word itself. The sort of questions one might ask oneself as reader will depend not only upon the translation, and its presentation in a monolingual or bilingual book, but also upon one's cognitive context. They might vary from 'Why has the German word (not) been kept?' to questions about one's own reactions: 'How would I feel about the German language if my mother had been murdered by the Nazis?' Or it may include questions about the effects of the poem, such as: 'Is this poem just a cry of anguish or is it making me think more deeply about what those events did to language?'

Cognitive poetics, then, is poetics that goes back beyond the text to the mind of the narrator in the text, and, by extension, often to the inferred author (also called the 'implied author'; see e.g. Stockwell 2002: 42), whom the reader might assume is speaking with the narrator's voice, and who could be the inferred original poet or the inferred translator, or both. It also goes forward from the text to consider the mind of the reader. Seen from the reader's point of view, the implied author is the author inferred by the reader. Both terms are possible: it is a matter of perspective.

Within cognitive poetics, the real historical and geographical context of a poem or set of poems (or other texts) is seen as having a cognitive counterpart. It is not just the fact that Celan's mother was murdered by the Nazis in late 1942 or 1943 (the exact date is not known; see Felstiner 1995: 16–17) that is most relevant to the reader but what Celan felt about it, what his lack of knowledge of the actual date of her death, and his sense of guilt about his own survival, meant for him and his poetry, as well as what the reader knows (and feels) about the events, and about Celan's responses. What affects the reader most is how the actual textual detail of Celan's poems reflects this knowledge or other possible knowledge that the reader may attribute to poet or narrator, in interaction with the reader's own knowledge of Celan's mother's death. As we saw in the example of 'Seasons in Buchenwald' in Section 1.1, the interaction can be described in terms of an interplay between 'bottom-up' processes that originate in the text itself and drive 'a reader's meaning-making faculties' and 'top-down' processes that include those faculties. Such processes include the forming of mental imagery, of mental representations, and the building up of the reader's cognitive context (Burke 2011: 3–13). However, I would always add as a third element the reconstructed choices, attitudes, mental dispositions and representations that the reader attributes to the author on the basis of textual information. In the cognitive poetic study of translation, we are concerned with what all these issues mean for translation. Typically, we will want to consider whether the effects on readers of an English translation could be similar to those on the readers of the original poem. Or whether, in the case of Celan, the peculiar density of his poetry and its integration of different linguistic and cultural traditions have consequences for its translation into a language where these traditions might have a different status in the cognitive contexts of readers.

I noted in the previous section that scholars of Holocaust writing have tried to reconcile ethical worries about the aesthetic representation of the Holocaust with the question of how such representation works in the large number of non-factual and non-documentary Holocaust representations that actually exist, by using terms such as 'awkward poetics' (Rowland 2005), or 'the poetics of silence' (Martin 2011) or 'traumatic realism' (Rothberg 2000); these are all aspects of what I am calling 'Holocaust poetics'. Its characteristics are seen as the violation of 'narrative logic' (Gubar 2003: 8), as prosopopœia, or speaking in the voice of another (Martin 2011: 98), as 'obscurity or ambiguity' (Felstiner 1995: xvii), or the use of gaps and 'dislocations' (Hamburger 2007: 29). For translation it is especially important to be aware that poetics is not just a scholarly activity that theorizes the link between poetic form, expressed attitudes and effects on the reader; it is also the sum of the poet's actual beliefs and attitudes that drive the writing of their poetry, the reconstruction of which is one of the main tasks of the translator. When we speak of Celan's poetics or Sachs' poetics, we mean the view of poetry, in interaction with textual effect, that was peculiar to Celan or Sachs, and which can be reconstructed from what we see as a particular mind-style common to the work of that poet. We cannot, of course, know what made either poet, or any other poet, choose to write in exactly the way he or she did. But part of finding meaning in a text, part of reading it, is to ascribe particular choices, made for particular reasons, to its author, just as we do with any other act of communication. I have argued elsewhere (e.g. Boase-Beier 2010b) that one cannot do anything and certainly one cannot write or translate without a mental representation – a theory – of what one is doing. This might be clearly formulated and expressed, or it might never be expressed at all. But it is still there. When we talk about Celan's or Sachs' poetics, we are, thus, not talking merely of a theoretical explanation of the poetry and its effects, held (and possibly expressed) by a scholar or a reader. We are also, and primarily, talking about those views, whether expressed or unexpressed, about poetry held by the poet. Poetics is a mental construct that is not dependent on its communication or expression, though we reconstruct it from the way it is communicated and expressed. Poetics in this sense is of particular importance for the translator. If translation as a practice (and the theory of that practice) aims to go beyond a focus on the text and what it represents, in order to consider *how* its poetic style achieves this representation and its potential effects on the reader, then it is not only a translation of poetry but also a translation of poetics (cf. Boase-Beier 2011b).

Questions of the poetics of individual poets will lead the translator to important areas of research that may include statements made by the poet, details of the poet's background and their relation to the Holocaust, of their development, which often involved a growing awareness of the unfolding of historical events, and of the ways they responded to discussions such as that around the statements made by Adorno. We must remember that this discussion was happening at the same time as many of the poets in question were writing, so that direct and indirect responses to the philosopher's words can be found in those of the poets, and vice versa. A fairly clear development from earlier poetry with more explicit Holocaust imagery to later poetry that characterizes what I shall call the 'post-Holocaust mind' can be traced in poets such as Sachs and Celan. By using such a term I do not, of course, mean to imply that everyone thought alike; I mean simply that the Holocaust and its effects had become integrated – in a variety of ways depending on an individual's background, cognitive schemata, attitudes and views – into the way that individual thought. The post-Holocaust mind is reflected in the mind-style of these later texts in particular. In Celan, for example, an increased use of compound words has been demonstrated (Neumann 1968), and in Nelly Sachs we see more diffuse imagery and less clear syntax.

Because the Holocaust led to the writing of poetry by (and about) so many different victims, factors such as religious and political beliefs, nationality, historical and geographical context, will all have a bearing on its poetics. The Holocaust was in many ways a peculiarly Jewish catastrophe. This was not only because of the vast numbers of Jewish victims or the Nazis' intention to annihilate them completely, but also because for Jewish victims (though one must be careful not to imagine 'the Jews', or any other group of people, were all the same), it called into question the existence of God. There was also the Nazis' intention to destroy the Yiddish language (see Rosenfeld 1980: 115–26). These factors had an important influence on Holocaust poetry. Yet if translators do not translate poetry by other victims, the overall picture of translated Holocaust poetry becomes distorted in the ways I suggested in the previous section.

In understanding and reconstructing Holocaust poetics as the poetics of individual poets to be translated, the translator must therefore be aware, as with any poetry, of the historical and geographical situation of the poets and their often complex cultural background. Celan's poetry, for example, was influenced by Jewish symbolism, the Hebrew and Yiddish languages, by Romanian poetic form (the poem 'Espenbaum' [Celan 1952: 15], 'Aspen Tree', is written in the form of a Romanian doină or lament), by his studies in linguistics, his interest in the names of flowers, as well as his grief at his mother's murder. Sachs' poetry was influenced by her work as a translator of Swedish Modernist poets, such as Johannes Edfelt, and their forerunners, for example Edith Södergran (see Sachs 1947). Władysław Szlengel, writing in the Warsaw ghetto, was influenced by earlier trends in Polish poetry, in particular the Skamander movement, which favoured experiment, colloquialism, irony and lightness of tone, and also by traditional poetic forms like the lament (see Aaron 1990: 4–5, 21). Yukiko Sugihara, wife of the Japanese Consul Chiune Sugihara, in Lithuania, wrote tanka, the traditional court poems of thirty-one syllables, about her husband's struggle to help rescue Jews (see Sugihara

1995). Reading poetry for translation requires research into such influences and a consideration of their effects on poetics. I shall return to these questions in Chapter 3.

1.3 Poetry, empathy and the reader

When Adorno spoke, six years after the end of the war (Adorno 2003: 30), of the barbarity of poetry after Auschwitz, he was concerned with the writing of it, focusing on what he saw as the act of a possibly or necessarily insouciant and insensitive artist, rather than upon the recipient. Yet there are many reasons why questions about poetry after Auschwitz need to focus on the reader. As Gubar (2003) explains, for several years after 1945 little was said or written in Europe about the Holocaust. Though many studies (e.g. Hoffman 2004; Rosen 2010) strongly suggest that survivors felt the need to communicate with those who would be prepared to listen, many of them found themselves unable to do so. Memoirs like Smith's (2010) recounting of the life of Treblinka survivor Hershl Sperling show this very clearly. This means that those who wanted to know, and would have listened, such as Hershl's children, also suffered from their inability to speak.

For rescuers, the situation was especially complex: many did not speak out because of the possible suspicion with which their actions might have been viewed by a community still showing many of the prejudices that led to the catastrophe in the first place (Hoffman 2004: 213). Literary representation was affected by prejudice, fear and uncertainty. Alain Resnais' 1955 film *Night and Fog*, about the concentration camps, did not mention the Jews (see Gubar 2003: 2), but Celan, in his translation of poet (and Mauthausen survivor) Jean Cayrol's script, put them back in subtly, also avoiding German words with Nazi resonances (Lindeperg 2011).

When archives and memorials were established later, writers and artists such as Wiesel (1990) and Lanzmann (1995) declared that the Holocaust could not and should not be understood, interpreted or represented (see Section 1.1). Then there arose through historical scholarship and the work of philosophers like Adorno a strong sense of the failures of art, of culture and of language itself, to work against the catastrophe (cf. also Gubar 2003: 4). Language had not only failed as an aid to resistance, but was implicated, in its misuse by the Nazis, in much of the repression and destruction of their victims (cf. Klemperer 2000).

But where does this leave the reader? Gubar (2003: 1–7) argues that all these factors have contributed to a literary silence that might be seen to parallel the silencing of the victims of the Holocaust. Here she cites and echoes literary and linguistic theorist Walter Benjamin, who saw that the key to preserving active memory lay in the confrontation of the present with the past, so that it could incorporate and rework it (see Benjamin 1992a: 247; see also Stone 2003: 1–2). Gubar is thus arguing, as many other scholars have done, for the importance of Holocaust writing, whether scholarship or literature: 'to indulge in silence is to court madness or death' (Rosenfeld 1980: 15). But writing is not only crucial for the writer or the subject of the work: it is also crucial for the reader.

And there have been other literary silences, less often noticed. Mintz explains how the literary silence in what was then Palestine in the immediate aftermath of the Holocaust arose from ignorance of the situation of the Jews in Europe, compounded by a strict Zionist interpretation that suggested catastrophe had been inevitable and by blame for the supposed passivity of the European Jews (Mintz 1996: 9–14). This situation changed as survivors like Dan Pagis and Abba Kovner began writing poetry in Hebrew and achieving a significant readership.

In Europe, there was little literary writing, as I noted earlier, that expressed the fate of the Roma. There was also little early scholarly work. An exception is the work of early Holocaust historian Poliakov (1956: 265–6). And I am not aware of any poetry by Jehovah's Witnesses, though they were a particular target of Nazi hatred, with many being transported and killed (see Garbe 1999).

To this day, little is known about whether the decision by Germany's government in 1939 to murder all disabled or otherwise unwanted children in the country's hospitals resulted in any literary output. These victims and their immediate families were at first condemned to silence by several factors, not least of which was the 'Medical "As If"', to use Lifton's term (1986: 54), that is the elaborate pretence that children were going to be treated, when in fact they were to be killed. This situation is an early example, within the Holocaust events, of the blend of 'mass killing of certain groups of people ... with ordinary bureaucratic frames to produce a blended concept of genocide' (Fauconnier and Turner 2002: 27). It was a blend that allowed everyone involved, as in any bureaucratic system, not to feel a sense of personal responsibility (Lifton 1986: 55). It is hardly surprising that few people wrote about it when almost everyone pretended it was not happening. Work by Lifton and other historians such as Burleigh (2002) and Friedlander (1995) has shown not only the extent to which the medical establishment sanctioned and carried out these murders but also, in the following years, the systematic murder of many thousands of adults deemed medically inferior. Here there was more protest, also by a few psychiatrists, such as Karl Bonhoeffer (the father of the theologian and poet Dietrich Bonhoeffer) and religious figures such as Bishop von Galen (Trautmann et al. 2012; see also Burleigh 2002: 171–4), though von Galen was silent on the murder of the Jews. There were also public protests (Lifton 1986: 89–90), so that the campaign was officially ended in 1941. This, too, was a pretence, for it continued in fact until 1945 (Burleigh 2002: 227–54). Presumably it was the disadvantages the 'Euthanasia' victims suffered, coupled with the poor support in their communities or families, that resulted in the absence of writing by the people affected. But there also does not seem to be much poetry about these victims. Until recently, had it not been for the few scholarly works (such as those mentioned previously and especially Evans 2010) that mention them, one might have thought they had never existed.

It seems that a lack of literary work is often paralleled by a lack of scholarly work. I mentioned in Section 1.1 that not much literary work by those persecuted because they were homosexual has come to light, but there has also been little scholarly work on these victims (though with exceptions such as Gellately and Stoltzfus 2001), and none, as far as I know, that mentions their possible literary output. Poetry by religious figures such as Bonhoeffer, though well known, is, as we shall see later, not usually subjected to critical reception, and neither is poetry by Roma victims.

All these various silences – by historians, writers and critics – are not just failures to speak but they result in failures to be heard. Lack of critical engagement can often mean that it is now hard to discover even what exists, and, if such work does exist, to make sure it is translated.

One of the dangers for future generations, and those outside the areas mainly affected by the Holocaust, is that they will not know whether and how such writing might have influenced later literature. In order to prevent the Holocaust from 'dying', to use Gubar's term (2003: 1–27), it is necessary for future readers to be able to read, hear and otherwise receive art that represents or engages with the Holocaust in all its aspects. It is not those who already know who need to know but those who did not experience the Holocaust at first hand and do not yet know. This is why translation of Holocaust writing is such a crucial activity in terms of both remembrance and understanding.

Literature, and especially poetry, differs from witness accounts, historical treatises and other documentary writing. I would argue that, as time passes and more is researched about the events of the Holocaust, as facts become better known, poetry not only serves to keep alive memory, but it also gives to its readers a stronger sense of the voices that the Holocaust silenced. Many of the Jews killed in the Holocaust were speakers of Yiddish: indeed, the majority of Jewish victims in Central and Eastern Europe, according to Schwarz (2013: 102). Schwarz points to the importance of Anglo-Jewish writers such as Irving Howe (who, with Eliezer Greenberg, first edited *A Treasury of Yiddish poetry* in 1969; see Howe and Greenberg 1976) and included there their translations of work by Yiddish poets such as Sutzkever, who had survived the Holocaust. It is clearly the case that translations of the works of Holocaust poets writing in Yiddish helped ensure the survival of the language, though Yiddish poets were plagued by the same doubts as Holocaust poets in other languages, and perhaps more so; Howe and Greenberg speak of their 'recurrent doubt, even guilt, about the very act of continuing to write verse, continuing to care about meters and rhymes, images and phrases' (Howe and Greenberg 1976: 53).

Reading poetry is a way of experiencing these very individual voices, especially of those who did not survive, whether they were murdered, like Bonhoeffer, whether they were transported and died of illness, like Selma Meerbaum-Eisinger, forced to live in ghettos, like Ausländer, or to flee their homes, like Sachs. All the more reason that translation should confront the question of what characterizes a particular voice, and how it can be recreated in another language. And all the more reason that we should question what it means to read in translation, whether it is 'Deathfugue' by Celan in Felstiner's English (2001: 30–3) or 'Death Fugue' in Hamburger's (2007: 70–3), for example.

In particular, the importance of translated poetry after the Holocaust is in its cognitive effects on the reader and how these are preserved for present and future readers, and for those who are geographically, as well as historically, far removed from the events of the Holocaust itself. In considering cognitive effects on the reader, besides taking into account empirical studies, the work of psychologists and other scholars of the mind is also of great importance. For example, Simon Baron-Cohen's research into empathy is potentially useful. Baron-Cohen describes empathy in neuroscientific terms as the action of several interconnected brain regions, and shows how it involves the perception not only of standing in someone else's shoes but also of feeling what they feel 'as if it had been our *own* sensation' (Baron-Cohen 2011: 16–28, 25). More than this, empathy also includes the ability to retain a 'double-minded focus of attention' (Baron-Cohen 2011: 10) so that we do not simply, as for example Sklar (2013: 24–5) maintains, lose ourselves in the other person's feeling. We are, in fact, able to reflect on it and respond 'with an appropriate emotion' (Baron-Cohen 2011: 11). I suggested earlier that empathy is more than just our immediate reaction when we read Celan's '*Wolfsbohne*' and feel sad, because the speaker is sad. Crucially, for Baron-Cohen, it also involves the 'explicit understanding of mental states, emotions, and how others are related to oneself' (Baron-Cohen 2011: 26). If a poem fails to trigger empathy in the reader, then one may still perceive it as a sad poem, but not oneself feel sad in response (cf. Tsur 2008: 100). However, an appropriate response might not only be to feel sad, but also to feel angry, or energized or guilty. If a person is generally low in empathy, he or she may see others as unimportant, and so commit crimes against them for personal gain or pleasure (Baron-Cohen 2011: 13). Or, a person low in empathy might find the poetry of a survivor simply meaningless, because the feeling it evokes cause no further response, or a response that is clearly inappropriate. Baron-Cohen also directly addresses the Holocaust. While not necessarily arguing that the Holocaust itself was not unique, he finds the view that the Nazis were uniquely cruel 'absurd' (Baron-Cohen 2011: 6). His view is supported by many studies documenting the vast numbers of people including administrators or functionaries at various levels and with various degrees of influence (cf. Fulbrook 2012), and the 45 per cent of medical doctors who joined the Nazi party (cf. Burleigh 2002; Lifton 1986), who were certainly not usually uniquely cruel. Their behaviour, in terms of both lack of empathy and its many other contributing factors such as ambition, fear, indifference or stupidity, is therefore all the more disturbing, because we can see so easily how aspects of it might be found in our own behaviour (cf. Kershaw 1983: viii). Poetry has an extremely important role to play here. Its ability to evoke empathy has the potential to cause us to re-set our reactions. Instead of the horror we feel at such statistics as the murder of 6 million Jews or 570 thousand (Jewish and non-Jewish) Hungarians, or the forced sterilization of 300 thousand people (Lifton 1986: 27), or the historical interest we might have in whether the Nazi destruction of the Sinti and Roma communities resulted in 25 thousand (Lewy 2000: 222) or 220 thousand (Winstone 2010: 10) deaths, poetry gives rise to other feelings. It causes us to feel both the grief and sadness that are automatic responses because of the 'mirroring' element of empathy (cf. Baron-Cohen 2011: 25–6; Oatley 2011: 20, 113; Goldman 2006: 3–22), and also, beyond this, the determination to act differently which is part of empathy (cf. Baron-Cohen 2011: 11). Empathy as an effect of Holocaust poetry is important and needs to be considered in more detail. Lack of empathy led to greater and lesser crimes in the Holocaust. Hoffman (2004: 11) calls it the 'perpetrator's utter failure to recognize the humanity of the victim', a failure she sees both compounded and confirmed by their later lack of remorse; see also von Kellenbach (2013). Failure to recognize the humanity of others is also noted by Lifton as crucial to the development of so many doctors from healers to killers, or those who acquiesced in killing (Lifton 1986: 113). For Hoffman, such lack of empathy is caused by 'numbing' (Hoffman 2004: 179), for Lifton, by 'doubling', which splits the self and allows the different parts, such as the moral person and the murderer (Lifton 1986: 418–19), to co-exist (see also Emmott 2002). Lack of empathy, furthermore, led the Nazis to blame the victims (Lifton 1986: 462): the ill were at fault for being ill, the Jews for living in ghettos and camps, the Sinti people in Germany for acting in such a way as to cause normal people to be prejudiced against them. Note that splitting the self in this way is the opposite of the integrated 'double-minded focus' of Baron-Cohen's empathy (2011: 10). Poetry can work to counteract lack of empathy, according to Gubar (2003: 241–7), by allowing identification with the speaker or those spoken about (cf. Franklin 2011: 13).

Poetry allows in the reader a sense of identification with the sufferer, a sense of 'if I were you' (Fauconnier and Turner 2002: 255–8), a conceptual blend crucial to empathy, and one of the common features of a response to literature (cf. Oatley 2011: 161; Stockwell 2009: 135–7).

We can see how such an empathetic response works if we consider the short poem 'Gustav!', translated from the Hungarian of András Mezei by Thomas Ország-Land (2010: 39). The poem starts by saying that a Jew from Memel (now in Lithuania), Feinstein, recognized his neighbour in an execution squad, and goes on:

And he cried out to him:
Gustav! aim
straight between the eyes!

This poem, which is in total just six lines long, represents what Miall calls an 'episode', that is 'a thematically distinctive topic requiring a shift in the reader's understanding' (Miall 2007: 148). The shift that occurs here is a sudden realization that one might appeal to a neighbour in such a situation, not to beg him not to shoot, but to ask him to shoot so as to kill. That is, it is a hopeless situation, from which there is no way out. That sense of hopelessness, acceptance of inevitable death and the juxtaposing of the neighbour's first name, which suggests a request for help (as indeed it is), with the request to be killed quickly creates a strong sense of what Miall calls 'decentering' (Miall 2007: 144). Decentring occurs when you are taken out of yourself and made to focus on someone else, in this case a character in a poem, by projecting yourself onto that character (Gavins 2007: 40; Stockwell 2009: 9). What happens is a conceptual blend: you, the reader, are both yourself and Feinstein, the Jew from Memel, staring at your executioner.

But projection onto more than one character is also possible, as Whiteley (2011: 23–42) has shown. This is what happens in this poem. Feinstein, the victim, is the character whose voice we hear, but he is only mentioned by his last name and the description 'a Jew from Memel'. Because Gustav is addressed by his given name (in fact, his *Christian* name), we also find ourselves taking his position, so that the victim is merely 'Feinstein, a Jew from Memel'. Feinstein is, of course, not an uncommon name. So the victim becomes depersonalized, as we shift our projection from victim to executioner.

To consider the role of empathy, of projection and decentring in Holocaust poetry is to focus on the reader. And a focus on the reader seems crucial because poetry 'wants to go to another', as Celan (1968: 144) said; it is essentially communicative. In saying this, Celan shows the particular influence of philosopher Emmanuel Levinas, whom we know Celan read (see Felstiner 1995: 310; Levinas 1990: 108–9). Poetry carries within it the possibility of its own translation, said Benjamin (1972: 9–10; from now on usually quoted in Rendall's translation as Benjamin 2012), and so it communicates across boundaries of language and culture, of time and place. When Benjamin (2012: 75) said that works are not aimed at their reader, what he meant (in my interpretation) is that works communicate by their very nature, irrespective of who the critic might think they are aimed at. Poetry communicates by its nature, as does the translation of poetry (or any translation), but trying to match the text (whether in original or translation) to an imagined reader endangers the work itself. All the more reason then, to make sure a translation is available to all potential readers, and that its poetic effects are not hampered by either its translation or the presentation of the translation, points I shall come back to in Chapters 3 and 4.

If Holocaust poetry encourages empathy in the reader, then we need to ask what is the point of this empathy? What can it do?

One thing it can do is cause readers to question their own beliefs and attitudes; inferences and emotions that arise in reading a poem like 'Gustav!' 'project back' (Stockwell 2002: 127) into our original mental models, so we are able to examine what we know and think. Many studies of the Holocaust point to the extraordinary capacity of human beings to both know and not know about something that is hard to accept (cf. Fulbrook 2012: 8; Lifton 1986: 489). For Lifton, this, too, like the inability to empathize with victims, can be explained by 'doubling' (Lifton 1986: 418–65), the capacity to keep incompatible ways of thinking in play at the same time. It was a capacity prevalent not only among perpetrators but also among bystanders at the time and among those who came after. I would argue that it is possible even today to know the facts about the Holocaust, and yet not to really know. Really knowing would involve the sort of examination of one's own thoughts and cognitive models that such projection makes possible. Von Törne's poem '*Beim Lesen der Zeitung*' (1981: 56), 'While Reading the Paper', is another poem that questions exactly what it means not to know (see Boase-Beier 2004). Its translation, therefore, requires an understanding of the levels of embedding of represented thought in the poem and the possibility for the reader of the translation to engage in working out who knew what; I shall return to this poem on several occasions.

Many writers have pointed to the absence of empathy as one of the factors that made the Holocaust possible. Arendt, originally writing in 1961 about the trial of Eichmann, one of the main organizers of Nazi deportations, notes how 'his inability to speak was closely connected with an inability to *think*, namely, to think from the standpoint of somebody else' (Arendt 2006: 49). This is a crucial point: if one cannot put oneself in someone else's position, empathy will fail, moral behaviour becomes empty phrases, and one is in danger of classing others as barbarians for not conforming to such phrases, a view that, as Todorov (2010: 13–21) explains, leads to barbarity in those who hold it. One way to counteract such barbarity of thinking is to recognize the humanity of others and another is to make sure we can all 'understand a foreign identity' (Todorov 2010: 22). Poetry and translation invite new readers to identify with the humanity of those they do not know.

Lack of empathy is often tied to an inability to use language: Eichmann could not speak because he could not think, language was manipulated by the Nazis so it lacked nuance and meant what they wanted it to mean. And it was used to mean its opposite whenever its opposite involved greater loss of power for the victim. Lifton notes that 'euthanasia', when applied to human beings generally means that they have the right to die, or the right to be assisted to die. But it was used by the Nazis to mean the right to kill (Lifton 1986: 46). Poetry always questions language and engagement with poetry always involves, for the reader, a questioning of language, more so (as I will show in Chapter 2) when the poem has been translated from a different language.

By drawing our attention to the plight of individuals whose voices we hear in the poems, rather than to the statistics that are a necessary part of writing history, poetry allows us, better than the statistics alone do, to reverse, even if in a small way, that aspect of the Nazi crimes which involved what Arendt, quoting philosopher Karl Jaspers in a radio interview of 1961, called a crime 'against mankind as a whole' (Arendt 2006: 270). Arendt saw this as the real nature of genocide. As Lifton (1986) has shown, when the dehumanizing of patients began with critically sick children, it became easier to extend the notion of non-humanity to sick adults, then to Jews, Poles and anyone one did not like. What is sometimes referred to as the 'slippery-slope argument' was not an argument: it was a strategy that involved a conscious repression of empathy, so this later became the norm. Poetry will not tell us anything *about* those circumstances that we do not already know. But it will, perhaps, work against the dehumanizing tendencies in us all.

Poetry demands much of the reader: thinking, questioning, critical engagement, empathy, understanding. In this way it can help counteract not only emptiness of thought as manifested by perpetrators like Eichmann, but also the emptiness of thought which meant that people in Germany in the 1930s allowed the medical profession to get away with murder, simply because they were in a position of authority (cf. Lifton 1986: 139; Weinreich 1999), thus paving the way for genocide.

But we also need to be aware of the dangers of empathy. In discussing trauma, Franklin (2011: 224–5), quoting Celan's concern with the reader or listener, points out that complete identification with victims (as discussed, for example, by Laub 1992) amounts to 'overidentification', which leaves the listener unable to help (Franklin 2011: 225). Such overidentification, which, according to Baron-Cohen's view of empathy would leave one unable to respond appropriately (cf. Baron-Cohen 2011: 120–4), is unlikely to happen with poetry, because the focus on the form of the poem caused by foregrounding, often achieved through poetic devices such as fragmentation of syntax, ambiguity or textual gaps, distances the reader just enough to make considered response possible. This effect is described by Tsur as 'disrupting (or delaying at least) the automatic transition from the *signifiant* to the *signifié*' (Tsur 2008: 5). That is, if we read '*Wolfsbohne*' (Hamburger 2007: 398–403) we are not immediately in the speaker's head; we are also considering what the Jewish symbolism (such as 'the seven-branched candelabrum', Hamburger 2007: 399) means, we are considering what the actual words spoken by the speaker's mother suggest and not just what a lupin looks like. And we are also susceptible to echoes of non-speech processing of the sound qualities of the poem, which are processed as though it were an acoustic and not a phonetic level of language (Tsur 2008: 11). Attention to the stylistic qualities of the poem can thus work against the automatic responses that Hoffman calls 'costless sympathy', and which are on a par with numbness from 'over-familiarisation' (Hoffman 2004: 178) because they are momentary. In Baron-Cohen's terms, they lack the element of reflection and awareness of one's own response that is a crucial part of empathy (Baron-Cohen 2011: 10–11).

Beyond the important aspect of empathy, understanding poetry entails further mental work that results in cognitive effects (cf. Boase-Beier 2006: 47). This was described by Celan's translator Hamburger as the readers experiencing at first a sense of being 'rewardingly baffled' and then needing to 'take such steps as they could take to emerge from the bafflement' (Hamburger 2007: 422; see also Gubar 2003: 20). As I have explained elsewhere (see Boase-Beier 2011a: 143–53), reading poetry involves not just emotions and a concern with the acoustic and other stylistic qualities of the language, but also a concern to find meaning. Meanings differ depending on the cognitive context of the reader; there is not *one* meaning, but every reader will attempt to find his or her own (cf. Oatley 2011: 175). The search for meaning, which helps build up contexts during the reading of the poem, is crucial to the possibility of contextual effects such as changing one's existing views, images and models (cf. Stockwell 2002: 127; Iser 2004: 8–9).

So how does translation deal with the question of reading and the reader? What I am arguing throughout this book is that the stylistic features of a Holocaust poem engage the readers, causing a decentring, to use Miall's term (2007: 144), that allows them to project and identify, and so to re-enact some of what is happening in the poem, thus giving direct rise to feelings that mirror those of the character or narrator identified with (cf. Goldman 2006: 17–21). At the same time, stylistic features encourage the reader to embark upon a search for meaning. Style is thus the central element in the translation of poetry, and especially of this poetry. Because of the cognitive effects of the style, poetry and its translation avoid what is sometimes seen as the commercialization or commodification (cf. Cole 2000) or even the parody (Erk 2012) of Holocaust memory. Rothberg discusses the dangers of commodification by noting that, in both Adorno's and Benjamin's thinking, culture, with its easy possibilities of reproduction, can make calamity more likely, rather than mitigating against it (Rothberg 2000: 31–5; see Adorno 2003: 30). It was Adorno's tendency to see lyric poetry as part of the uncritical cultural production to which he ascribes such terrible potential that made him wary of it. This view is not, in fact, unusual: it is the view that making aesthetic objects such as poems is a form of making ugly reality beautiful. However, if the translation of poetry and the effort to read translated poetry tell us anything, it is that such poetry does not make the Holocaust beautiful. It does not commodify or simplify events and emotions, nor stultify its readers. By placing great demands on them, it works, in fact, against such a possibility.

The questions that arise for the scholar concerned to understand how Holocaust poetry achieves its cognitive effects are thus the same as those that will be asked by the translator of such poetry. These are questions about its stylistic features and how such features are processed by their readers, and will be addressed in more detail in the next two sections, and in Chapter 3.

1.4 The silences of Holocaust poetry

'The silence of artistic integrity "after Auschwitz" is a real thing', said Ted Hughes (1994: 232). What he meant, in my view, is that the poetic silence is a real thing, inscribed into the poetry in ways that affect us. What stylistics, and especially cognitive poetics, can do is to describe precisely how poetic silence is expressed by the text and how its expression relates to potential effects on the reader.

I have been arguing up to now that Holocaust poetry is of central importance for the way we keep the memory of the Holocaust alive in a productive way, a way that includes the possibility, and, indeed, the necessity, of its translation. Its poetics – the way its poetic style reflects a mental state or set of beliefs, attitudes or values which we attribute to the poet, and expresses these in the text in a way that has effects on the mind and emotions of the reader – depend on the stylistic detail of the text, and it is thus this detail that translation needs to work with.

I will argue in this section that the notion of 'silence' as applied to the Holocaust, and seen in the titles of books on Holocaust writing (*The Poetics of Silence*, by Elaine Martin, 2011; *The Language of Silence*, by Ernestine Schlant, 1999) or on language after the Holocaust (Steiner's *Language and*

Silence, 1985, written in 1958), a notion now in danger of becoming rather commonplace, has real and describable counterparts in the style of Holocaust poems. 'Silences' can serve as an overall term for something that is reflected in Holocaust poetry, wherever it was written, by whomever it was written, and under whatever circumstances. The notion of stylistic 'silence' is the stylistic counterpart of Rowland's 'awkward poetics' (2005). That is, Holocaust poems engage their readers not just, or indeed not primarily, through content, but through the various stylistic devices (if seen to be intentional; more neutrally, they are simply stylistic features) that register death and destruction, upheaval and ending, and the mixed emotions of grief, despair and guilt. These stylistic features can often be noticed as textual gaps. They include syntactic gaps, often particularly noticeable in the ending of poems mid-sentence, as in Sachs' *Vergebens* (Holmqvist 1968: 268) ('In Vain'), which ends '*Es war*—'('It was —'), or Pagis' famous poem 'Written in Pencil in a Sealed Railway Car' (Mitchell 1981: 23) with its final line 'tell him that i'. Such gaps are instances of what is usually referred to as 'iconicity' (cf. Leech and Short 2007: 187–96; Fischer and Nänny 2001), that is, they resemble the events they are describing: the burning of letters that are cut off but do not destroy love, in Sachs' poem; the abrupt change (perhaps death) in the life of the transported writer in Pagis' poem. Iconicity can be seen as 'form enacting meaning' (Leech and Short 2007: 195; see also the articles in Nänny and Fischer 1999; Sonesson 2008). But iconicity is not merely (or perhaps, in some cases, not at all) in the text; it is in the mind of the reader, who has to work out the significance of the echoing of burning letters or unfinished statements in a poem. Iconicity plays an important role in all poetry, and it is something the translator needs to be aware of.

Gaps within words, caused by their morphological or syllabic fragmentation, are also common, especially in Celan's poetry. Such examples as '*Cor- // respondenz*' ('cor- // respondence' in Hamburger's translation, 2007: 374, 375) or '*über- // sterbens- // groß*' ('more- than- // death- // sized', 2007: 370, 371) lead the reader to consider not only the different parts of the word, for example, the substitution of 'death' for the usual 'life' in a compound that would usually mean 'larger than life', but the actual gaps themselves and their possible meanings. In the example of 'cor-respondence', the gap echoes that which German writing and printing rules would insist on at a line end, and thus underlines the context of letter writing the poem suggests, as well as artificially creating the morpheme '*cor*'- (heart), which is not present in a normal morphological analysis of the word, that is, an analysis which divides it up according to the smallest parts that possess meaning (see Crystal 2013 for a good description of morphology). Normally, the word divided morphologically would be '*Co-(r)-respond-enz*' (the process of responding mutually), so the division in the poem is foregrounded for the reader.

Other stylistic devices or features that create or rely upon gaps in the text include the use of ambiguity, homonymy, polysemy and connotation, so that not only is it impossible to read the poetry without considering meanings that are absent, as it were, from the text, but poetic language itself also becomes a metaphor for the slipperiness of everyday language and the possibilities of its manipulation to serve malevolent ends. This is again especially the case in the poetry of Celan, where, for example, the word '*weggebeizt*' ('cauterized'), in the poem of that title (Celan 1982: 27) suggests '*beißen*' ('to bite'), with which it is etymologically connected, but also 'bitter', also etymologically related, and a word used often by Celan, with connotations of the 'bitter herbs' traditionally eaten at Passover, the 'bitterness' that results from affliction, for example in *Lamentations* 3.15 (*New King James Bible* 1982: 335), and also of bitter almonds, which contain Prussic acid, used in the production of the gas Xyklon B used in Auschwitz and other camps (cf. Felstiner 1995: 64, who says it might also possibly be suggested by Celan's use, in other poems, of the image of almonds). But '*weggebeizt*' is also related, via the assumed Indo-Germanic word *'*bheid*' ('to hit', 'to split'), to words meaning to cut or wound (e.g. in Swedish '*bita*') and to '*Beil*' ('axe'). The consequences of such a wealth of connotations are that the reader sees various possibilities of interpretation and understanding, which, of course, makes such poetry especially difficult to translate. Though Celan's poetry provides perhaps the best examples of ambiguity, both lexical and syntactic, other poets also use it. Ausländer's ambiguity is less etymologically based than Celan's and more dependent on the semantics of words such as '*wenn*', which can mean what in English would be 'when', or 'if' or 'if and, if so, when'. Such ambiguities are almost always reflected in the fact that different translators translate them differently. A line from '*Am Ende der Zeit*' (Ausländer 1978: 104), 'At the End of Time', reads:

wenn	es	sein	wird
if/when	it	be	will

This line is translated by Ewald Osers (1977: 55) as 'when it happens' and by Eavan Boland (2004: 23) as 'if and when that happens'. I shall return to this poem in the next two sections.

Particularly in the case of Celan, the use of homonymy and polysemy not only highlights the misuse of language by the perpetrators of the Holocaust, by foregrounding its etymology, but also suggests the impossibility of freeing language from sinister connotations.

Rowland noted a similar use of gaps and fragmentation in English poetry influenced by the Holocaust, which is in 'direct dialogue' with earlier Holocaust poetry as well as with the 'worries that Adorno expounds' (Rowland

2005: 2, 10). Poetry such as that by Celan or Ausländer or Sachs, or others writing in the immediate aftermath of the Holocaust, is also to some extent developing a dialogue with its own earlier poetics. Thus both Celan's and Sachs' poetry becomes less explicit over time, leaving more to the reader in what I designated in Section 1.2 as the style of the post-Holocaust mind. As the poetry of an individual poet becomes less explicit, it also becomes more self-aware, not only engaging in dialogue with both earlier work and the discussion about the Holocaust and poetry, but also representing life lived in the knowledge (which, for many poets, became greater almost by the day) of what the Holocaust had actually meant. In the case of Sachs, in particular, since she did not lose close family members, this meant a shift from the observer role of an early poem like 'O the Chimneys' (Sachs 1988: 8), written in 1947, to the internalized pain, which she felt as the pain of the whole Jewish people (Holmqvist 1968: 37–8), in a later poem such as 'Sie schreien nicht mehr' (Sachs 1971: 28), 'They no Longer Weep and Wail'. The later poem refrains from evoking typical Holocaust imagery such as the chimneys and the smoke, and instead uses the position of words in the line to create parallels: thus she places the words *Wunden* and *Wolken*, 'wounds' and 'clouds', in the same position in different lines, subtly suggesting that wounds become insubstantial, but are no less present. Clouds are like a less substantial form of the smoke of the early poems and, indeed, also feature in metaphorical expressions in both languages: a (dark) cloud on the horizon, to be under a cloud. When Celan, echoing Adorno, spoke of poetry with a 'tendency to fall silent' (Celan 1968: 143), he was also describing exactly this development that we see in many Holocaust poets. The poetry does not literally fall silent, but it speaks less, thus leaving more to the reader as well as echoing the traumatic internalization of catastrophe, that is, it represents the post-Holocaust mind more than the events themselves.

Gubar is quick to point out that 'a sincere expression of grief' (Gubar 2003: 24) (as in Sachs' earlier poem) should not be merely dismissed as banal. But it does not automatically guarantee good poetry. Good Holocaust poetry is appropriate poetry, and what is appropriate in the senses discussed is often bound to be the opposite of what is usually associated with lyricism: 'clumsy, under- or overstated … stymied by stutters or by untranslatable words; thwarted interruptions, caesurae, and hiatuses' (Gubar 2003: 24; see also Young 1993: 550). All these stylistic silences suggest feelings of grief, lack of understanding, the break with what was known, the brutality of events and people. But they also help to engage the reader, thus functioning as gaps in Iser's sense (1974: 280) that draw the reader into the text. These are the sort of silences I am especially concerned with; they potentially pose special problems for translation. They are the silences found in these various stylistic features of the text.

Schlant, explaining what she means by her term 'the language of silence' (Schlant 1999: 7), notes that she is concerned not with the gaps and silences caused by the Holocaust (cf. Lang 1988: 15), that is, the silences *of* the Holocaust, but with what she calls literature's own 'blind spots': the literary silences I mentioned in the previous section, which she calls silences *about* the Holocaust.

In talking about 'the silences of Holocaust poetry', I mean primarily the first of these types of silence: the silences of the Holocaust, as they are reflected in the style of Holocaust poetry, and as they affect translation. However, the concern of translation cannot be just with the stylistic features of the poetry but also with the question of what is translated, or what is not translated, and so literary silences matter, too.

In studying translation, then, we need to consider both types of silence. And they interact: because much of the later, more subtle poetry of those poets who are widely translated, such as Celan and Sachs, with its representation of life and thought after the Holocaust, is not very well known in the English-speaking world, the greater degree of engagement this poetry requires of the reader goes unrepresented and what readers usually know as Holocaust poetry in translation can seem predictable in its clearly recognizable imagery.

1.5 Lost worlds, longed-for worlds, impossible worlds and deadly worlds

Holocaust poetry reflects the silences of the Holocaust in its style, through gaps and hiatuses and ambiguities. But another important characteristic is the way it conjures up worlds that do not exist. These worlds may have existed in the past, as in Ausländer's lines:

Die Zeit im Januarschnee versunken.
Der Atem raucht. Die Raben krähn.
Aus Pelzen sprühen Augenfunken.
Der Schlitten fliegt ins Sternverwehen.

The lines may be translated as:

Time buried deep in January snow.
Breath smokes. Ravens crow.
Eye-sparks spray out from among the furs.
A sledge flies into a drift of stars.

These lines are from '*Bukowina I*' (Ausländer 2012: 13), one of several poems that evoke Czernowitz as it was in the days before the war: an important centre of culture, a city where fashionably dressed middle-class people like Ausländer's family wore furs to protect them against the cold (as many photographs of Czernowitz in the 1930s attest), and there was time for sledging. There are hints, though, in the apparently idyllic scene, of the horror to come, and I shall return to this.

Or the poet may imagine future worlds as an escape from the horrors of the Holocaust events. Thus Ausländer again, in the poem '*Am Ende der Zeit*' (1978: 104), 'At the End of Time', mentioned in the previous section, says:

Wenn der Krieg beendet ist
am Ende der Zeit

When the war is ended
at the end of time

Ausländer wrote that some of Czernowitz's Jews, expecting to be killed, lived 'in dream-words' (Ausländer 2012: 10) as a way of surviving. These 'dream-words' were used to create an imaginary world that did not actually exist, either because it had been destroyed or because it lay in an uncertain future. Indeed, Ausländer described the realm of dream-words as 'traumatic' (Ausländer 2012: 10), partly playing on the near-homonymy of dream ('*Traum*') and trauma ('*Trauma*'), which, though the words are not etymologically related, are clearly related for Holocaust poets: the latter led to a need to escape into the former. Turner remarks that someone 'trapped inescapably in an actual story of suffering or pain may wilfully imagine some other, quite different story, as a mental escape from the present' (Turner 2003: 118). Sometimes the imagined world is one that by definition cannot exist in the situation the poet depicts, that is, it is impossible in the fictional world just as it would be in the real one (see e.g. Ronen 1994: 48–61 for the difference). An example is the situation suggested by Celan's expression '*als schliefst Du auch jetzt noch*' ('as though you were still asleep'), which suggests powerfully the way in which the mind inhabits worlds that have no counterpart in reality. That line occurs in Celan's poem '*Heimkehr*' ('Homecoming'), written in 1955 (Celan 1980: 94), some years after his mother had been murdered by the Nazis. It is usually assumed that the poet is addressing his mother here, especially given that an earlier poem with the same title was sent to his mother when he *was* coming home to her in 1939 (see Felstiner 1995: 97). '*Als schliefst Du auch jetzt noch*' suggests the persistence of the feeling that it might be possible for her to wake up. It is of course not possible for her to wake up, and it is also not possible to talk to her (as it would not be even if she were asleep) in any meaningful sense, though speaking to the dead is commonplace (see Fauconnier and Turner 2002: 204–6). What such images do is to transport the reader (cf. Stockwell 2009: 87) not only into the world the poem describes, which in this poem is a world of snow and ice, but also inside the speaker's mind, and, depending on the amount of background knowledge the reader has, the poetic narrator is more or less likely to be identified with Celan (see Semino 1997: 38). The world we enter is known as a text world, which is 'a readerly mental representation of the alternate world' (Stockwell 2009: 7). In this case, the text world is a counterfactual world: it has no existence except in the speaker's mind, in which knowledge of the mother's death and longing for her to be merely asleep and able to wake are able to co-exist (cf. Boase-Beier 2014b). Such imagined worlds rely upon the cognitive process of blending (see Fauconnier and Turner 2002), mentioned briefly once or twice already in this chapter. Intuitively, it is clear what blending is because it is a common process used in everyday thinking, to enable us to combine two or more different 'mental spaces' that may be perceived to have certain elements in common (Fauconnier and Turner 2002: 40–1). The human mice in Art Spiegelman's comic-form Holocaust memoir *Maus* (Spiegelman 2003) are a good example. In the example just given, the speaker knows his mother is dead but combines that mental representation with one in which she is alive but asleep. Clearly sleep and death have things in common. Coming home triggers, perhaps in remembrance of the earlier situation, which the earlier poem described, a sense that the mother might be asleep. All the examples given above involve an element of blending. Ausländer's description of the Bukovina includes hints of what one only later knew was at the earlier time about to happen. At the time itself one would not have known. And the poem about a time when the war will have ended involves the speaker placing herself in a time when it had not ended and imagining a future time.

Other poems by Celan use conceptual blending of a more complex nature. The poem '*Espenbaum*' (Celan 1952: 15), 'Aspen Tree', mentioned briefly in Section 1.2, compares the speaker's mother with an aspen but, in fact, the comparison is repeatedly negated (for example, the tree's leaves turn white, but the mother's hair did not), so that a world in which the mother behaves as naturally as the tree simply does not exist, because the mother is (unnaturally) dead. A further example is Celan's poem '*Weggebeizt*' (Celan 1982: 27), also mentioned earlier, in which the worlds of medicine (evoked by images of radiation, cauterizing, wounds and breath), of snow and ice (snow, glaciers, crystal) and of speaking (language, tongues, witness) are blended together. To the reader who is aware that Celan studied medicine in Tours in 1938–9 (Chalfen 1979: 77), the medical imagery will be particularly striking. The result of such blending is that the reader must mentally visualize a world in which, for example, a wound and a crevasse in the ice are blended, in which body and landscape are fused. This is achieved in this poem not just through the use of ambiguous words such as '*Schrunde*' ('wound' or 'crevasse'), or '*Zunge*' ('tongue' or 'language') but by a whole pattern of lexical elements in the poem that conjure up the three different worlds and fuse them. The resulting world is not a possible one but a poetic one in which nature echoes the body and the mind.

Whenever a poetic world that exists in the narrator's mind is created, it is a sub-world of the world of the poem itself, often referred to as an 'epistemic world' or a 'knowledge world' (cf. Semino 1997: 72). There are various stylistic markers in the poems that indicate we are entering such a world-within-a-world. They include the conjunction '*als*' and the subjunctive verb form '*schliefst*' (from '*schlafen*', to sleep) in the phrase '*als schliefst du*' ('as though you were asleep'), in '*Heimkehr*' (Celan 1980: 94), 'Homecoming'. Such structures suggest that the speaker in the poem operates in a world in which the mother is not asleep, but is able to imagine a world in which she is. The reader also has to enter this imaginary world, which echoes the state of mind of someone living with the knowledge of disaster, but unable to fully accept it: a traumatized state that is characteristic of the post-Holocaust mind. It results from an 'event that is not fully assimilated or experienced at the time' (Caruth 1995: 4). And indeed, acceptance of death often requires what Fauconnier and Turner (2002: 204–6) call a 'material anchor' – a corpse, a grave, ashes – which Celan, in common with so many family members of Holocaust victims, did not have.

Stylistic markers that indicate a sub-world also include words such as '*wenn*' ('if and when') in '*Wenn der Krieg beendet ist*' in the poem by Ausländer mentioned earlier, which introduces a hypothetical extension to the knowledge world of the poem's narrator (cf. Semino 1997: 72), a future world that may not come about. German is able to do this much more powerfully with the concept of 'if, and if so, when', expressed by '*wenn*', than is possible with the English 'when', which suggests the future world will come to be (Boase-Beier 2010a).

For the translator, a crucial question will be how to render such stylistic features that mark the entry into worlds which exist only in the mind of someone who has suffered (or is expressing suffering) in the catastrophic world or aftermath of the Holocaust. The subjunctive mood (as in '*Heimkehr*') has no clear verb form in English, and the word '*wenn*' (as in '*Am Ende der Zeit*') has no counterpart.

What is particularly striking in Holocaust poetry, though, is its suggestions of the Holocaust world, often without being an obvious description of that world. Ausländer's poem '*Bukowina I*', quoted earlier, might seem to evoke an idyllic pre-war world of furs and snow and sledges, but the connotations of 'ravens crow' are associations with death, as the bird's black feathers in myth frequently suggest it is a harbinger of death, in which sense it is also used by Edgar Allan Poe in his poem 'The Raven' (Poe 2008: 92), and by another Czernowitz poet Meerbaum-Eisinger in her poem '*Du, weißt du ...*', asking 'Do you know how a raven cries?' (Meerbaum-Eisinger 2013: 39). Ravens are also, however, in Ukrainian legend, the birds that were turned black for feeding on carrion and 'only in the new paradise at the end of time will their former beauty be restored' (Biedermann 1996: 281). Thus ravens could be seen, in Ausländer's poem, to suggest both death and a future beyond death (as in the poem 'At the End of Time'). The association of ravens with death might also lead the reader to see the furs as not only an image of luxury, but also one of death.

'A drift of stars', on the other hand, evokes images of items such as shoes and glasses piled up high as Jewish victims were taken to be exterminated in the death camps. Some witness reports have said that the stars they had been forced to wear were removed from the clothing after the people who wore them had been killed so that the clothing could be reused by non-Jewish Germans (cf. Smith 2010: 101). It also suggests a drift of snow, a common Holocaust image, which blends memories of actual hard winters, especially in the camps, with connotations of apparent purity, of temporary covering up. References to the Holocaust can thus be inferred by the reader. Readers might indeed want to argue that these inferences are based on strong textual evidence, that they are the result of implicatures, that is, intentionally communicated implications to be found in the text (see Sperber and Wilson 1995: 10–12; Clark 2014: 162–3).

To return to Celan's poem '*Heimkehr*', his images of silence, invisibility and deafness ('*Stumme*' (literally 'dumbness'), '*unsichtbar*' ('invisible'), '*tauben-*' ('dove' or 'deaf')) as well as his images of injury and loss ('*das Verlorene*' ('the lost'), '*weh tut*' ('hurts')) all imply or conjure up a world beyond or beneath the snow-covered landscape he describes. This is the world that has been left in the wake of the events of the Holocaust.

The image of the aspen tree, which, as we saw earlier, works as a potential but unrealized counterpart for Celan's murdered mother in '*Espenbaum*', can itself also evoke the Holocaust, because the aspen is associated with fear, since its leaves tremble. And the fusing of medicine and the body with landscape that I have described in the discussion of '*Weggebeizt*' works partly because it points to the Nazi ideology of healing the body, and its warped view of the Jewish community, and others, as illnesses or injuries upon the body of the German *Volk* (cf. Lifton 1986). Even poems such as those of the young poet Meerbaum-Eisinger, all written before 1942, and apparently conjuring up an idyllic world in which the only fear is of rejection by a lover, cannot help but be influenced by the historical context, and, when read today, by the knowledge of what was happening at the time, much of which only came to light in its full extent later. An apparently joyful poem like '*Den gelben Astern ein Lied*' (Meerbaum-Eisinger 2013: 14), 'A Song for the Yellow Asters', seems prescient (and can be read as though it was meant to be prescient) when we consider that the flower name 'aster' is from Greek '*aster*' ('star'), and that these asters are yellow. Reading the poem in retrospect today, we thus might interpret the following lines as ironical:

Und gar nichts von des Regens Trauer kann
die leuchtend gelbe Freude mir verletzen

These lines could be translated as:

And nothing of the rain's mourning can
spoil for me the shining yellow joy

Here we notice an important point for the way the original poem is read and translated today, and the way its translation will be read: even if the original poet meant not irony but rather the conscious shutting out of fear, today the irony that arises from the contrast between the image depicted, the feelings expressed, and the knowledge that forms part of the cognitive context of its readers, is an inevitable part of the way this poem is read. Whether we know Meerbaum-Eisinger's actual state of mind at the time of writing is immaterial: the state of mind the poem conveys is one of consciously achieved joy. The fact that it *is* achieved consciously (for the speaker mentions the rain's mourning, which she does not allow to dampen her mood) already paves the way for another world to be visualized, in which the mourning is no longer anticipated but real and inevitable. Thus, even this poem carries hints of what might be yet to come, and which later events show were to come, and which today's reader knows did come. Clues in the poem to the world of the Holocaust thus always require the active participation of the reader, and the activation of the reader's knowledge of the Holocaust, which will vary across historical and geographical location; what might have seemed, to a reader at the time, to be merely a possible implication, would be taken by today's reader as an implicature, so a translator today might well translate '*Trauer*' as 'mourning', just as I did earlier, to make the implication stronger. The published translation by Silverblatt and Silverblatt (2008: 11), in fact, opts for 'sadness', seeing the implications of the Holocaust events to come as less strong.

One of the ways the world of the Holocaust is conjured up in the poems is through their use of metaphor. In a cognitive poetic view of metaphor, it is not just a stylistic figure found in the text but, first and foremost, a way of thinking and thus is, in fact, conceptual metaphor (Lakoff and Johnson 1980). Conceptual metaphors (usually represented in small capitals to show they are mental rather than textual entities) are shared by and across communities. Most studies of metaphor as it is used in literary texts suggest that they regularly take common conceptual metaphors and change them slightly (Lakoff and Turner 1989: 67). This makes it harder for the reader to understand, requiring greater engagement and triggering a number of cognitive effects, such as re-thinking and new ways of seeing. For example, Celan's poem '*Espenbaum*' (1952: 15), 'Aspen Tree', combines the common conceptual metaphor PEOPLE ARE PLANTS (Lakoff and Turner 1989: 5) with specific features. The comparison is negated, emphasizing that the mother was not able to live out her life in a natural way, and the specific connotations of aspens, mentioned earlier, are implicated. The conceptual metaphor PEOPLE ARE PLANTS suggests, especially to the post-Holocaust mind, a common complex blended image in which death (often already a skeleton) is a reaper of souls, who are thus implicitly compared with plants (cf. Fauconnier and Turner 2002: 291–5).

Both Celan and Ausländer, in common with many Holocaust poets, use images of snow and ice. Lakoff and Turner (1989: 18) count DEATH IS WINTER as a conceptual metaphor; such images thus always suggest death to the reader. In the world of the Holocaust, snow also suggests the actual conditions of hardship in camps and ghettos, much worse in winter, and also, especially for Celan, an image of purity (GOOD IS WHITE; Lakoff and Turner 1989: 185), which, however, is not to be trusted as it is just a covering; this is the image of snow in 'Homecoming', a poem to which I will return in Chapter 3.

The Holocaust world was in many ways a manufactured one, relying on a number of blends. We have already seen the degree to which perpetrators and public, and those in between, such as doctors, collaborated in a world of make-believe in order to avoid uncomfortable truths. But in the camps themselves, there were also elaborate pretences. If the 'if I were you' blend of empathy was totally lacking here, it was replaced by what Lifton calls the 'as if' situation of the camps, with their pretend stations, gardens and deadly showers (Lifton 1986: 236, 444; cf. Poliakov 1956: 205). This was the world of the 'concentrationary universe' (a term Rothberg 2000: 105 attributes to David Rousset who wrote a memoir with this title; see Rousset 1946). In this world, the perpetrators themselves only had a stake with a split-off part of their mind that felt nothing. This split-off part of the mind enters into the most terrifying blend of all: that between 'bureaucracy and murder' upon which Fauconnier and Turner comment (2002: 27–8; cf. also Mithen 1996: 224; Rothberg 2000: 36, and see Section 1.2). Bureaucracy involves part of the mind of the perpetrator in just doing his (or occasionally her) job (cf. Lifton 1986: 496). Murder is aligned to it and becomes killing on someone else's (the state's) responsibility. Victims of murder become dehumanized names in bureaucracy's files. When Holocaust survivor Eva Schloss, Anne Frank's step-sister, at a public talk in Norwich on 20 January 2014, showed us her passport with the added name 'Sarah', which the Nazis gave to each Jewish woman, as they gave the name 'Israel' to each Jewish man, she described such an act as 'childish' (cf. also Schloss and Kent 1988). It is indeed childish in that it allowed the perpetrators to avoid the real world and live solely in the world they had created. Such inappropriate childishness, a blend of 'rational means and irrational ends' (Rothberg 2000: 36), like other forms of what Arendt called 'grotesque silliness' (Arendt 2006: 252) and Bonhoeffer referred to as dangerous stupidity (Bonhoeffer 2010: 43), also led perpetrators to avoid responsibility after the Holocaust (cf. von Kellenbach 2013: 187). To understand the poetry, though, the reader is called upon to activate constantly a process of empathetic blending – a feeling of 'if I were you' – with the poem's speakers. So reading Holocaust poetry can be a small, but at least a conscious, act of reparation. Because translation also involves a similar act of empathetic blending of the translator's mind with that of the original author, it, too, is a small step in this direction.

1.6 Beyond the text: The translation of Holocaust poetics

In this chapter I have been presenting a view of Holocaust poetry from the position of cognitive poetics. That is, the style of the poetry is a key to the poetics behind it, including attitudes and mental representations in the poet's mind. The style in the text mediates between such elements, which are not directly accessible to the reader but which will be constructed as part of the reading process, and the effects on the mind of the reader herself or himself, as cognitive context is built up and altered during reading. For translation, such a view means that we are always, as translators and as translation scholars, concerned with what is behind the text and what comes after it. This is also a view of poetry explicitly subscribed to by several Holocaust poets; Celan, for example, saw it as the way to avoid the poetry of simple description and stylistic embellishment that Adorno had criticized (see Englund 2012: 15). The translator's task is never going to be exhausted in the linguistics of textual transfer, and so stylistics will need to be formulated broadly in order to be equal to the task.

Stylistic devices such as ambiguity, syntactic gaps or odd metres have at least potential counterparts in English. The difficult task for the English translator in most cases is not to render them but to recognize and understand them; reading for translation will be discussed in Chapter 3. But what happens when the devices that signal the imaginary world are recognized but appear to be specific features of the source language that cannot easily be rendered? I mentioned earlier the difficulty of translating 'wenn' in poems by Ausländer, since English does not have a word comparable to 'wenn', which can mean 'when' and be used to suggest something definitely predicted to happen in the future, as well as 'if', when it indicates uncertainty as to whether the events described will happen, as well as 'if, and if so, when'. It is not merely that such a lexical item does not exist in English; the concept of a time that is about to be located and described, but that might not actually come to pass, is not expressed easily in English, though of course it can be expressed, as it has been, somewhat clumsily, earlier in this sentence. A strong view of the Sapir-Whorf hypothesis (see Crystal 2003: 15) is usually taken to be the view that if a language does not express something, it has no concept for it and so the word cannot be translated into that language (Boase-Beier 2011a: 29–35; Malmkjær 2005: 48–50). If such a view were to be held, there would be seen to be no possibility of even conceiving of a state of affairs that might be expressed by 'if, and if so, when' in English, and so there is no point in the translator's trying to represent it. Not only this discussion but also Boland's translation of 'wenn' as 'if and when that happens' (Boland 2004: 23) show that the hypothesis in its strong version cannot apply. However, the heavy-handedness of Boland's translation, while ensuring conceptual accuracy, does mean that the reader has less interpretative work to do than the reader of the original. From both a religious and a philosophical point of view, the reader's engagement is crucial in Ausländer's poem: there are various possible interpretations of the poem's beginning 'If/when the war is over // at the end of time'. It could suggest that the war will never be over because as long as time persists, so will the war. Or it could signal a firm belief in a future world, when the current time has passed. The point is that 'wenn' does not tell us.

What instances like 'wenn' show is that translation needs to go beyond such notions as textual equivalence. Of course, no modern discussion of the translation of poetry, whether by practising translators or by scholars, would suggest anything else (cf. Hermans 1999: 47–8). Indeed, many studies of the translation of poetry, as well as many descriptions by translators, express very clearly that what is at stake is not what the poem says but what it suggests: 'the inner core of his message and its mode of expression', says Csokits (1989: 11), explaining what Hughes tried to capture in his translations of Pilinszky (Hughes 1976).

This is especially true of Holocaust poetry with its silences, gaps and indirections. Here translation is going to be as much the translation of what is not said – what is implied or what the translator deems to have been implicated – as of what *is* said (cf. Boase-Beier 2011b: 176).

In order to fully understand the consequences of such examples as the translation of 'wenn' in Holocaust poems, we need to understand how models of language have changed and how these changes affect translation. One particular change is especially crucial. This is the increased emphasis placed, since the 1990s, on the role of inferences in making meaning from texts. Early structuralists such as Jakobson (see e.g. his 1959 essay; Jakobson 2012) or Havránek (and others in Garvin 1964), writing in the 1940s and 1950s, who wrote not only about linguistics, but also about stylistics and translation, and had a great deal of influence in all these areas, worked within a framework in which language was assumed to be a code, with a meaning that could be found by a process of decoding. For translation, this meant that, once the original text had been decoded, the meaning could be transferred into and re-encoded in the target language to make a target text. This view can be seen clearly expressed in models like Jakobson's, where he speaks of 'code-units' and says the translator 'recodes and transmits a message' (Jakobson 2012: 127). The view of language as a code and the assignment of meaning as decoding is evident in the terminology used – 'sender', 'receiver', 'code', 'interference' and so on – and in the metaphors used, which combined wireless imagery (the radio had become commercially viable in the first decade of the century) with the 'path' image schema and the 'container' image schema, basic 'minimal knowledge structures' with which we mentally represent common experiences (Semino 2008: 92, 95, 7).

All these images are part of an overall 'CONDUIT metaphor for comm-unication' (Kövecses 2002: 34), which informed the model of language with which early structuralism worked, in both linguistics and literature. It was also the view of language that was around at the time many of the Holocaust poets such as Celan or Ausländer were writing. Of course, the degree to which this element of the historical intellectual context affected their poetry will vary. Celan, for example, studied French and Russian languages and linguistics in Czernowitz in 1939 and 1940, and English in 1944, and there are clear traces of code, path and container imagery, especially in his critical writing: the poem is '*unterwegs*' ,'travelling', along '*Wege einer Stimme zu einem wahrnehmenden Du*' (Celan 1968: 144, 147), 'paths of a voice towards a perceiving you'; a poem is '*eine Flaschenpost*' (Celan 1968: 128), 'a message in a bottle'.

As a structuralist understanding of literature moved towards a post-structuralist one in the 1950s in France and about ten years later in the English-speaking world, the interest in literary convention and the (conscious and unconscious) structures in language and literature that produce meaning and effect shifted towards the understanding that structures are not 'out there' in the world or the text, but are created by writers and readers. This is an understanding that already pervades Jakobson's work (see the essays collected in Jakobson 1978). This development was paralleled not only by the questions about aesthetics and responsibility that philosophers like Adorno prompted but also by questions about the role of political views, especially given that several modernist writers in the 1920s and 1930s had been drawn to Fascism (see Potter 2012: 177–81). Meaning was seen to be less fixed and to depend particularly on the reader or listener. Iser, as we have seen, wrote about gaps in the text and the reader's role in engaging with them (see Iser 1971, 1974). Such a view, like Celan's messages in bottles, places emphasis on the recipient: we do not know where the message will go or who will receive it. But it is there to be received. In this, Celan was following the tradition of the Kabbalah, to which I shall return several times, for its interactions with structuralist thinking are highly interesting. Not only literary studies in the 1970s but also linguistics began to place more value on inference and what is not actually said, and the work done by the recipient (cf. also Riffaterre 1992). Even in theories that placed less emphasis on the insubstantiality of meaning than, for example, literary deconstruction, language was seen to greatly underdetermine its meaning, so that the reader needed to supplement whatever could be arrived at by processes of simple decoding with complex inferences based on what it is assumed the writer is saying: the implicatures already mentioned earlier. This was put most clearly by Sperber and Wilson's groundbreaking *Relevance* of 1986 (see Sperber and Wilson 1995, 2012), which initiated the development of Relevance Theory, the inferential theory mentioned in Section 1.1 (as used e.g. by Pilkington 2000), and its later applications to translation theory (e.g. Gutt 2000). The effects of such developments on translation are that interpretation can be seen as more flexible, the creativity of the act of translation has space to flourish and, most crucially, the reader of the target text (and the translator as reader of the source text) takes on much greater responsibility for the meaning of the text (as in, for example, Scott 2012).

There are many ways in which this historical development has affected the various disciplines that impinge upon translation (cf. Boase-Beier 2006: 12–30); one particularly important way is that a focus on the broader context of writing and interpretation includes the view that mental representations and all that affects them are part of the cognitive context of the poet, of the translator and of the readers of both original and translation.

Seeing Holocaust poetry against the background of this current under-standing of linguistics, literature and translation means that the distinction between poetry and other types of writing can be more clearly expressed. While the language of poetry may not differ in significant ways from the language of non-literary texts (a common view in stylistics, see e.g. Fowler 1996; Stockwell 2002), it seems clear that there are characteristics of certain texts which we would want to define as literariness (cf. Pilkington 2000: 15–21; Attridge 2004: 2–4) and that 'literariness is manifested by the special nature of the interaction between reader and text' (Miall 2007: 3). That is, literariness is what predisposes the reader to read the text as literature. In the case of Holocaust poetry, the poets were clearly writing something very different from documentary or witness accounts: they were communicating their own experiences or those of others, and their thoughts, attitudes and reactions, in such a way that the reader has to work, and feel, and think, is 'decentred' (Miall 2007: 144), transported out of herself or himself into the world of the poem, building up a context whereby existing knowledge, thought and feeling interact with the text, so that existing cognitive structures are changed. Because the difficulties of the style of these poems, as an expression of a reflection upon poetics before the Holocaust and after, are not merely mimetic of the horrors and dangers of the Holocaust, but have the effect of placing greater cognitive demands on the reader, translation needs to concern itself with the preservation of such possibilities of involvement, so that the reader of the translation can also experience cognitive effects.

An example of how this might work is in von Törne's poem '*Beim Lesen der Zeitung*' (1981: 56), 'While Reading the Paper', mentioned briefly in Section 1.3. This poem is particularly interesting in terms of translation, because it both contains several layers of reporting on thoughts and appears to do something that is untranslatable. For this reason, though I have discussed it elsewhere (Boase-Beier 2004, 2006: 122–7, 2011a: 155–7), I shall mention it again several times in this book in order to consider different aspects of reading it and translating it. Von Törne was the son of a member of the SS (Hitler's private military police force) and he found it extremely difficult to come to terms with the place his nation and his own father had played in the Holocaust. Much of his anguish and self-questioning is common to many of his generation, as can be seen, for example, in interviews conducted by Gitta Sereny in 1990 with the children of perpetrators (Sereny 2001: 289–308). He devoted much of his life to work of reparation for damage inflicted by Fascism and Fascist regimes with the group *Aktion Sühnezeichen* ('Action for Atonement'), and died, probably of overwork, at the age of forty-six. Both in terms of its subject and in terms of its potential effects on the reader, it seems important to consider such poetry as Holocaust poetry, though someone like von Törne was not himself a victim of the Holocaust, or, if so, only indirectly, in that he inherited feelings of guilt and responsibility.

Here is the poem in question (von Törne 1981: 56):

Ich	lese	in	der	Zeitung,	daß	die	Mörder
I	read	in	the	paper	that	the	murderers
von	Mord	und	Totschlag		nichts	gewußt.
of	murder	and	manslaughter		nothing	known
(Meine	Schwester	nähte	damals			
my	sister	sewed	at-that-time			

ihren	Puppen	gelbe	Flicken	auf	die	Brust.)
to-her	dolls	yellow	patches	on	the	chest

(The first two lines translate roughly as: I read (present tense) in the newspaper that the murderers [did? allegedly did?] not know anything of murder and manslaughter.)

At the end of the second line there is a missing auxiliary, marked here by two possibilities in square brackets: '*Ich lese in der Zeitung, daß die Mörder von Mord und Totschlag nichts gewußt* [*haben? hätten?*]'. In the semi-literal translation given below the poem, we can see that there is something missing before 'not'. (In German the auxiliary '*haben*', 'to have', is used rather than 'to do'.) As a reader of the English translation, does one insert 'did' or does one insert 'allegedly did' in the space before the word 'not'? The corresponding auxiliaries would be indicative ('*haben*') and subjunctive ('*hätten*') for the German reader. And yet the German is more complex still: a subjunctive auxiliary for 'did' ('*hätten*') can certainly imply scepticism ('allegedly') on the part of the reporting speaker, but it can also simply be a grammatically correct way of indicating reported speech or thought, because, in reporting, German always indicates distance in a way that English does not. There are, then, three possible ways of reading these first two lines:

(a) 'I read in the newspaper that the murderers did not know anything of murder and manslaughter (and I accept this)'.

(b) 'I read in the newspaper that the murderers did not know anything of murder and manslaughter (and I report this neutrally)'.

(c) 'I read in the newspaper that the murderers allegedly did not know anything of murder and manslaughter (but I don't believe it)'.

The poem is important as a poem about living with the Holocaust because it does not let the reader off lightly. It gives rise to a number of questions: Does the speaker in the poem, and, perhaps, by extension, the average newspaper reader, believe what it says or not? Does he believe that the newspaper journalist believes what the murderers say (or think) or not? Is the distance signalled by the subjunctive auxiliary in reported speech or thought enough to allow the journalist not to think any further about whether he or she believed what he or she reported? This very short poem thus becomes, in the German reader's mind, a question about responsibility for beliefs and thoughts. Do we take on those of others unquestioningly (whether they are those of a Nazi murderer, or a journalist or the newspaper the journalist writes for, or, indeed, of a poem's narrator, or a poet), or should we not always consider our own relation to views or beliefs expressed by others? For the translator, it seems crucial to capture the gap after '*gewußt*' in the poem that can give rise to such questions, because, though English does not have the same linguistic means (indicative *versus* subjunctive) to indicate reported speech, exactly the same question arises, of responsibility for what we do with what we read, and also of what it would mean to be a German faced with these questions.

What this poem illustrates, and what it suggests for translators of Holocaust poetry, is not that one needs a large amount of historical or biographical knowledge about the poet in order to understand the poetry, but that understanding the poetry involves a dynamic process of questioning, so that the context is built up as one does so. Relevance Theory, in keeping with most cognitive and inferential approaches to literary texts, suggests that cognitive effects arise from the work needed to understand the poem. In my interpretation of the theory for literary reading and literary translation (see Boase-Beier 2006: 39–49), not only will there be more such effects the more one has to engage, but the reader is also likely to continue re-reading and re-analysing the text so long as new effects are felt. It is this process that the translator aims to make possible for the new reader.

It should be clear from the examples discussed thus far, however briefly, that the point of translating Holocaust poetry is, on the one hand, to give voice to those silenced, or who speak for those silenced and, on the other, to make sure those voices can resonate in the minds of new readers in a different language. I mean this in an entirely practical and concrete way. Poems like all those hitherto mentioned will not of themselves add to the factual knowledge we have about the events of the Holocaust. There are other sources for this. What they can do instead is to give rise to a response of empathy and a reliving in the reader's mind of the questions that lie at the heart of the Holocaust, about why and how it happened and, above all, about what our response today should be. They ensure, in translation, that the response, and the thinking about the response, and thinking through the consequences of our responses, can continue.

This book is partly about how we read Holocaust poetry in English, taking into account the fact of its translation, regarded not as a necessary though potentially obscuring factor in its communication to new readers, but as part of a dynamic process of renewal that was begun when it was written. These questions will be examined in Chapter 2, where I will also consider how readers might reconstruct the act of translation as just such a dynamic process, by taking on the role of comparative readers, that is, rather than by seeing the translation as though it stood in place of the original, by reading through the translation to the original, irrespective of whether they speak the language of the original. This is what all reading of translation should aspire to, but, in the case of Holocaust poetry, it seems especially important. I go on to address the second main concern of the book in Chapter 3: what it means to read a poem for, rather than as, translation, and what it means to translate it. I will then consider in Chapter 4 what these observations about the nature of Holocaust poetry, and its translation, and the possibility of reading it *as* and *for* translation, suggest for future translation and presentation of Holocaust poetry. In this way I hope to demonstrate how the translation of Holocaust poetry can aspire to the creation of an enhanced reading experience, and can potentially have upon its readers the full range of effects that the original poetry was able to have, and more.

2

Reading Holocaust poetry in and as translation

2.1 Holocaust poetry and the reader

In English-speaking countries, most Holocaust poetry (like eye-witness accounts and fictional writing) is read in translation. Yet its readers do not, in general, seem to be conscious of this fact. Where they are aware it is translated, as anecdotal information from a public exhibition and workshops on the translation of Holocaust poetry, held in Norwich on 4 and 5 November 2013, suggests, most readers assume that they are reading poetry translated from German, Polish or possibly Hungarian, because the Holocaust is mainly associated with the countries where these languages are spoken (see also Winstone 2010: 2). Most of those who commented on the exhibition had never considered what it might mean to read such works in translation beyond a hope that the translation was 'correct' (this concern was expressed several times) and did not falsify the experience of the poet, who was generally assumed to be someone directly involved in the events of the Holocaust.

In work on Holocaust writing, including poetry, translation itself is rarely mentioned. For example, Clendinnen (1999), in discussing the ways in which we can and should represent the Holocaust, mentions the many languages spoken in concentration camps (see also Rosen 2005), the use of subtitles in Lanzmann's film *Shoah* and the need for writing (presumably English writing) which engages the reader, but she never mentions translation *per se* nor discusses its effects. Her subject is mainly the writing of history and memoir, and she is aware of the mediating effect of memory (Clendinnen 1999: 23–5). And yet her discussion of Filip Müller's memoir, translated from Czech into English in 1965, though noting the difference between this translation and the literary collaboration that resulted in *Eyewitness Auschwitz* (Müller 1979) in the

United States, along with simultaneous British and German versions, does not once mention the mediating effect of translation itself. It is as though writing is an interpretative act but translation is entirely transparent. When speaking of poetry (see Clendinnen 1999: 164–8), she mainly discusses English language poets such as Plath. She quotes Pagis in Mitchell's translation (Mitchell 1981: 23), as though Pagis himself had written it in English (Clendinnen 1999: 165–6). This is the situation Even-Zohar described in 1978, saying that translations are often associated with 'major events in literary history', and there is often no distinction made in the receiving literary system between original and translated works (Even-Zohar 2012: 163). Even-Zohar, together with Toury, was one of the pioneers of a view of literature as a dynamic system of systems in interaction with one another, a view that came to be known as polysystem theory (see Hermans 1999: 106–7; Munday 2012: 164–90). The danger of the lack of recognition of translation is partly that the translator's work is made invisible, as Venuti complained in 1995, and he still feels, in the second edition of his book several years later, that translation occupies a 'marginal position' in the Anglo-American literary system (Venuti 2008: vii). The aim of his theory of foreignization, which he describes as an ethical attitude towards constructing 'an image of the foreign that is influenced by the receiving situation but aims to question it by drawing on materials that are not currently dominant' (Venuti 2008: 19, 20), is to ensure that 'translations can be read as translations' (Venuti 2008: 13). In this book I am also arguing for the importance of reading translations as translations, and part of my reason for this is that I share Venuti's concern for the marginalization of translation and the translator's role as writer of the translated text. But I have another concern, as well. The effect of treating Mitchell's work as though it were Pagis' also renders invisible Pagis' decision to write in Hebrew after emigrating from Czernowitz to Israel. Clendinnen, in discussing Pagis, does, of course, mention this decision, but we have no sense at all that we are reading not Pagis' words but (probably) Mitchell's.

Rosen's 2005 book on Holocaust writing deals in great detail with the importance of language in Holocaust representation, and specifically with English language Holocaust writing since the end of the Second World War, and is one of the very few studies that address translation as something that does not merely provide a 'poor substitute' for the source language but is actually 'a necessary mediating step' (Rosen 2005: 36). Most only mention translation in passing, and seem unaware of its mediating and interpretative nature: see also Waxman (2006); Schlant (1999); Young (1998). They are aware (at most) that what we read are the products of translation; the process is not considered.

In general, most studies of Holocaust writing implicitly assume the transparency of translation, and, with the exception of Rosen (2005), where it is referred to at all, it is generally seen as something negative: 'translated poems are an impossibility', says Young (1993: 549), quoting Ausubel and Ausubel (1957), who are, she says, quoting Franz Werfel. Young (1993: 549) says that the translation is always 'secondhand', that there is a 'distance never quite bridged' between the original and its translation, as though distances of time, place and culture did not already require bridges. Similarly negative remarks are made by Langer (1995: 553). And Carol Ann Duffy notes that Primo Levi's translated poetry has a 'universality that translation cannot restrict' in a strangely contorted view of translation that seems to see it as a process that usually makes the literary text less, rather than more, universal (Feldmann and Swann 1992: back cover).

Yet the fact that Holocaust poetry has usually been translated ought to be clear enough. As with all writing about the Holocaust, we know that the events that lay behind the poems happened to a large extent in other countries; thus we know (if we give the matter even a second's thought) that the original poems were usually not in English. Schiff's 1995 anthology, though not mentioning translation in the 'Introduction' with more than a passing reference, does at least give the translator's name in each case after the original poet's name. Nevertheless, there seems to be an assumption in the book, which 'includes ... the voices of 59 poets' according to the back cover, that there is no issue about how those voices are heard through the voice of the translator, and what this means for the new reader.

Translators themselves are, not surprisingly, more aware of the issues, though they tend not to engage with translation as an academic discipline, as Venuti (2008: 274) points out. Hamburger wrote on many occasions about the translation of Celan (see, e.g., the various statements in Hamburger's 2007 collection) and Felstiner discusses in many published articles (e.g. Felstiner 1992), and especially in his 1995 study, the details of the interpretative work of translating Celan, making it clear where he has found rhyme a problem, or the imagery 'difficult to grasp' (Felstiner 1995: 11). The very fact that Celan has been translated by both Hamburger and Felstiner makes it impossible for readers not to be aware that there are different ways of interpreting and translating the same poem. Later translations by Fairley (2001, 2007), among others, have added to even the casual poetry reader's understanding of this fact, just as the several recent translations of other major poets such as Dante (e.g. Ellis 1994; Dale 1996; Carson 2004) have confronted readers of poetry with the implications of translation more widely and highlighted the differences in interpretation that poetry makes possible.

What I will call 'comparative reading', that is, in its most obvious sense, reading a translated text, in this case a Holocaust poem, in a number of different versions, provides interesting insights into the process of translation, and the choices made by different translators. Even to a general reader, who reads to experience the poetry, rather than to reconstruct the translation process, the differences between, say, Felstiner's translation of Celan's 'Deathfugue' (Felstiner 2001: 30–3) and Hamburger's translation of the same poem, as 'Death Fugue' (Hamburger 2007: 70–3), will be apparent. Consider, for example, the following line, translated by Felstiner (2001: 30; here JF) and Hamburger (2007: 70; here MH):

> we shovel a grave in the air where you won't lie too cramped (JF)
> we dig a grave in the breezes there one lies unconfined (MH)

Both translations appear in bilingual presentation; the original line (Celan 1952: 37) is as follows:

> wir schaufeln ein Grab in den Lüften da liegt man nicht eng

The striking differences, apart from the rhythm, are in the verb 'shovel' or 'dig' (for '*schaufeln*'), in 'air' or 'breezes' (for '*Lüften*') and in 'cramped' or 'unconfined' (for '*eng*'). One way of thinking about the differences in these two English lines is to consider the definition of what Jakobson, in one of the most famous statements on poetic language, called 'the poetic function'. Jakobson, who was very influenced by the poetic theory of Gerard Manley Hopkins (see Jakobson 1960; Jones 2012: 56–69), said the poetic function of language (that is, the way language is used in poetic utterances) 'projects the principle of equivalence from the axis of selection into the axis of combination' (Jakobson 1960: 358). If we take this statement seriously, we might conclude that the translator's choice of 'dig' or 'shovel' for '*schaufeln*' becomes a possible factor in aiming for equivalence (not of meaning but of register or form), in the choice of translation for '*Lüften*'. Furthermore, if we take Jakobson's term 'projects' (not to be confused with cognitive projection, as described in Section 1.3) in something like its modern linguistic sense that features of a structure are carried on to later ones that depend upon them (see Ouhalla 1994: 92) or that, as in more recent developments, the syntax does not interfere with the internal structure of the lexical elements that are integrated into syntactic structures (see Chomsky 2008: 138), we can see that there are interesting consequences for how one might read the line. Understood in this way, Jakobson's 'projection' suggests that, when the reader reads the line, those earlier translation choices that have been made in a paradigmatic sense (between 'dig' or 'shovel'), are potentially recoverable from the final syntactic combination in the line one reads. Indeed, such an understanding of Jakobson's term 'projects' is compatible with his insistence (according to Winner 1987: 266) that diachrony (past and future development) is always there in any synchronic (present and systematic) view of structure.

A similar view of persistence of earlier stages of language can also be found in Benjamin (cf. 2012: 77–8). Both Jakobson and Benjamin were writing at a time when the strict division between diachrony and synchrony, as proposed by Saussure in 1916 (see Saussure 1959), was a common view. But their views of the internal structure of language differ. Whereas Benjamin saw syntax as a barrier to understanding the word (Benjamin 2012: 81), Jakobson is arguing that the syntax should not stop us from having access to what was in the word, and what preceded the word in the choices from which it resulted. If we read, through Jakobson's eyes, Hamburger's line with 'dig' and 'breezes' and 'unconfined', we can see there are other choices at each point that might have been made. This process of considering what paradigmatic possibilities lie behind, and contained in, the line as read is, in fact, common in our understanding of style as choice (see Leech and Short 2007: 9–32), because style is assumed to result from optional aspects of language determined by choice, and not from those aspects determined by the grammar, such as the presence of a subject or the agreement of the verb. But it is particularly important in reading a translation to consider choice, because translation presents us with two possible comparisons: the comparison with what other translators chose, or might have chosen, or the translator in question might have chosen, on the one hand, and the comparison with what was chosen in the original language, on the other. Projection thus understood would suggest that the translator's choices carry those of the original text: there were original words behind the translator's words, which influenced their selection. This means that a line such as Felstiner's line quoted earlier can be read comparatively in two ways, which do not exclude one another but are mutually enhancing:

(i) 'shovel', 'air' and 'cramped' might be read in relation to 'dig', 'breezes' and 'unconfined', especially given that Hamburger's version had already been published when Felstiner wrote his. A contrast that emerges in the comparison is that Hamburger's interpretation suggests freedom. Lack of confinement is only possible outside, when working, even though one might be digging one's own grave. Felstiner's 'shovel a grave', by comparison, suggests moving earth that has already been set aside for a grave, and '(not) too cramped' suggests an ironical contrast to the living conditions in the barracks rather than freedom as such. Digging one's own grave, as noted by Fauconnier and Turner (2002: 131–4), is a potent blended image. Usually used metaphorically to suggest someone is making a mistake that will cause (metaphorical) death, the reality of the Holocaust was that people were forced to actually dig their own graves, and the only way to make sense of this is to imagine that, though alive, they were regarded by the perpetrators as already dead (see Lifton 1986: 47). 'Shovel a grave', in Felstiner's version, suggests also the pointless and repetitive work (one digs a grave or trench, but shovels earth or ashes) that camp inmates were required to carry out.

(ii) Felstiner's 'shovel', 'air' and 'cramped' can be read as retaining something of the original poet's choices: 'shovel' is etymologically related to '*schaufeln*' and both are related to '*schießen*' ('shoot'), to '*Schlinge*', a noose, and to '*schwingen*' ('swing'), which occurs thirteen lines later in the poem. The choice of 'shovel' rather than 'dig' could thus be seen to take the etymology of the German original into account. However, this sort of detailed reading is more likely to be undertaken by someone trained in linguistics or etymology, or with a particular knowledge of German; it is unlikely to be possible for the general reader. I shall return to this difference in the next section.

Such comparisons are, of course, by no means a new idea for the translation scholar; comparisons of a source text with several translations (Nida 1964) or with one translation (Toury 1980, 1995) have been part of translation studies for a very long time. However, my particular interest here is not in classifying the sort of changes that occur in order to discover trends or propose norms, as did Toury (1995; see also Chesterman 1993; Hermans 1991). Instead, I am concerned with a specific way of reading that sees the style of a translated text as the result of choices made by a translator, just as the style of any text results from choices made by its author. Toury, in fact, also said, as I have suggested here, that reading in this way does not demand the presence of the source text (Toury 1995: 35). My argument is that a comparative view of a translated poem is in essence available to any reader of translations, who is much more likely than is the reader of original poetry to be aware not only of patterns that are visible in the text but also of those suggested by the language of the text (as in the etymology of its lexical elements) and of the consequences of stylistic choices made by both original writer and translator. Celan said of poetry that 'the person who writes it is passed along with it' (Celan 1968: 144), and the way choices reflect both the etymological (that is, the historical) and the interlingual relationships of words is particularly foregrounded by translation. The general reader may have no interest in explaining such things, but this does not mean that general readers have no interest in knowing such explanations exist. Comparative reading in its most obvious sense is a practice carried out with a number of translations and, usually, a source text. But it has a less obvious, though equally important, sense: it is an attitude, available to any reader of translated poetry.

   The example of Celan's '*Todesfuge*' (1952: 37–9), 'Death Fugue', in translation suggests that statements such as that made by Young (1993: 549), quoted earlier, which have in any case long been rejected in this simplistic form by translation theorists (see e.g. Steiner 1992: 316; Gaddis Rose 1997: 9) and world literature theorists (see Damrosch 2003: 289), need to be given special re-consideration in the case of poetry, and that clichés such as 'verse "resists" translation', repeated by Langer (1995: 553) in his Holocaust anthology, are not helpful to the general readers at whom, presumably, such anthologies are aimed. In Holocaust poetry, with its deep concern for the way words are used, the need to see what translation has brought to the text seems especially pressing. This is perhaps the need of scholars rather than the general reader, but it is important that more nuanced thinking about translation becomes part of the general discourse, because then it will play a part in translators' introductions, in reviews and the words of wisdom that appear on the backs of books. I will return to this point in Chapter 4.

Celan wrote many times about the need to communicate and the place of poetry in such communication (e.g. Celan 1968: 133–48). Communication cannot only be with those who already know what is to be communicated. His own work as translator – even in the work camps in Romania in the years 1942–4, he translated Shakespeare, or at least kept his translation work with him (see Gellhaus 1997: 48–50) – suggests that he saw translation as an important activity, as do many reports of conversations with Celan about translation (see e.g. Daive 2009). For Celan, the poem itself partakes of the more obvious act of transference the translation embodies: a poem, for him, is always '*unterwegs*' (Celan 1968: 144), that is, on its way from one place to another (see also Fioretos 1994).

Benjamin, whose work greatly influenced Celan (see e.g. Felstiner 1995: 96), wrote of translation as that which arises from the translatability or the potential for afterlife in the original text (Benjamin 2012: 76). This potential is there in great literature, says Benjamin. Presumably this is not, or not merely, because of the notion that such literature tells some sort of universal truths, but because of the text's own truth: because the relationship between its language and what it says is clearly thought through and appropriate. It is that relationship which is both expressed and read in the style of the text, and this understanding of literary writing is the basis for stylistic approaches to translation (see Boase-Beier 2006), and especially for the cognitive poetic approach of this book. If poetry is seen, in the sense in which Celan saw it, as communication, then it is not surprising that it contains within it the possibility of translation, and that translation will be potentially enhancing, because a layer of further communication will have been added. A similar argument is made by Herman for the importance of embedding stories within other stories told by other narrators in helping enhance 'distributional reach' and thus adding to understanding, especially of events that happened in the past (Herman 2006: 360, 368). Seen in the present context, such a view suggests that the addition of a translator's work, including the translator's choices, stance, attitude and interpretation, and the implicit endorsement of the original text through translation, make the original poem more interesting, more understandable (because of the addition of another interpretation) and more likely to engage the reader's thought processes. Just as the process of translation itself needs to be seen not as the action of an individual but of many different agents, so, too, do the understanding, interpretation and reception of a translated text (see Jones 2011: 191–5). I shall return to this point in Chapter 4.

If a translated poem is an enhanced poem, in the sense that it bears the weight of the translator's added interpretation which increases the potential for engagement by and effects upon the reader, this is in part the case because of its blended nature. (See Section 1.5 for a discussion of blends.) As I explained in an earlier book (Boase-Beier 2011a: 67–72), a translation can usefully be represented as a blend: it takes the source text, with its author, as one input space, and the target-language text, with its author, as the other, and the resulting blend has elements of both. Crucially, though, it also has elements that are in neither; they result from the 'emergent structure' of the blend (Fauconnier and Turner 2002: 42–4). Seeing a translation as a blend helps us explain why, in the case of the poem discussed earlier, we are likely to say things such as 'I know Celan's "Death Fugue"' and also to say 'Felstiner's "Deathfugue" is different from Hamburger's'. That is, our understanding of Felstiner's poem is that it both is and is not Celan's poem. Felstiner, in fact, enhances the blended nature of his translation of this poem by gradually integrating words from the German original (especially 'Deutschland'). This is a strategy that has occasionally attracted censure (see e.g. Friedlander 1987), but it serves very clearly to signal both the linguistically hybrid nature of Celan's background and the blended nature of translation itself. Because blends always have additional emergent elements and are not just the sum of the two originating mental spaces, a poem like Felstiner's – and, one might argue, any translation – allows us to hear the German while reading the English, giving the reader an enhanced reading experience. Additional cognitive effects include connotations such as a sense of invasion and gradual displacement of our own language. In fact, Felstiner is not doing anything particularly unusual: in spite of Venuti's contention that translated texts tend not to show they are translated (Venuti 2008: 1–34), devices that signal the translated nature of the text are common: a recent English translation of a fictional account of the Łodz ghetto, for example, keeps many phrases in Yiddish and Polish (Death 2011). Such devices always lead to enhanced possibilities of engagement by the reader, and this is what reading a text as a translation means.

The reader's enhanced understanding of and engagement with the translated poem depend to a great extent upon trust: the reader must have trust in the translator's linguistic skills and also in his or her abilities as a reader of the original text. If either skill is lacking, or if the reader thinks one or the other is lacking, the blend will be lopsided: a good English poem that does not do justice to the original or a close rendering that is not poetic (indeed, this is Friedlander's complaint about Felstiner's 'Deathfugue'). Translators seek to enhance the likelihood of trust through the use of paratexts such as translators' prefaces, or footnotes, or accompanying articles and scholarly monographs in which they set out their approach, as in Felstiner's and Hamburger's many scholarly works about their translations, already mentioned. Hamburger, for example, no doubt influenced by the same debate that influenced Celan's writing, pointed out that he had been careful not to normalize the poetry, or rid it of ambiguity, because 'better no translation at all ... than one that makes a merely aesthetic game of the existential struggle' (Hamburger 2007: 421). By putting his cards on the table, Hamburger, with such statements, makes it easier for us to trust his sincerity, whether or not we agree with the implications of 'a merely aesthetic game'.

Part of what is involved in trusting the translator is trusting that the emotional effects of the translated text on the reader are not completely different in kind from those of the original text. The reader wants to be decentred, to feel identification with the narrator or characters in the poem: the 'empathetic understanding of others' emotions' (Oatley 2011: 115). These effects, in the case of Holocaust poetry, often depend upon the fact that we read the poems as expressing the direct experiences of the person speaking, who is often, in this poetry, equated with the poet, as I explained in Section 1.2 (see also Stockwell 2002: 42). This is what Celan meant by saying, as quoted earlier, that the poet gets passed on with the poem. It is often intensely personal poetry. In order to respond with empathy, the reader needs to feel that the translator is 'performing the identity of the poet' (Jones 2011: 196). When the reader is willing to trust the translator, translated poetry can be a powerful tool for experiencing the voice of the poet, especially important if he or she died in the Holocaust, as in the case of Radnóti, or Meerbaum-Eisinger, or Gertrud Kolmar, the German-Jewish poet assumed to have been killed in Auschwitz (see Smith 1975). In most such cases, there are no recordings of the voice of the poet.

However, a performance always adds an interpretation and a new voice (cf. Schiavi 1996) and I would argue, as did Benjamin, that it is this that ensures the potential afterlife of the text can be realized: it is the 'transformation and renewal' (Benjamin 2012: 77) of the original text. The changes themselves, as they appear in the translated text, are not, however, Benjamin's primary concern, just as he is not primarily concerned with the reader (Benjamin 2012: 75). Benjamin does not say that the reader is unimportant, but only that the poem is not shaped (which for Benjamin meant created) by the concern for particular readers. This view is in line with Benjamin's well-attested interest in the Kabbalah (see e.g. Alter 1991), a tradition of Jewish mystical thought concerned with how religious knowledge or a sacred text is *received* ('*kbl*' is the Hebrew verb meaning 'to receive', cf. Dan 2007: 3), and how it is reshaped by the receiver. That reshaping is essential because 'the holiness of the texts lies precisely in their capacity for such metamorphosis' (Scholem 1996: 11–12). For Celan, the reader was particularly important: writing poetry was, he said, like shaking someone's hand (Celan 1983: 177); it was a communication with and passing on of thoughts to another person (see Olschner 1985: 57–9), but it always carried the risk of contamination, or misinterpretation, a risk of which Celan was acutely aware: 'whose hand did I shake // when I went with // your words to // Germany?' he asks his dead mother in '*Wolfsbohne*' (Felstiner 2001: 383). The reader's interpretation is central to this view of poetry, as it is to cognitive poetics and cognitive approaches to culture (cf. Sperber 1996: 16–17). In this view, the survival of texts through their translation depends not, or not only, on some intrinsic quality, some spirit, as Pope called it (Lefevère 1992: 64f.) that gets passed on from original to translation, but on its reception and the perception that it is similar to the original (cf. Pym 2010: 165). This is a view that goes well beyond that of Benjamin or of the more recent translator and theorist Scott. Though critical of Benjamin's insistence on the derivative nature of translation with respect to the source text (see Scott 2000: 76–9), Scott argues that the way round it is to relocate the source text in its literal translation and work creatively with this. His main concern is to explore the '*projective* collaboration' (Scott 2000: 82; Scott's italics) of target and source texts, because both share creative status, not the similar parallel status of the translator and the reader. But there is no reason, in my view, why a reader of the target text should not be enabled to experience some of what the translator experienced, even without the translator's bilingual background, by being attuned to the fact that it was preceded by another text, from which it differs. Considering such differences, by focusing attention on the translation process behind the text, leads the reader to adopt a multilingual mind-style (cf. also Scott 2012: 11). We see an example in poems translated from Yiddish into German. By their very existence, they remind the reader that Yiddish was almost destroyed by the Nazis. For a German reader, the closeness of Yiddish, which, according to one view, developed from a fusion of Jewish Aramaic with Medieval German as spoken in Bavaria (see Katz 2004: 24–46), to Modern German, enables the original to be read in a bilingual presentation with transliteration such as Ajchenrand's *Aus der Tiefe* (Witt 2006), 'From the Depths'.

The first (untitled) poem (Witt 2006: 5) is just five lines long; like all the poems in this book, it is presented first in Ajchenrand's Yiddish, written in its Hebrew script, then in the Yiddish transliterated into Roman script, and then in Hubert Witt's German. The final two lines of this short poem read, first in Yiddish, then in German, and then in my English:

sol sej onchapn a grojl
far sich alejn.

Soll es ihnen vor sich selber
Grauen.

they'll recoil in horror
at what they are.

The German reader, who is the most likely reader of the Yiddish-German book, would have little sense of how German related to Yiddish if the poem were only given in Hebrew script and in German, because the Hebrew script would not be accessible to most German readers, given that most of those who spoke Yiddish were killed. By providing a transliteration as in the first version above, the German reader is able to reconstruct the Yiddish: '*sol*' must be '*soll*' ('should', 'will'), '*a grojl*' is probably '*ein Greuel*' ('horror'), and so on. Such an experience of reading engages the reader in many ways. It demonstrates how easy it would be to read Yiddish if one were to learn Hebrew script, it dispels the stereotypical belief that Yiddish is an incomprehensible secret language, and it also leads the reader to consider exactly what Witt has done with the original.

A similar emphasis on reading the translation as a translation, rather than merely an impoverished version of the original, will be achieved by translations into German of English poems by Holocaust survivors or their family members, such as the translations of Wind's poetry by Gabriel (Gabriel 2004). Translations into German, like the original poems of German-speaking Jewish poets such as Celan, or Sachs, or Ausländer, also go some way towards suggesting a possible reclaiming, for these poets and translators at least, of a mother tongue that had been so misused (cf. Felman 1992a: 28), that had, as Celan put it, gone through the 'thousand darknesses of death-bringing speech' (Celan 1968: 128). It is important in such cases that the readers are German and that they are enabled to read the translation in full awareness that it is a translation.

We saw in Chapter 1 that a focus on reading and the reader was emphasized by Iser, one of the proponents of what became known as reader theory or reception theory (the latter a misleading term in English as we tend to think of reception as criticism and review rather than, as in French or German literary theory, the process of reading). See Iser (1974); Jauss (1982), or Tompkins (1980) for examples of reader-orientated theories. The focus on the reader is something these theories share with stylistics, and especially with cognitive poetics. According to Iser, focusing on the reader allows the scholar to take into account the nature of a text as 'open-ended', as a 'cascade of possibilities' (Iser 2004: 14). Meaning in poetry is not fixed (cf. Attridge 2004: 79–93) because it is in the nature of poetry to evoke different reactions and give rise to different feelings in its reader. The meaning is not to be found on the page alone, but in what happens in the mind of the reader. When Wilfred Owen, speaking of his First World War poems, said 'the poetry is in the pity' (Owen 1990: 192), what he meant was that poetry is what happens in the mind, not what is said on the page. If we take empathy to involve both feeling what someone else feels and responding with an appropriate emotion (as Baron-Cohen 2011: 11), then an empathetic translator will have experienced his or her own emotions, not just those he or she identifies as being expressed in the poem. Consider, for example, Hamburger's translation of Celan's '*Wolfsbohne*' ('Wolf's-Bean'; Hamburger 2007: 398–403), a poem discussed briefly in Chapter 1. The second stanza in Hamburger's translation begins thus:

> (Far away, in Michailovka, in
> the Ukraine, where
> they murdered my father and mother

The original version, presented alongside, is as follows:

(Weit,	in	Michailowka,	in			
far	in	Michailovka	in			
der	Ukraine,	wo				
the	Ukraine	where				
sie	mir	Vater	und	Mutter	erschlugen	
they	to-me	father	and	mother	beat-to-death	

Celan's phrase '*wo sie mir Vater und Mutter erschlugen*' is glossed here as: 'where they to-me father and mother beat-to-death', but '*erschlagen*' is often used more generically, simply to mean 'murdered'. '*Vater und Mutter*' is, in fact, grammatically ambiguous. It has no article or possessive, so it could be simply an idiomatic expression suggesting possession, similar to such uses in English: 'I emigrated with husband, child and library to Australia'. Alternatively, the lack of determiners could suggest what someone (especially a child) actually calls his or her parents when speaking to them and when speaking colloquially about them: 'they murdered Father and Mother'. Such usage is not very common in adults unless they are speaking to someone they know well, so its effect is striking here. Because the absence of determiners indicates both these uses, they become blended for the reader of the original: the phrase both sounds childlike and carries the sense of possession. Hamburger's translation has opted for the clear expression of possession, presumably to capture the German '*mir*', which indicates that the speaker feels to be the recipient of the action. This usage is possible, though rare, in English: it occurs, for example, in Arthur Hamilton's song 'Cry Me a River'. In the case of the line in Celan's poem, though, it is difficult to translate: 'They killed me my father and mother' sounds colloquial to the point of being flippant.

Hamburger's translation is not merely a question of linguistic possibilities. As an engaged translator, and one who knew and championed Celan, it also carries evidence of his own emotional response to the childlike expression of grief in the original. And his response is to create a little more distance. The voice in Hamburger's poem has become a little more adult and considered. Readers of Hamburger's poem, in turn, have their own emotional responses. Because they are less likely to hear the voice of a child, feelings such as protectiveness are less likely.

It is worth recalling here what Tsur (2008: 100) has said about emotions in poetry: a sad poem is not necessarily one that makes you feel sad. Owen's war poetry does not *express* pity; it evokes it in the reader, and this evocation is the poetry, according to Owen. Similarly, whatever emotions the reader of Hamburger's translation will feel are not necessarily those expressed in the poem. But those Hamburger felt are also, by the same token, not those expressed in the original poem. While we will trust Hamburger not to make us feel amused, or bored, or irritated, or to experience any other inappropriate response, we should not expect him to make us feel as we would if we read Celan's original.

The important thing, then, here, in reading a translated poem, is that the reader is able to engage with the poem and to experience appropriate emotions; it is only through experiencing such emotions that there will be any change to the reader's cognitive structures. And these will also vary according to the reader's background and circumstances. A reader reading Hamburger's translation might, for example, be particularly struck by the fairly unemotional tone and be moved to consider what situations might be hidden behind other such unemotional expressions of the effects of murder.

If the reader reads a different translation, his or her responses may be different. I would probably translate the lines from '*Wolfsbohne*' thus:

(Far away, in Michailovka, in
Ukraine, where
they murdered Father and Mother.

There are several differences, but the omission of the possessive and the use of capital letters for 'Father and Mother', because it suggests a more childlike speech, might, for example, cause the reader to reflect on the effects of trauma, and how they make traumatized people constantly re-live the circumstances in which they found themselves at the time the traumatic event occurred (Caruth 1995: 4).

Other poems may give rise to feelings of nostalgia or premonition, which are more likely to be experienced when the translated poem is interpreted, perhaps momentarily, to fit the reader's own background cognitive context, so that he or she can identify with the speaker; such might be the case with Ausländer's poem '*Bukowina I*', discussed in Section 1.5. Empathy involves readers imagining themselves in the impossible position of being both themselves and the narrator or figure in the poem; this is a counterfactual blend. But many of the emotions expressed in the poem or experienced by the reader are in themselves conceptual blends (cf. Fauconnier and Turner 2002: 27–8). Grief is a blend of knowledge of what once was with knowledge of what now is, as is a sense of loss. Horror arises in cases like András Mezei's poem 'Gustav!' (Ország-Land 2010: 39), discussed in Section 1.3, because of the blend of the everyday world of the reader (one spots a neighbour in a group of strangers, usually a welcome sight) with the extreme situation of the Holocaust (the neighbour is part of an execution squad and the speaker of the final words is the man about to be executed). Many of the feelings embodied in Holocaust poems are blended feelings. The danger of blends is that they can disintegrate: when we cannot fully integrate the once alive mother with the dead person she now is, we continue to address her, hopelessly, as Celan does in '*Wolfsbohne*' and many other poems. When we cannot integrate different stages in our development, we experience a disintegration of personality. Many of Celan's poems suggest that such states of disintegration can momentarily be overcome by acceptance: 'and who I am forgives the one I once was', as he says in '*Totenhemd*' (Celan 1968: 51). To forgive oneself as one was earlier is to achieve integration, whereas to retain feelings of guilt is to remain fragmented. I shall return to this question in Chapter 4.

Richards, writing in 1924 (see Richards 1960: 82–6), argued, in a foreshadowing of current cognitive poetic understanding of literature, that the emotions and cognitive changes that reading a text gives rise to in the reader persist beyond the act of reading itself (cf. West 2013: 15). According to Richards (1960: 82–6), such emotions can lead to later action (see also Baron-Cohen 2011: 12). If the emotions are not felt by the reader of the translation, there is no possibility either of a change in cognitive models or of any other sort of action, because the poem will probably be forgotten. But the emotions the reader feels will be affected by the knowledge that the text is a translation. Consider the following example, the final stanza of Richard Dove's 'On Abstraction' (Dove 2010: 115), his translation of Steinherr's poem '*Von der Abstraktion*':

in one heap
the gold wrenched out
of their teeth

This is also a bilingual collection; the original (Dove 2010: 114) is as follows:

auf	einen	Haufen
on-to	one	heap

das	Zahngold
the	tooth-gold

The poem is a series of six short stanzas that begins with a discussion of 'neat-and-tidy' abstractions, such as women to the left and men to the right, and culminates in the above lines, which follow images, in stanzas 3, 4 and 5, of other heaps: of coats, of shoes, of glasses. The Holocaust context is unmistakable, but, in fact, the poem is likely to be read not only in reference to the Holocaust. The earlier phrase 'on the left women // on the right men' makes the reader transfer some of the horror that is felt at the heaps of shoes and glasses to the sort of 'neat-and-tidy' thinking that divides women and men into their stereotypical groups, especially given what we now know about the views the Nazis held of what men and women should be like, and what they did to those who did not conform. But being aware that one is reading this poem as a *translation* leads the reader not just to see the violence of 'the gold wrenched out // of their teeth' but also to look for that violence in the original. The original poem simply has 'tooth-gold' ('*Zahngold*'). The difference, obvious even to the reader without knowledge of German, leads one to speculate about German: if there is tooth-gold, are there other sorts of gold? That is, is tooth-gold gold destined for teeth, in one of the 'neat-and-tidy' terms that German allows, and that the poem highlights? Or is the view that Germans favour such neat-and-tidy categories because their language allows them itself a prejudice? Especially if this poem is read in conjunction with Howard and Plebanek's translation of Tadeusz Różewicz's '*Złoto*' ('Gold'), also presented bilingually (Howard and Plebanek 2001: 32–47), with its '*złote cegły, złote sztaby, złote sztabki, złote monety … złote zęby*' ('gold bricks, gold bullion, gold bars, gold coins … gold teeth'), the difference between '*złote zęby*', 'gold teeth', and '*Zahngold*', 'tooth-gold' becomes clearer. Tooth-gold is a dental material and was never intended to be used for anything else, and yet it later became the gold coins about which Różewicz writes. Perhaps the German compound, by conjoining 'tooth' and 'gold' so closely, is an instance of iconicity (see Section 1.4): the gold should be an inalienable part of the tooth. Here the horror the reader might feel at 'gold wrenched out of their teeth' leads to a consideration of misuse: teeth become coins, humans become part of machinery, healing becomes killing (Lifton 1986: 14–18). An understanding that this is a translation, and has a relationship to its original text, thus allows for further cognitive effects.

Reading translated Holocaust poetry depends, then, on an awareness that it is translated and on having sufficient trust in the translator to be able to feel that one's emotional responses are appropriate (cf. Myers 1999: 269). The fact that a translator whose work one knows has chosen to translate particular poetry is also likely to inspire trust in that poetry itself, in the same way that we trust reported accounts when we trust the reporter. Gutt (2000: 105–7) noted that translation was like reported speech, it is 'saying what someone else said', or at least, what the sayer thought the other person meant (see Boase-Beier 2004), and, of course, we must trust the sayer to judge what was meant.

Beyond the trust we place in the translator, which can be enhanced by knowledge of the translator's other works and an understanding of their approach, as set out in prefaces or notes, media interviews and so on, an empathetic response to the translated Holocaust poem is more likely where the reader has some understanding of the historical context. One factor that can help the reader identify with the speaker or characters is a realization of the extent to which the survival or destruction of particular human beings, of particular poets and of particular works was a matter of accident (see also Felman 1992a: 25). Any reader can sense how easy it would have been to have become a victim oneself; this, in turn, depends on a highly developed sense of 'if I were you', a sense completely lacking in Nazi perpetrators and many bystanders. Reading poetry depends on projection and identification, on being decentred, and poets have ways of making it easier for the reader to identify: think of Celan's '*Du*', the 'you' he constantly addresses, or von Törne's use of common idioms to make one feel one is having a conversation. Such devices allow the reader to construct what in text-world theory (see e.g. Gavins 2007) is considered to be a counterpart – in both these cases the addressee – in the world of the poem, and the construction of such a counterpart, like an avatar in a digital virtual world, allows the reader to experience genuine emotions (cf. Stockwell 2009: 134–67). We can fall in love with a character in a film, or believe ourselves transformed or feel, momentarily, the grief of a poem's speaker.

If we read a poem as a translation, there is always the danger that particular elements of the discourse world, that is, the 'situation that surrounds human beings as they communicate' (Gavins 2007: 9) will be foregrounded to such an extent that they will make it more difficult for the reader to construct a text world, a mental representation or model of what is happening in the poem (cf. Gavins 2007: 10). This is, of course, not merely a problem for translated texts; it can be a consequence of the language of a text drawing attention to itself to such an extent that projection or the sense of being in the world of the text rather than the world of discourse (cf. Gavins 2007: 40) is hampered. This might be why many publishers, and even translators, feel the urge not to focus on the additional discourse layer that comes with translation. The resulting attempt to play down this additional discourse layer is, therefore, not 'weird' (Venuti 2008: 7) but understandable, if misguided. It is misguided because there is no real reason why the reader should not be able to process an added layer of discourse.

Background knowledge is crucial to identification and projection into the world of the poem, which are likely to fail if the world described is too bizarre, or distant or simply incomprehensible. It is almost certainly the case that, because of the vast number of studies, literary works, memoirs, films and reports that have appeared in recent years (cf. Gregor 2005: 1–2), most English readers know something about the Holocaust; they will have a schema (or several schemata) associated with it. This means that the background context necessary for empathetic reading is already given. However, it cannot be expected that the reader will know further details, for example that Ausländer lived in the ghetto in Czernowitz or that the Sachs family were important in the business world of Berlin, having invented the elastic exercise expander (Fritsch-Vivié 1993: 20). In fact, not only could it be argued that knowledge is a prerequisite for engagement, but also that part of the engagement poetry demands of and enables in its reader is the wish to increase knowledge. Kuiken calls this being responsive to the 'unsayable "more" that is implicit in the felt sense of a situation' (Kuiken 2008: 53; see also Iser 2004: 13–15; and cf. Levinas 1990: 181).

We can see how this works if we consider the reading of a translation of Celan's poem '*Espenbaum*' (Celan 1952: 15), briefly mentioned in Chapter 1. The first two lines are as follows (cf. Boase-Beier 2011b: 169):

Aspen tree, your leaves glance white into darkness.
My mother's hair did not turn white.

On reading these lines, the reader will understand several things. The mother of whom the poet speaks must have died; in fact, the poem later makes it clear that she was shot. The fact that the mother's hair did not 'turn white' suggests that she was not particularly old and it also implies that, had she had time to respond to the shock of what was happening to her, it would have turned white. The aspen tree in the first line has connotations, in English, of trembling and thus of fear, and this might lead the reader to find out whether the same connotations exist in the original language, German. The fact that the two lines suggest a common conceptual metaphor PEOPLE ARE PLANTS makes it highly likely that particular plants will be associated with particular (though possibly different) characteristics in both languages. In the third line of the poem, there is a reference to Ukraine, and this might lead the reader to explore both the current geographical location of Ukraine and its borders at the time of writing (the 1940s). The mention of a well later in the poem sounds like a symbol or a reference to a myth, so the reader might follow up the reference (and find the story in Genesis 10 of Rachel weeping at the well (*New King James Bible* 1982: 4), or other references to Rachel in Jewish religious tradition (cf. Cort 2011: 67–9). Furthermore, the form of the poem, as preserved in the translation, may remind the reader of the sort of comparisons familiar to many from the study of literature and known as pathetic fallacy (after Ruskin 1863: 16), where nature appears to echo human concerns. Researching pathetic fallacy and similar figures will lead one to a tradition of folk poem and song in many languages and cultures (such as, for example, the Romanian lament called *doină,* which almost certainly influenced this poem; see also Jakobson 1960: 370).

Reading Ausländer's poem '*Bukowina I*' (Ausländer 2012: 13), discussed in Section 1.5, might cause the reader more difficulty. Because an English reader is unlikely to know either the Bukovina of the title, or the town of Czernowitz, mentioned later in the poem, it is not easy to relate to the situation described, though its sinister hints ('The ravens cry') are, as explained earlier, comprehensible in many different cultures. Because of the importance of background to the possibility of entering the text world, it is worth considering the way translated poems such as this are presented; I shall return to this in Chapter 4.

One of the most important aspects of reading poetry, then, is that it engages the reader sufficiently to give rise to cognitive effects of various types: it causes the reader to experience emotions, it prompts rethinking and it triggers the need to find out more.

New insight or knowledge (which Cook described as 'schema-refreshing', 1994: 192) may tell us, for example, that unconsidered phrases and expressions, and the corresponding abdication of real thought, are dangerous. Such emptiness of language, in which expressions used to describe the Nazis' intentions were called '*Sprachregelung*', that is, the application of language rules, was noted especially by Arendt when she wrote about the Eichmann trial (Arendt 2006: 85). Words such as killing were avoided and 'special treatment' used instead, deportation was 'resettlement' and so on (cf. Lifton 1986: 445–6). Of course, for the perpetrator, such phrases were far from empty: they were used as a code, and the meanings were clear. They were also used with deliberately malicious intent and often with gleeful irony, as in the phrases '*Arbeit macht frei*' or '*Jedem das Seine*' – 'Work brings freedom' and 'To each his own' – written over or on the gates of concentration camps. But it was all too easy for bystanders to take up such phrases without thinking, or as a way of refusing to think. Probably the most common such phrase was the often-recorded statement by those on the periphery of the atrocities that they had 'known nothing about it' (Fulbrook 2012: 9, 27, 349). But all areas of German society were pervaded by empty phrases. Whittock records how youth camps had to daily repeat such things as 'Hitler is Germany and Germany is Hitler' (Whittock 2011: 143). Such phrases are given in what sounds like direct speech (or thought) in von Törne's poems: phrases like 'The Jews are our misfortune' ('*Die Juden sind unser Unglück*'; von Törne 1981: 163), a saying attributed to historian von Treitschke (Lifton 1986: 35), or 'Didn't know' ('*Nichts gewußt*'; von Törne 1981: 56) or 'Then we'll speak plain German' ('*Dann wird deutsch gesprochen*'; von Törne 1981: 189). Many of von Törne's poems explore the danger of such unthinkingly repeated phrases. In 'Drinking Song' ('*Trinkspruch*'; von Törne 1981: 31), he ironically explains the Holocaust as the result of Hitler's teetotalism. Although this is not an explanation usually offered, other equally facile explanations were common (Hitler was simply mad and no one could influence him; Hitler kept everything a secret; Hitler didn't know about the 'final solution'). It is these that von Törne's poem satirizes. Set phrases are dangerous because they indicate set thinking; they allow one to avoid real thinking. They also allow perpetrators to put people into groups, categorize them and dehumanize them. Anyone could be labelled as part of a group by the Nazis if they were perceived as posing a threat. If one were mentally or physically ill, or just appeared to be so, one would be labelled 'life unworthy of life' (Binding and Hoche 1920); if one were politically left-wing or religious, one would be seen as an enemy of the state (cf. Evans 2005: 80).

Many of these phrases, such as 'life unworthy of life', have become known in their English translations through historical writing (e.g. Lifton 1986 and Burleigh 2002 in this case). Even those that are not known in English tend to be recognizable in translated poetry by similar equivalents: to 'speak plain German' is, in fact, a translation of the original rather than a substitution of a supposed equivalent ('to speak in plain English') but the presence of 'plain' is enough to make its status as an idiom clear so that von Törne's ironical intent can be appreciated by the English reader. Von Törne's poetry is thus on one level a subversion of the empty speech representing empty thoughts documented by Arendt (2006: 85) and also, by its incorporation into poetry, it demands the reader's engagement. Von Törne's concerns are born out of the necessity for what Stonebridge calls 're-imagining the relation between language and thought' (Stonebridge 2011: 59), as Arendt saw at Eichmann's trial, but it is a re-imagining that in von Törne's poetry has yet to be learned nearly twenty years later. To date there is no published translation of von Törne's poetry, though one is to appear in 2016; see Boase-Beier and Vivis (forthcoming). Reading these poems in translation seventy years after the end of the Second World War and more than fifty years after Eichmann's trial and the Frankfurt Auschwitz trial (see Pendas 2006), the English reader will lack some of the background that was still present for von Törne as he wrote the poems, in an era when the statute of limitations for Nazi murders, which had been extended to 1979, formed the basis for important discussions leading to the exemption of genocide from such limitations altogether (see von Kellenbach 2013: 119). Much of the reader's engagement and the resulting cognitive effects on the reader will thus come about through stylistic indicators of idioms in generalizing phrases such as 'the Jews', 'we Germans', through obvious references to the Holocaust and the War in proper names such as 'Hitler', 'Leningrad', 'Göring', through references to German and the international consumer culture of the late 1970s, in most cases recognizable even today: 'Doktor Oetker', 'McDonald', 'Wienerwald'. Above all, signals for direct speech such as italics or using a separate line or exclamation mark, can help the reader see when phrases common in the 1970s are being criticized.

As we have seen, Holocaust poets avoided the possible barbarity of poetry after Auschwitz that Adorno warned against (Adorno 2003: 30), by eschewing straightforward lyricism and using the various stylistic means of distorted, fragmented syntax, gaps, silences and ambiguities already noted. Their translators, aware of this, were then careful not to create such lyricism in their translations, as Felstiner (1995) or Hamburger (2007: 23–40) explain. Von Törne takes a different route, using words and phrases that are indeed barbaric, but embedding them in poems to give an ironical distance, and translations will carry this irony if the stylistic distinctions are clear to the reader.

Poetry such as von Törne's, read in translation, thus challenges the reader to see the state of mind, reflected in the mind-style of the poem, that is able to accept such easy categorizations and set phrases without question, and in doing so to question it. Von Törne, who felt that he had taken on the sins of his forebears ('And mine was the guilt… ', von Törne 1981: 68), used poetry to issue such challenges. The very fact that the empty phrases have been translated into English serves to suggest to the reader the ease with which language can be made to express such unthinkingness and undifferentiated characterizations.

Poetry of guilt such as von Törne's is particularly important in translation because, though the guilt of survivors is well documented (see e.g. Felman 1992b: 196), the guilt of the children of those who might have been involved in atrocity and who almost certainly were complicit in crime is the driving force behind so much modern German policy (Ferrar 2012: 241–54). Hoffman (2004: 118) discusses the need to sympathize with the guilt and the deprivations of the children of perpetrators. Von Törne's poems, and their translations for readers unlikely to be in this position, make it possible not just to understand this need in an abstract sense, but also to feel it.

Another thing we might learn from reading Holocaust poetry in English translation is the importance of responsibility. In one sense, responsibility is a natural consequence of having seen the emptiness of thought portrayed by von Törne. If we cannot change what happened, we still have a responsibility to the rest of society for the future (cf. Sacks 2005: 113–29). Ambiguity and gaps in the poems often force the reader to make choices in interpreting and, thus, such stylistic devices mirror the need to make other choices, including moral ones, and their cognitive effects might be the consideration of what choices we would make ourselves. Even years later and in another language, the process of interpretation will still demand responsibility on the reader's part, even if the context has changed. For example, the need for the reader of von Törne's 'While Reading the Paper' to decide who actually believes that the murderers did not know what was happening, discussed in Section 1.5, not only calls for responsibility in terms of assigning the expressed opinion to the newspaper, the murderers, or the reader (within the poem) but also, because such assignment might be impossible, leads the reader to reflect on issues such as collective guilt and moral responsibility, issues that are important beyond the immediate context of the poem that is suggested by the reference to the 'yellow patches' the speaker's sister sewed on her dolls' clothes.

Both these insights, or cognitive effects, in the reader arise because engagement is required: in seeing the irony in the use of fixed phrases or in interpreting ambiguity. In both cases, the interpretative procedures needed to draw attention to the language itself and its potential for manipulation, or uncertainty, or distortion. Thus one could argue that the proper response to Adorno's concern about the barbarity of poetry after Auschwitz is poetry that encourages the reader into what Attridge has called 'creative reading' (Attridge 2004: 79–83, 2011: 2), that is, reading with responsibility. Creative reading is possible for any reader, and there are ways of encouraging it; I shall consider some of these in Chapter 4.

Such engagement is possible with the translated text whenever it avoids an exclusive focus on semantic content that ignores or demotes to the background the style of the text and the translation process it has undergone. But the translator needs to know how to avoid doing this; this will be taken up in Chapter 3.

Those who read translated poetry, whatever their understanding or knowledge of translation, will have certain expectations, though some (such as the common notion that the translation is a transparent reflection of the original; cf. Venuti 2008: 1–13) will be misguided. Their reasons for reading it are likely to be similar to the reason Schiff gives in the 'Introduction' to her anthology: to come 'as close as one can to entering psychologically into those unique events as they were actually felt by those individuals who experienced them' (Schiff 1995: xiv). Not facts, then, but feelings and a sense of psychological closeness to sufferers, are the main reasons for reading Holocaust poetry in translation. Reading it in awareness of its translated status, in what Venuti (2008: 20–1) calls a 'symptomatic reading', enhances this sense of closeness. This is because reading in this way focuses on the language, the differences between target and source language and culture, and above all is conscious of the role and intervention of the translator, rather than assuming some sort of 'semantic unity … intelligibility, transparent communication' (Venuti 2008: 21).

2.2 Translated poetry and analytical reading

I suggested in the previous section that reading Holocaust poetry in full awareness of the fact that it is translated could be expected to involve, at the very least, some sense of the task undertaken by the translator and the effects that has had, or might have had, on the poem in question, a sense of trust in the translator's ability and integrity, and a self-aware empathetic engagement with the poems. This could be expected to apply even to the general reader who reads in order to experience the poetry rather than to imaginatively reconstruct the translation process. Philosopher Mary Midgley has noted a similarly enhanced understanding of philosophy when reading translated texts (Midgley 2014: 48).

But Holocaust poetry is not only read by general poetry readers, that is, those who are used to reading poetry and who are attracted to the idea of translated Holocaust poetry because they have read some Holocaust poetry before, or because they have an interest in the Holocaust or because they know the name of the original poet or the translator. It is also read by scholars, who will inevitably have a different background and approach to reading. And it is also, of course, read by those who will themselves go on to translate such poetry, a point to be taken up in Chapter 3. Even within these three broad categories – the general reader, the scholarly reader and the translator – there will be different types of reading. Stockwell makes a clear distinction (which may indicate different modes of reading rather than different readers) between the 'natural everyday activity of reading and the scholarly and scientific activity of analysis' (Stockwell 2013: 264; see also Hall 2009), whereby the latter activity can illuminate effects that cannot necessarily be explained during the first type of reading but are nevertheless felt. I will refer to this second type of reading as 'analytical reading', irrespective of who the reader is.

Studying translation makes differences in these two types of reading very clear. Translators are, of course, readers and we would not expect them to be the former type of 'natural everyday' readers. Yet the fact that translation scholars or even translators themselves read with a greater awareness of translation is denied by Venuti; he argues that such 'elite readers, whether scholars or reviewers, writers or translators' in fact 'rarely, if at all' (Venuti 2008: 124) read translations as translations. Though this is true to some extent, Venuti possibly overstates his case; such pessimism is not borne out by statements such as this one by poet and translator Ciaran Carson: 'some of us expect translations to sound like translations' (2004: xix). By 'some of us' he means the translator, but he must feel confident that the same applies to his reader.

Scott (2012: 1), in insisting that 'translation should preoccupy itself with readers *familiar* with the source language' (his italics), is making a somewhat different point: a translation is not a substitute text for the reader ignorant of the source language, who consequently only has access to the translation. While, as I have argued in the previous section, reading a translated text as translation always involves thinking about its relation to its source, it is clearly not the case that most (if any) readers of Holocaust poetry will be familiar with all of the source languages. If such familiarity were a prerequisite, reading Holocaust poetry in anthologies that include work by German, Polish, Norwegian and Japanese poets would make little sense. Reading Holocaust poetry not only as translation, but also as Holocaust poetry, is bound to shift the focus somewhat from a reading undertaken solely to find out more about the original poetry. Of course, reading a translation of a fairly accessible and well-known poet like Celan together with its original in one of the many bilingual works such as Hamburger (2007) or Felstiner (2001) will tell us much that is interesting about the original poems, as I hope to demonstrate in this section, but the translation will also (if translation is essentially a communicative undertaking, as it is in my view, though not in Scott's) need to be concerned with its reader so as to be not only a commentary on Celan's (or another poet's) work, but also a way of making the poetry available to those with no knowledge of German. This is, of course, a less important consideration in the case of a poet like Celan who has been so much translated than in the case of, say, a Yiddish poet such as Abraham Sutzkever (e.g. Mayne 1981). And a poet like Szlengel (see Aaron 1990: 20–7), who died in the Warsaw ghetto, will most likely be read in translation by those who want to understand what it meant to write poetry in a ghetto, and to experience 'a spectrum of the stages of a poet's consciousness in its relation to those events' (Aaron 1990: 21) rather than by those who want to better understand Szlengel's original Polish poetry. Again, this does not mean that by reading his work in translation they will *not* learn and understand more about the originals, because those very issues of writing while catastrophic history unfolds themselves inform the poetics of the work. Nevertheless, it seems unlikely that most of Szlengel's readers in English translation would also be readers of Polish. However, general readers, ignorant of the source language and of the discussions surrounding translation, can be encouraged to consider both the source language itself and what it means to read translated poetry as translation, and I shall return to ways in which such encouragement can be given in Chapter 4.

At this point we need to recall the discussion in Section 2.1 about the consequences of Jakobson's view that poetic language projects the principle of equivalence from the axis of selection to the axis of combination: in reading a poetic translation, we are aware that the lexical elements are the result of choices and that other choices could have been made by the translator, and, indeed, have been made by other translators. But there are further consequences to consider now. Besides possible equivalences of register, we can assume that repetition, defined by Jakobson's student Kiparsky as 'recurrence of equivalent linguistic elements' (Kiparsky 1973: 233), and including all manner of sound similarities, is what Jakobson meant by equivalence at the syntactic level. Thus, for example, a verb may alliterate with its object or rhyme with its subject. But if 'projection' is seen as that which carries over information from an earlier to a later stage, then we could potentially, as analytical readers, also try to reconstruct the translation processes that have produced these elements of repetition.

Consider the following lines from Celan's '*Stumme Herbstgerüche*' (Celan 1980: 24; 'Speechless Smells of Autumn'):

		Die
		the
Sternblume,	ungeknickt,	ging
star-flower	un-bent	went

If the translator has translated '*Sternblume*' with 'aster', as Felstiner does (2001: 153), this choice at the lexical level will have influenced the choice at the syntactic level of the following verb. Felstiner has

The
aster, unbent, passed

and it is likely that the assonance with 'aster' determined the choice of 'passed' for the original '*ging*'. I translate this line as:

The
starflower, unbent, went

where the choice of 'went' rather than 'passed' is determined in part by the preceding adjective. This is an apparently simple example: of course, in reading the English poem analytically we see the assonance and, therefore, trace back word choice (in our reconstruction) not merely along the lexical paradigm but also in interaction with the syntagm. The example is interesting, however, in the light of Benjamin's view that the syntagmatic relationships in a sentence form a wall blocking access to what is central in language, and that the latter lies within the word (Benjamin 2012: 81). By seeing what drove the choice of the word as projected onto the sentence, Jakobson (1960: 358) effectively shows how, in poetry, the word, with all its backward connections to the mind (cf. Benjamin 1992b: 33) breaks through the barrier of the sentence. Or, to put it from the analytical reader's perspective, the combinatory choices (of 'bent' – 'went' or 'aster' – 'passed') allow us to follow back the traces of choice in the words themselves: 'aster' not only combines with 'passed' but also has a history of its own selection in distinction from 'starflower', 'marguerite' (Hamburger's translation; 2007: 192) and so on.

In analytically reading this translated poem, then, we need to be aware that equivalence is not only equivalence on the phonological level of words in the assonance that we see in the syntactic and poetic line before us but also on the lexical level of those words not chosen. The interaction between phonology, lexis, syntax and the poetic line highlights the essence of poetry. Indeed, Jakobson said, twenty years after his statement on projection, that it was in fact a tautology, because the definition of poetry already depended on such projection (Jakobson and Pomorska 1983: 131–2; see also Liberman 1987: 144). Jakobson was not speaking of translation here, and therefore did not use the term 'equivalence' to mean something with the same meaning or function in different languages. Though the term when used in translation studies is fraught with controversy, not least because of the impossibility of deciding whether lexical items or syntactic expressions can possibly mean the same thing, or phonological elements carry the same connotations, in different languages, it could still be considered to be the basic notion upon which translation rests (see Pym 2010: 165). It seems possible, in reconstructing choices made by a translator, to understand equivalence not just as in the example given, that is, as the equivalence between 'starflower', 'aster' and 'marguerite', but also as the equivalence between all three words and the original 'Sternblume'. If equivalence is thus 'projected' (in the sense of being recoverable to analysis) across texts, from the source-text selection onto the target-text combination, and not merely within one text, as in original writing, then the phrase that does appear, in any given translation, must also potentially contain, or at least connote, the various equivalent potential choices that were not made. In 'aster', that is, we read the alternative 'starflower', partly because of its equivalence to the German 'Sternblume', in that it refers to the same flower, but also because 'aster' comes from the Greek 'aster', a star.

Such considerations seem crucial when reading translated poetry analytically, and are related to the concern of cognitive poetics to consider not only what is on the page but also what went before it, as reconstructed in the reading, and what comes after, in the effects it has on the reader. If that reader is a scholar of literature or literary stylistics, or of literary translation, one of the most interesting effects of reading a poem such as 'Mute Autumn Smells'

(Felstiner's translation of '*Stumme Herbstgerüche*'; Felstiner 2001: 153) in the knowledge that it is a translation is the focus on the language as well as on the preceding process of translation which the knowledge that it is a translation demands.

If in translated Holocaust poetry the role of language is foregrounded, this is in part because language is always foregrounded in poetry. Poetry differs from documentary texts in that it does not relate facts. Nor does it primarily, like narrative fiction, tell a story. Nevertheless, I would argue (as does Semino 1997: 86–8) that it still creates a fictional world in which the reader (reading in whatever way) becomes immersed. It does this by demanding the reader's engagement to make sense of the text, thereby leading the reader to experience emotions and empathetic response. 'Making sense', it should be noted, is not (unless one is a literary theorist of an unusually narrow-minded school) the same as trying to determine a fixed single meaning in the text. If poetry works by allowing different meanings to be made by different readers, then 'making sense' is to read the poem in a way that produces cognitive effects. I assume, in line with normal assumptions of cognitive poetics and text-world theory (see e.g. Stockwell 2002; Gavins 2007), as discussed in Section 1.5, that a reader reading a poem constructs a text world, which arises from the interaction of the reader's mental models, including their knowledge schemata, beliefs, experiences and attitudes, with the language of the poem (cf. Stockwell 2009: 190). If we are aware that the poem is translated, the role of language becomes correspondingly more foregrounded, because the awareness of its translated status also draws attention to how it came into being.

Besides being particularly foregrounded by the fact of translation, the foregrounding of language is a common characteristic of Holocaust poetry because it is a poetic response to the fact that language was in itself problematic. It had been subject to National Socialist manipulation, which changed the meaning of words, and it had also itself been used as a tool of repression (cf. Celan 1968: 128; Klemperer 2000; Lifton 1986: 445; Levi 2013: 94–114). For the analytical reader of Holocaust poems in translation, some of the connotations that can be recovered from words and expressions in the poems, depending on the reader's existing cognitive schemata, might be different from those available to the general reader, because they will require knowledge of German, and the way words such as '*Lager*' ('camp'), '*Heim*' ('home'), '*frei*' ('free'), '*Heil*' ('healing') acquired different meanings in the Nazi period. Many of the connotations of words used in Holocaust poems have particular Jewish resonances, for example, 'light', 'clay', 'earth'. And much of the imagery is based on Jewish symbolism: 'word', 'star', 'cloth'. (See Frankel and Teutsch 1995.) This is, of course, only true, on the whole, for poetry written by poets with a Jewish background. Almost all Holocaust poetry uses typical Holocaust images – ashes, smoke, snow, dark – which come from the realities of the Holocaust events, though most poets used explicit imagery less as they developed towards a poetic representation of the post-Holocaust state of mind, as we saw in Section 1.1. Indeed, language and images are necessarily closely related. Thus, for example, it is possible for Spiegelman in *Maus* (2003) to have the father, Vladek, refer to the son's cigarette ash as 'ashes', thus signalling both his Polish-Yiddish background and his memories of the Holocaust.

The analytical reader of translated poetry will always be a comparative reader, at least in the second sense outlined in the previous section: he or she will be aware that a relationship exists between this translation and others, and between this translation and a source. This is possible even when other translations or the source text are not actually available, and so do not allow comparative reading in the first, more concrete, sense. Comparative reading in this second sense makes use of what Malmkjær (2004) called 'translational stylistics', that is, stylistics that takes the source text into account. It should be recalled that comparative reading in both senses is used here to mean reading that consciously (if analytical) takes into account the relationships between languages and texts, and not in the sense of literary reading that considers cross-cultural influences nor in the sense of classificatory analysis carried out by proponents of Descriptive Translation Studies (see Hermans 1999: 55–71 for an overview of such comparative models).

Different translations are readily seen, in scholarly and critical work that relies on stylistic analysis, as representing different interpretations. In the case of '*Stumme Herbstgerüche*', for example, an analytical reader might want to argue that Hamburger used 'marguerite' for '*Sternblume*' in order to link this poem to other poems by Celan, and especially his best-known poem '*Todesfuge*' (discussed in Section 2.1) where the name '*Margarete*' is used, ironically, as a typical German name, a symbol of bravery and purity, partly no doubt in allusion to the character in Goethe's *Faust* (cf. Felstiner 1995: 36). The fact that Celan makes many references to German literature, for example, to Hölderlin in '*Tübingen, Jänner*' (Celan 1980: 27), 'Tübingen, January', and to many other European literatures (see Felstiner 1995: 173–4), would support this view. Or the analytical reader might argue that, in the first words of his translation of '*Stumme Herbstgerüche*', Felstiner chose to translate '*stumm*' as 'mute' because the cognate 'dumb' has, in American English, connotations of stupidity, which it does not have in British English, and which it could not have had in the original; this is not a connotation of '*stumm*' in German, despite the Nazi view of those who could not speak as less than human (cf. Evans 2010: 66). Comparative reading can thus make possible the study of particular translators' choices and allow stylistic analysis of the translated poem that pays attention to the translator's style as well as the original poet's.

But comparative reading, especially when it forms part of an analytical reader's approach, can also help provide important insights into the original, and it is here that we see perhaps the greatest difference between the general reader and the analytical reader. Such insights are perhaps especially likely with a poet like Celan for whom the etymological origins and connections of words were an important means of signalling the roots of language as a way of achieving a 'return' ('*Heimkehr*') of language through poetry from the manipulation and distortion it had suffered (Celan 1968: 147).

To see how comparative reading might play a role in analysis or criticism, let us recall from Section 2.1 the translations of line four of '*Todesfuge*' (Celan 1952: 37), 'Death Fugue', by Felstiner (2001: 31) and Hamburger (2007: 71):

we shovel a grave in the air where you won't lie too cramped (JF)
we dig a grave in the breezes there one lies unconfined (MH)

I add now my own translation for further comparison:

we shovel a grave in the air there you won't lie so tight

Not only are the differences in translation, which point to the translators' different interpretations, important, but also the actual fact of the difference. It has been noted before (e.g. by Parks 1998: vii, 2007; Boase-Beier 2014a) that differences between original and translation signal particularly significant points in the style of the original. But differences between translations also signal such points.

Work with students and non-student participants in translation workshops[1] confirms that the line is, indeed, seen as significant for translation, based on the differences in the translations alone. In an earlier article (see Boase-Beier 2009; also 2011a: 137–9), I argued that such points often correspond to what can be identified as 'the eye of the poem', the central and significant 'point on which the poem turns' (Freeman 2005: 40). Such points correspond to 'convergences' of stylistically important figures, to use Riffaterre's term (1959: 172). And they often are exactly the points of divergence between the translated text and its source, as those students who were able to compare the translation with the original text in this case noticed. While my earlier article suggested that such a point might often be about two-thirds of the way through a poem, this is clearly not the case here. However, this poem has the form of a fugue, that is, repeated sections come in, causing previous ones to 'flee', and any consideration of a line's or an expression's position in the poem needs to take this repetition into account; indeed, one would expect several such 'eyes'.

Reading any of the translations analytically takes into account that there is a relationship between the poem (and in this case the line in question) and its rendering in other translations and the original. The differences in these three different translations can, therefore, not only suggest the particular interpretations of the translators, but also give clues to what is so important about the line in the original text. If we do have access to the original:

wir	schaufeln	ein	Grab	in	den	Lüften	da	liegt	man	nicht	eng
we	shovel	a	grave	in	the	airs	there	lies	one	not	narrow

whether or not we intend to translate the poem, we will, therefore, want to explore this line further. In particular, the word '*Lüften*' seems to signal such a point in the source text: Felstiner and Hamburger, and also Christopher Middleton, who has 'sky' (Hamburger and Middleton 1972: 33), all translate the word differently. It is the plural of the word '*Luft*' ('air'), and is in itself rather unusual, because air is not generally countable. Thus it does not usually have a plural in German, except in literary usage where it can mean either skies or breezes. Translating it as 'breezes', as Hamburger does, is clearly a recognition of its plurality, and perhaps also suggests both the transience of the graves, their insubstantial nature, and, as mentioned earlier, the contrast between the freedom of outside work, though it is digging graves, and the confinement in the camp. Felstiner has kept it singular, as I have, thus assuming that Celan simply meant 'air'; Middleton's translation has suggestions of afterlife. This comparison leads the analytical reader to ask why the original was plural. One possibility is that the dative plural '*Lüften*', with its – '*en*' ending, suggests the verb '*lüften*', which means 'to air', but can also mean to speak out about something concealed, or to shed light on it, as in '*ein Geheimnis lüften*', literally 'to air a mystery'. Thus the reader inevitably sees a connection with the 'frightful muting, ... the thousand darknesses of deathbringing speech' (Felstiner 2001: 395) through which, for Celan, language had to pass before it could re-emerge. In fact, what Celan said in the 1958 speech in which he used these words was that language had to pass through such a silence in order to emerge '"*angereichert*" *von all dem*' (Celan 1968: 128). It is a curious and ambiguous expression, which Felstiner translates as '"enriched" by all this' (Felstiner 2001: 395), because not only do the inverted commas suggest irony, but they also suggest the particular irony of being affected by the *Reich*, as Felstiner has also noted (Felstiner 1995: 115). In the poem, once we consider both the plural of '*Luft*' and the verb '*lüften*' (related to English 'lift'), the other common meaning of '*Reich*', 'kingdom of heaven', becomes clearer.

The very fact that there are these striking differences suggests this line is crucial. And, indeed, a re-reading of the original German line shows other significant stylistic features. We see that in the German line the register changes between '*Lüften*' and '*da*', perhaps suggesting a change of speaker. It is not a clear break: we wonder whether the second half of the line is an echo, in free indirect speech (that is, where no speaker is mentioned but no one is directly quoted either), of something a guard has said. Or it might be a thought, or words, attributed to the guard, but not something that had actually been said. And if so, who is attributing the thought or words? Is it the 'we' of the first half? Fragments of the line are repeated several times in the poem and the whole line also recurs, integrated into another. Later in the poem there occurs the line (followed here by my translation):

da habt ihr ein Grab in den Wolken da liegt man nicht eng
and you'll have your grave in the clouds there you won't lie so tight

Because this time the first half is in the second person informal plural, there is no doubt that this is the guard speaking, though we still do not know whether these are words heard, or that might have been heard, or words or even thoughts that are attributed, in the world of the poem. However, the difference between this line and the earlier one is that the earlier line began in the first person plural and so the impersonal phrase '*da liegt man nicht eng*' could also be thoughts that the narrator in the poem has about himself (or herself). The second person address at the beginning of the later line just given strongly suggests that the impersonal '*man*' here is used of those spoken *to*: a guard addressing the prisoners.

The point is that there is fragmentation: different voices speak at different times throughout the poem. But there is not only fragmentation; there is also a curious amalgamation of the guard's voice with that of the narrator, whom one assumes from the first line 'Black milk of morning we drink it at evening' to be a prisoner. Amalgamation always occurs in free indirect speech because, by definition, it is a mixture of the features of direct and indirect speech (Short 1996: 288–319). Reporting of thought is more complex, but it always carries a contamination of the thoughts reported by the reporter, because there is no direct access to the thoughts of another (cf. Short 1996: 315), though of course a text that is fictional, such as a poem, can always attribute thoughts to another, presenting them as what Palmer (2004: 53–7) calls 'free direct thought'. The amalgamation of perspectives is underlined here by the small changes in the repeated phrases and by the resulting different possible interpretations of the impersonal '*man*', 'one'. This impersonal form could be used by Nazi bureaucracy, just as it can by any bureaucracy, to blur the boundaries between you and me, the prisoner and the state, the thoughts I give you and the ones you really have, and so on.

What this means is that, on the one hand, when we read the later line we are inclined to think the earlier one also featured the voice of the guard. But we are not sure. And the voice of the guard, if that is what it is, in this earlier line, is being ironical: you've complained about the overcrowding so let's see how you like the alternative. We know from accounts of inmates that concentration camp guards often made these little jokes. Lifton quotes witness reports directly, and one of these records Mengele, the Auschwitz doctor, who led 'selections' of prisoners for life or death on the arrival ramps, as saying, when a woman asked him to spare her father that 'father would be very well and the air would make him healthy' (Lifton 1986: 343). Lifton points out that these reports did not become widely available until the late 1950s, long after Celan is assumed to have written the poem (cf. Felstiner 1995: 26–32) but, as Felstiner notes, Celan would have had direct access to similar reports, from other camps. The sayings such as '*Jedem das Seine*' ('To each his own') above concentration camp entrances, are further examples, as mentioned in Section 2.1. The voice of the guard (just like Mengele's in the example given) is ironically expressing empathy with the prisoners; false empathy was commonplace in a world in which the prisoners were not real people.

All these considerations arise from seeing that the original line has led to divergent translations. These divergent translations send us to the original (or to commentaries on it, and glosses, if we cannot speak German), and the consideration of the original leads us through stylistic analysis to changes of voice and perspective, as we see that this line represents the first time in the poem that we experience such a shift of perspective, which will become stronger and more confusing as the poem progresses: there appear not only phrases that are in the second person, but also the imperative phrase 'cut the earth still deeper you lot' though this phrase is not expressed colloquially, thus suggesting reported rather than direct speech. And we also have the direct lines the guard writes, the cliché 'your hair of gold, Margarete'. One of the differences between reading analytically and reading in the 'everyday' sense of the previous section is that our intuitive sense of 'voice' as representing a character or narrator or inferred author speaking is supplemented by stylistic analysis. I was using the intuitive sense in Chapter 1 to speak of Holocaust poetry preserving the voices of those who did not survive. A stylistic understanding of voice considers how minute differences in style or register point to different mind-styles. (See also Bennett and Royle 2004: 68–76.)

What happens in comparative reading when the reader has access to the original is that differences like 'cramped', 'unconfined' and 'tight' point to the difficulties of identifying who is speaking, or who is attributing words or thoughts to whom. This apparently small difference thus suggests the importance of voices and the way voices can be combined.

Reading a text in this way involves thinking of the target text as a blend, a translated text conceived of as containing within it elements of comparison with its source, and with other translations, all of which constitute its input spaces. It has a shared generic space containing common elements of style and meaning – those elements in which many translation theories locate equivalence (cf. Pym 2010: 6–24). But the blend also allows us to think of elements not in any of these, such as Felstiner's interpretation of Celan in conscious difference from Hamburger's, for example. Diagrams of blends can become very complicated, and the interested reader can follow up the possibilities in Fauconnier and Turner (2002) and later works such as Dancygier (2012). A simplified representation of the above blend is given in Box 3.

One way to understand Celan's reference to 'deathbringing speech' and the need to pass through it in relation to translated Holocaust poetry is to see that such poetry also has to represent, in another language, the struggle of German to emerge from the Nazi contamination of earlier language and earlier literature. This is the struggle that results in Rowland's 'awkward poetics' (2005): not just a break with and comment on poetic style but also a break with and comment on earlier poetry, which is retrospectively felt to be tainted.

Box 3 Analytical comparative reading of a translated text

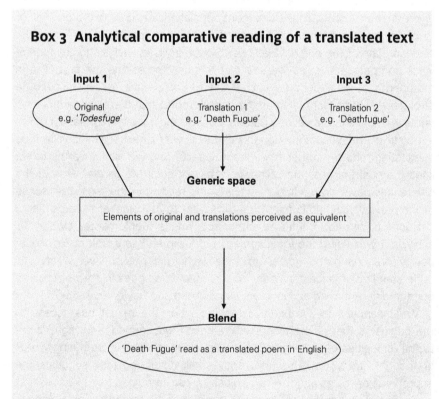

| Input 1 | Input 2 | Input 3 |
| Original e.g. 'Todesfuge' | Translation 1 e.g. 'Death Fugue' | Translation 2 e.g. 'Deathfuge' |

Generic space

Elements of original and translations perceived as equivalent

Blend

'Death Fugue' read as a translated poem in English

Reading 'Death Fugue' as a translated version of 'Todesfuge' is to run the blend: to think about it as a blended entity, a new structure, with some features of each of the inputs and some new ones (such as the combined voice of the original poet and translator).

Consider the example of Ausländer's poem '*Biographische Notiz*' (2012: 145–6) 'Biographical Note'. In this poem, Ausländer writes of the landscape of her youth in images that superficially seem to recall an earlier tradition of nature poetry such as that of Joseph von Eichendorff (see e.g. 1988):

Ich rede
…
von Trauerweiden
Blutbuchen
verstummtem Nachtigallensang

My translation of this poem reads

I speak
…
of weeping willows
blood-beeches
silenced nightingale song

The reader reading 'blood-beeches', where the normal designation for what in German is '*Blutbuchen*' would be 'copper beeches', will experience the 'blood' in the designation of the beeches as foregrounded. This can be read merely as an emphasis on the changes that the Holocaust has brought to one's perception of the landscape: the 'blood-beeches', together with the 'weeping willows' and the silence of the nightingale, could simply represent a damaged and degraded landscape that one can no longer invest with the positive qualities of the German Romantic poets. This is a time when, as Brecht put it, '*Ein Gespräch über Bäume fast ein Verbrechen ist // Weil es ein Schweigen über so viele Untaten einschließt!*' (Conrady 1977: 836) that is, when 'talk of trees is almost a crime // since it involves silence on so many horrors!'. The reader will thus be able to use this particular rendering of '*Blutbuchen*' as a clue to what I have been calling the post-Holocaust mind.

The end of the Nazi period and the war has been described as the '*Stunde Null*', the 'zero hour', in German literature (cf. Schröder et al. 1995). But most literary scholars describe the rejection of earlier trends in a much more nuanced and complex way (see Hamburger 1969: 267–314; Friedrich 2006: 19–23, Culler 1989). An analytical reader, reading the poem as a translation and focusing on the language itself as well as on what it describes, and on the fact that the poem begins 'I speak', will see in the translation, especially if read together with the original, not merely a beech whose leaves are red like blood but one that in German is called '*Blutbuche*'. This, together with '*Trauerweiden*', causes the reader to see in the original poem the word '*Galle*' ('gall'; 'bitterness') in the archaic '*Nachtigallensang*', which replaces the more usual '*Nachtigall-Gesang*'. The morphological division of the German that results in '*-sang*' furthermore suggests the French word for blood, '*sang*'. Such a reading of the translation is aware both of English-German differences and of links with French, and thus echoes the multilingual sensibility of the vast majority of Holocaust poets (cf. also Olschner 1985: 47); it reads in the mind-style of the text a representation of a post-Holocaust mind that is both traumatized and multilingual. The possibility of such reading can be brought closer for the general reader, too; it is made much more likely in a bilingual presentation of the text, a point to which I shall return in Chapter 4. But it is above all the foregrounding of 'blood' in 'blood-beeches' that makes this possible. So analytical comparative reading has consequences for the translator, too, and the next chapter examines some of them.

The focus on the language of the poem, which is enhanced by a reading in comparison with other translations, or with the original or with both, allows the scholar to reconstruct the poetics of the text. Assuming that poetics is both the study of what makes literature literary (Stockwell 2002: 1) and a system of poetic thought that drives the writing of poetry (cf. Boase-Beier 2011b: 167), the style of the translated text seen in comparison with its original makes it possible to reconstruct the choices made by the original poet. And it also enables the analytical reader, such as the critic or scholar, to situate the poetics of an individual poet or poem within Holocaust poetics in a wider sense.

Thus, for example, a comparison of Ausländer's '*Am Ende der Zeit*' (1978: 104), 'At the End of Time', discussed in Section 1.5, with its translations, shows differences in the way the following lines are translated.

es	wird	schön	sein
it	will	lovely	be

wenn	es	sein	wird
if/when	it	be	will

This poem has been translated by Osers (1977: 55) in a version marked (EO) below and by Boland (2004: 23), marked (EB):

It will be good
when it happens (EO)

It will be wonderful
if and when that happens (EB)

This difference in the translation of '*wenn*', in turn, points to the differences mentioned in Section 1.5 between '*wenn*' in German and both 'if' and 'when' in English (cf. Boase-Beier 2006: 119–20). Of course, it is interesting to speculate about the reasons for the use of 'when' in Osers' translation: it might be that Osers, before his immigration to England a bilingual Czech-German speaker, preserved some of the uncertainty of the German '*wenn*' in his use of the English 'when' (cf. Boase-Beier 2010a).

A further consequence of the difference between Osers' translation and the original, especially when seen in conjunction with Boland's translation, is that the use of '*wenn*' in Ausländer's poetry is highlighted *per se*, just as we saw earlier with Celan's '*Todesfuge*'. That is, the focus on '*wenn*' caused by comparatively reading two translations together with the original, and noting the difference, points to the significance of the word in the original, where it could be seen to suggest exactly this ambiguity between a temporal and a conditional meaning. If one has confidence in the future, the two meanings come together; if one has none, they remain separate. Furthermore, the interesting use of '*wenn*' in Ausländer's poem, together with the fact that she uses the word ambiguously in many other poems, such as '*Wenn wir auferstehen*', 'If/When we Arise from the Dead'; '*Wenn der Tisch nach Brot duftet*', 'If/When the Table is Scented with Bread' (Ausländer 2012: 93, 137) and that she wrote several poems, in both German and English, on the subject of time, such as '*Eh die Zeit anfing*' (Ausländer 2012: 26), 'Before Time Began'; '*Es ist an der Zeit*' (Ausländer 2012: 178), 'It is Time'; or 'Time Incognito' (Ausländer 2008: 186) and 'The Whitest' (Ausländer 2008: 207), will lead the analytical reader to consider what this interest might mean, and to look at the philosophy that most influenced her, such as that of Constantin Brunner, who saw time as that which could only be conceptualized in relation to physical (including natural) objects, and the changes they undergo (Brunner 1968: 59–77).

Thus reading that takes into account that a poem is translated gives insight not only into the translator's poetics but also, via the comparative analysis it makes possible, into the original, as well as into the possible context of the original. Such enhanced insight into the original then becomes part of the reader's cognitive context and can feed into a new translation process, a possibility to be discussed in Chapters 3 and 4.

3

Translating Holocaust poetry

3.1 Reading Holocaust poetry for translation

In Chapter 2, the discussion focused mainly on the different ways we might read translated Holocaust poetry as translation, depending on our cognitive context, including knowledge schemata, and our purposes as readers: whether we read out of general interest or because we want or need to analyse the poetry.

Analytical reading of translated poems might happen automatically, because our background and training makes it impossible to read in any other way; in this case, schemata for comparative analysis already exist in our minds, and come into play when we are reading translated poetry. But we might also read the original poem analytically, for example, if we intend to translate it. Reading for translation is certainly a type of analytical reading, but it is clearly not the same as reading a translated text analytically. I would argue that it includes what I have been calling 'comparative reading', but what does this mean if we are reading the original text rather than the translated text? We saw in the previous chapter that comparative reading of a translated poem compares different existing (or potential) translations of the poem with one another or with the original. A schema for comparative reading can be called into use by the reader of the translation, I argued in Chapter 2, even without the original text, as in a monolingual edition of the poetry, or without detailed knowledge of the original language, as is the case for a monolingual reader. This is because it relies on a multilingual sensibility, which includes a recognition that other languages and cultures exist and formed the context of the original poem. And a multilingual sensibility can be part of anyone's cognitive make-up, irrespective of whether they ever read analytically.

Reading *for* translation is different in several ways. Not only is it a reading of a source text, rather than a translated text, but the translator almost always has access to, and is competent in, the original language. 'Almost' because it is possible – though such cases tend to be exceptions – to translate without knowing the language of the source poem. In the theatre this is more common: the 'translator' whose name goes on the translated version of the play that is produced might have worked from a literal version in the target language produced by someone else (see Brodie 2012). The purpose of the literal version is both to provide access to the meaning of the original and to indicate something of its style. This process might also happen with poetry, as in the case mentioned in Chapter 1, of Hughes' translations of Pilinszky's Hungarian poetry, done together with Csokits (see Hughes and Csokits 1976), where, as Hughes explains in his 'Introduction', Csokits wrote 'rough drafts' in English first (Hughes and Csokits 1976: 13). A process that involves an intermediary in this way is not based on reading for translation in the sense in which I am using the expression here. Apart from a few such exceptions, though, most Holocaust poetry is translated by those who can read and understand the original, and so the language and culture of the original form part of the reader's background knowledge. As suggested at the end of Section 1.2, reading a poem in order to translate it involves, like any analytical reading, constructing against this background a sense of its poetics, that is, how the stylistic features of the poem lead back to what the translator takes to be particular choices on the part of the original poet that can be related to particular effects but that also always leaves the text open to the individual reader's engagement.

But reading for translation goes further. In the same way that it has been argued, for example by Slobin (2003: 164), that there is such a thing as 'thinking for translating', where the translator, as part of the translation process, is able to envisage different ways of thinking more appropriate to the target language and culture, I would argue that there is also a type of reading which is particularly geared towards translating (see Boase-Beier 2006: 23–5). Though it is difficult to find (or to implement) empirical studies of such phenomena, there is some evidence in think-aloud protocols (TAPs) discussed by scholars such as Jääskeläinen (2000) or Jones (2011), or Jones' interviews with practising translators (Jones 2011: 85–107). Like the comparative reading of translated texts I described in Chapter 2, reading for translation is also comparative, but the comparison is between a source text and a translated text that does not yet exist but is imagined. The possibility of such reading is seen by a translator as inherent to the source text, and depends on what Benjamin (2012: 76) called the 'translatability' of the text. In cognitive terms, as represented in Box 4, the source text and an imagined target text (and possibly existing translations) are the input spaces to a generic space with common stylistic features and then to a blended space of reading for translation in which these two texts, one real and one imagined, co-exist and are compared, possibly along with other existing translations. From the blended space emerges (see Fauconnier and Turner 2002: 42–3) an enhanced understanding, a 'comparative analysis', of the text. This can be fed back to the source text input space, and fed through the blend again, and so used to help produce an actual translation, represented in Box 4 as an object rather than a mental space.

Jones (2011: 35) points out that reading for translation is not a homogeneous procedure, because translators read to decide which poets to translate, or to compare a target text they have already produced with the source, depending upon the stage of the process. There may also, as Jones' use of Actor Network Theory suggests, be many other factors that influence the translator's reading

Box 4 Reading an original text for translation

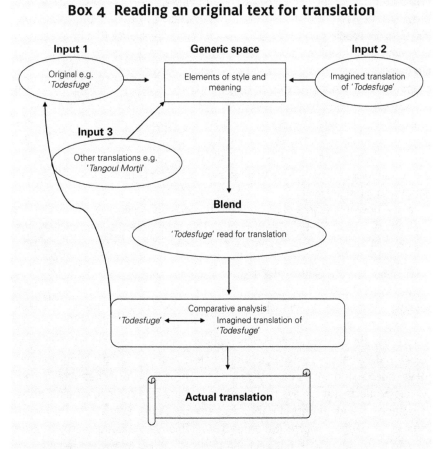

The blend is not the actual source text but the way we think of it when we read it for translation. The resulting comparative analysis may be largely conscious. The actual translation is represented here as an object in the real world, that results from the analysis.

and subsequent translation: deadlines, the nature of the commission, cultural expectations in the target language, personal working preferences and so on (see especially Jones 2011: 173–200). Actor Network Theory, as applied to the translation of poetry, envisages a situation whereby 'poetry translators enter and form a community of shared actions and values', where 'teams and their translations interact with a social, political, literary and cultural context that spans the worlds of the source and receptor language' (Jones 2011: 4). These insights will be particularly important when considering, in Chapter 4, how changes to the way we translate and present Holocaust poetry might be made.

The term 'reading for translation', then, is shorthand for various possible ways of reading, one of which is illustrated by the diagram in Box 4. But all have in common what I would call 'translational poetics'. Alongside Malmkjær's term 'translational stylistics' (2004: 16), mentioned in Section 2.2, which accounts for reading and stylistic analysis of the translated text in relation to its source text, I use the term 'translational poetics' to account for a reading and comparative stylistic analysis of the source text based on its relation to a target text that is not yet written; I am thus using 'poetics' in the sense I gave in Section 1.2, to emphasize the concern with writing a new text. The cognitive context the translator builds up during such a reading already encompasses the future translated text, so reading the original poem for translation, like reading the translated poem as translation, always happens in a blended space. Translational poetics is what allows the 'comparative analysis' on the diagram to happen.

To see how this works in practice, let us consider again line four of Celan's 'Todesfuge' (1952: 37–9), 'Death Fugue'. This time, though, we consider the original:

wir schaufeln ein Grab in den Lüften da liegt man nicht eng

Reading 'Todesfuge' for translation might involve some of the same considerations that play a role in reading translated versions, but it is far more complex. It starts from an analytical reading of the source text, as we see in Box 4, and will always envisage, while one is reading, a translation that has not yet been made. In the case of poems that have previously been translated, I would argue that it always makes sense for the translator to consult those translations, represented on the diagram by Petre Solomon's Romanian translation, 'Tangoul Morţii' (Solomon 1947). This is not because they provide clues to how to translate but because they offer clues to how to read: in the diagram in Box 4, we see that they feed via a shared generic space into the blended space of reading for translation. Such comparative reading is the only way to do full justice to the translational possibilities of the original. What I am suggesting here is that, far from first reading and then translating, as some writers on translation (e.g. Díaz-Diocaretz 1985: 21; Barnstone 1993: 49) seem to feel is the norm, reading for translation, in fact, is not only analytical but it is also already comparative, a reading that aims to understand the translational poetics of the original text.

Because reading for translation is always comparative, it sees the cross-linguistic potential in an original poem, and appears especially apt in the case of the poetry in question here. Holocaust poetry is not simply written originally in German or Italian or Polish, but in addition is almost always written from a multilingual sensibility, and the English translator needs to take this into account. Poets like Celan or Meerbaum-Eisinger or Pagis grew up in a multilingual environment; the particular circumstances of the Bukovina, in these three cases, ensured that this was so. Especially for poets with a Jewish background, their multilingualism was enhanced by the Yiddish often spoken at home and, usually, Hebrew learned at school. The vast majority of Holocaust poets were themselves translators, and the Holocaust, as discussed in Section 2.1, both involved and affected a large number of languages (cf. Clendinnen 1999; Rosen 2005). The circumstances of many annexed or occupied areas, such as Poland, Romania, Ukraine or Belgium, were multilingual, as were the ghettos, as Jews from Germany or already annexed countries were moved further east, to be followed by Jews and other people from the occupied countries. (See Gilbert [2009]) for very clear maps of these events.) In the concentration camps, inmates from many different linguistic backgrounds were forced into close cohabitation. Indeed, Yiddish flourished in many camps as the language of communication for Jews from different countries. And Levi (2013: 99) quotes Maršálek (1977), who says that in Mauthausen a truncheon was known as an 'interpreter' ('*Dolmetscher*'): everyone understood it.

Only a reading of the original poetry that is done in awareness of its inherently multilingual context will allow the translator access to its poetics. And a comparative reading, which envisages the movement of the poem across a language boundary, which takes its 'translatability' (Benjamin 2012: 76) into account, is the way to an enhanced understanding of its poetics.

Reading for translation, I would argue, leads to a deeper analysis of the style of the original poem as the translator's cognitive context is built up, for a number of reasons:

(i)   As with analytical reading of translated texts, the translator's
      focus shifts from linguistic reference onto language, symbolism,
      connotation, metaphor and other aspects of the style of the poem.

(ii) Any number of potential translations can be considered; that is,
      not only translations that already exist and the translator's own
      emerging or imagined target text, but other possible ones (including

those in other languages than the intended target language) can be taken into account.

(iii) Cross-linguistic differences and connotations implied or suggested in the original poem can be considered.

In the example from '*Todesfuge*', a reading for translation, in considering the irony of '*da liegt man nicht eng*', which I discussed in Section 2.2, will consider the fairly colloquial register of *eng* and also, in line with (i) what the connotations of '*eng*' might be: in what other circumstances (for example, concentrated ghetto living or transports in cattle trucks) would one speak of things being '*eng*'? What else does it suggest? Felstiner notes here the relevance of '*eng*' to Celan's view of poetic constraint (Felstiner 1995: 35), an echo of which is perhaps present in Hamburger's translation: 'unconfined'. Other connotations that the original poem may carry, and that the translator's focus away from reference might make clearer, could be particular symbolic or cultural or philosophical traditions in the poet's background. On one level the poem can be read as representing 'plain fact' about the concentration camps, as some reviewers maintained on its publication in 1952 in Germany (see Felstiner 1995: 27). But, of course, it is a poetic representation of fact, and the context in which it was written will, therefore, have affected its writing, and will be of concern to the translator. Felstiner has undertaken meticulous research into the poem and given a great deal of thought to the possibilities of translation (Felstiner 1995: 22–41), finally rejecting the possible rhyme of 'tight' with 'night' in an earlier line: that 'rhyme would prettify' (Felstiner 1995: 35). There have been many translations of this poem, and my own translation, from which I gave this line (which does use 'tight') in Section 2.2, is not in any sense intended as an improvement on previous ones but simply as another interpretation.

Reading for translation, one might also consider, as in (ii), not only the connotations of '*eng*' in German in contrast with the possible connotations in English of words used in other English translations (Felstiner's 'cramped', Hamburger's '(un)confined', my 'tight') or that might be used – 'narrow', 'constricted', 'packed' – but also words that might be used in French, for example '*serré*', or Romanian, for example '*strâmtă*' (as in Solomon's translation), and so on. One could consider translations into any language, but those that Celan spoke, and that, therefore, will have influenced his lexical choice here, seem most likely to be helpful.

The translator will also, in seeing the cross-linguistic possibilities of the original, as in (iii), consider etymology. The latter concern arises particularly for the translator because the word is loosened, by the need to cross language boundaries, from both its obvious referents and its original language, as Benjamin (1972) appears to suggest and as Jakobson stated (see 2012: 126).

The translator might, therefore, consider (or indeed discover) that 'eng' in German, from Middle High German 'enge', assumed to derive from Indo-Germanic *'anĝh', is related to Middle High German 'ange', whence we get Modern German 'bang' ('fearful'), 'Angst' ('fear'), 'bangen' ('to be afraid' or, in Middle High German, 'to drive into a confined space'), but it is also related to English 'angina', 'anger', 'anguish', 'strangle' and words with similar form and meaning in many other languages, as indeed Felstiner noted (1995: 119). It is unrelated to 'Engel', 'angel', but the echo, given the images of air, stars, graves, clouds and golden hair, is unavoidably there as soon as etymology sets one on the track of homonymy, of real, spurious and supposed connections.

One reason for translators to use their knowledge of those etymological connections that a concern with the word itself leads them to acquire, is that, in this case, it must be important to the translator because it was important to the poet. There is no doubt that Celan was fascinated by etymology, partly as a result of his study of French language and linguistics in Czernowitz after the outbreak of war in 1939 prevented him from returning to his study of medicine in Tours. During his studies in Czernowitz, he also became aware of Saussure's general linguistic principles (Chalfen 1979: 87). That Celan was very interested in the problems of language and reference that Saussure discusses is documented by the linguist friend who introduced him, around 1944, to Ausländer (Chalfen 1979: 87–8). Hamburger (2007: 21) notes how much he liked dictionaries. And his study of linguistics would have given him new insights into Yiddish: speaking Yiddish inevitably leads one to the earlier stages of German. His concern for etymology was also both an attempt to find a language that was not tainted by the Nazis' manipulation, and a need to show that this was, in fact, impossible.

Another reason for following up etymology when building up one's cognitive context while reading Celan for translation is based on the point discussed in Chapter 2 in relation to Jakobson's notion of the projection of selection (the paradigm) onto combination (the syntagm): since projection includes choices made or not made by the original poet, it will also include earlier stages of the German language, because of the influence of these earlier stages, via etymology, on Celan's lexical choices. Thus the words used in the poem carry with them their earlier history as surely as they carry connotations, symbolic meanings and possible translations.

The result of such considerations for the translator into English might be a reading that seeks the connections between German and English in the roots of the two languages, using words in the translation that particularly resonate in this way. Though both 'cramped' (Felstiner's word) and 'tight' (my own) have Germanic roots, 'tight', for me, is etymologically more interesting here because of its direct connection to German 'dicht' (used often by Celan, as in 'Heimkehr'), and also because of the connection between 'eng' and both German '*Angst*' and English 'anguish', 'strangle' and 'angina', all of which involve tightening. 'Tight' thus carries similar connotations of fear, and of the exclusion of air. It might, in fact, be impossible to distinguish connotation or symbolism from etymology, because words can carry connotations from earlier stages of the language; these may constitute fairly passive linguistic knowledge for the reader but are likely to persist in colloquial expressions and idioms, such as '*jemanden in die Enge treiben*' ('to leave someone no way out', for example in an argument), or '*sich beengt fühlen*' ('to feel confined, constricted'). It is this persistence of connotation in idiom that Benjamin may have had in mind when stressing the importance of idioms and what Brecht called '*das plumpe Denken*', 'rough thinking', for an understanding of language (cf. Benjamin 1966: 90; Arendt 1992: 21). The importance of these habitual ways of thinking, because they demonstrate reliance on basic conceptual metaphors (see Section 1.6) as seen in idioms and sayings and so-called 'dead' or conventional metaphors, has been underlined by every writer on conceptual metaphor (see e.g. Lakoff and Turner 1989).

Reading a poem for translation, as works such as Felstiner's 1995 book on Celan illustrate particularly well, leads the translator into the background and autobiography of the poet in a way that reading a translated poem critically – even if that reading is done in full awareness of the fact that what is being read is a translation – generally does not. Indeed, one would not expect it in the case of translated poetry, because we usually trust the translator to decide what is relevant in terms of context, and to provide this in prefaces or notes. But the translator reading a poem in order to translate it will focus on the background not merely as part of the cognitive context of the poet and the original readers, but also for the way it might resonate in the language, that is, have become part of the poetics of the original poet. Whereas a reader of Celan in English might or might not consider the etymology of the English words and their links to German and other languages, the translator reading the original poem has no choice but to consider etymology, because this is how translation works. It is impossible to consider how to render '*eng*' in English without thinking of the common roots of English and German.

Reading for translation thus always involves research, not just into the source and target languages and the poet's background, but also into the various systems of belief that influenced the poet, or were likely to have done so. It is useful to know that Celan read Blake and Benjamin, that Sachs, when living in Sweden, learned more about her Jewish background and studied the Kabbalah, that Ausländer was influenced by the philosophy of Brunner, with whom she studied in Czernowitz before co-founding the Brunner Circle in 1923 (Braun and Sprick 1999: 17).

We can illustrate, using the case of Ausländer, how this impacts on the reading of her poems for translation with the example of '*Als gäbe es*'

(Ausländer 2012: 289), translated as 'As If' (Boase-Beier and Vivis 1995: 20). Here is the first stanza with a gloss:

Als	gäbe	es
as	gave (subj)	it
einen	Himmel	
a	heaven	
und	eine	aufblickende
and	a	up-looking
Erde		
earth		

(As though there were a heaven and an earth looking up.)

The poem could be read as a meditation on Brunner's view that 'the common egoist's popular wisdom about humanity consists of ... black-and-white thinking' (Brunner 1919: 6; 283–300); that is, the making absolute of what is relative. In Brunner's vast work *Der Judenhass und die Juden* ('Anti-Semitism and the Jews'), from which this quotation is taken, he shows how the inability to relativize leads to all manner of evils and, particularly, the characterization of the Jews as wholly different from the rest of humanity (or, at least, from the section of humanity the anti-semite considers himself to belong to). Recall Steinherr's '*Von der Abstraktion*', 'On Abstraction' (Dove 2010: 114–15), discussed in Section 2.1, which expresses similar fears. Ausländer's poem goes on after this first stanza with three more, each beginning with '*Als gäbe es*'. This expression, a common one in German, is usually translated as 'as though there were', because '*es gibt*' (here in the subjunctive) is the expression for 'there is' or 'there are'. Each stanza suggests a further possible contrast: between lighted-up blue and dull brown, between earth-words and above-earth ('*überirdisch*') words, and finally between your word and my word. It is an apparently simple poem, expressing scepticism about what might seem to be contraries. When I translated this poem in the early 1990s with Anthony Vivis, this is exactly how we saw the poem. Here is the translated poem (Boase-Beier and Vivis 1995: 20):

As if there were
heaven
and earth
looking up

As if there were
dull brown
and radiant blue

As if there were
heaven-words
and words of earth

As if there were
your words
my words
you and me

We noticed at the time the striking lack of parallelism in the original between the (spurious) contrasts in each stanza. Stanza 1 of the original has heaven and earth, in that order, stanza 2 has blue and brown, stanza 3, earth and the supernatural, so the order here has changed, and stanza 4 has you and me. It seemed to us at the time, and it seems to me now, preparing a revised version (Vivis and Boase-Beier, 2014), that the break in parallelism, in a poet so attuned to repetition, must be significant. Perhaps, we thought, it was an iconic representation of the fact that the two things in each case were *not* separate, so that keeping the order would have falsely emphasized a separateness that was not intended. So we also changed the order, but in stanza 2.

In fact, what happened when we translated was that the style of the poem led us to see the change in the order of the heaven – earth elements as foregrounded: in one stanza, they are different. This meant the pattern was disrupted, and we kept the disruption, but without knowing anything about the philosophy behind it. It was clear to us, as readers and translators, that the poetic shape of the poem was making a philosophical point, and it seemed clear what it was, but not what its background might be.

The thing about reading for translation is that it is not exhausted after the act of translation. On the diagram in Box 4 we can see that the resulting comparative analysis feeds back into the source text and goes through the blend again. Furthermore, 'translational stylistics' in the sense in which Malmkjær used it (Malmkjær 2004), as a simple comparison, has not been supplanted, but has been incorporated into a reading of the source text and forms part of translational poetics. As mentioned earlier, some theorists and, especially, some practitioners have argued that reading comes first. The important point I want to make here is that reading goes on afterwards. Reading for translation, because it involves cross-linguistic thinking that recognizes the extraordinary and far-reaching power of the language, always sends the translator to the point of difference between languages and what that difference means. Here the simple pattern of disrupted parallelism, so easy to reproduce in English, (even though we varied it slightly to fit the monosyllabic 'dull') draws attention to what is not simple: the phrase, also repeated at the start of each stanza *'als gäbe es'*. *'Es gibt'* ('there is', 'there are', literally 'it gives') is, to an English speaker, an extremely odd way of expressing things. It takes an accusative in German in the following noun phrase; '*es*' is singular and the verb '*geben*' ('to give') always agrees with it, not with the noun phrase itself. What, then, is 'it', and why does it give?

Pursuing this linguistic question leads the translator to the common origins of '*geben*' ('to give') and '*haben*' ('to have') in the Indo-Germanic root *'*ghabh*', and the fact that Southern dialects of German, in particular Bavarian, say '*es hant*' ('*es hat*' or '*es haben*') for '*es gibt*' (though '*es hant*' is also used for '*es sind*', a possible alternative, also in standard German, to '*es gibt*'; see Merkle 2005: 64). Both to give and to have suggest that there is agency in German where English has none (cf. also Joseph 2000). This might also lead the translator to consider Benjamin's term '*Aufgabe*' ('task') of the translator. 'Task' (related to 'tax') is a neutral way of expressing what is to be done, or rendered (thus possibly to someone else) but '*Aufgabe*', with its root in the verb '*geben*', includes the perspective of whoever has assigned it, passed it on to the recipient, and in this is a clue to what Benjamin saw as the sacredness of such an undertaking and the possibility of achieving insight into 'pure language' (Benjamin 2012: 78) by translating. The task of translating, in this view, has been given to the translator by a higher agency, and the translator must receive it, pass it on, and be judged on how she or he has done so.

The poem by Ausländer also contains a sense of what has been given to us, expressed in the contrast between heaven and earth. Interestingly, this makes the final contrast – '*Deinwort // Meinwort*' ('your word // my word') – much more suggestive of a contrast between divinity and humanity than between simply other and self, and so seems an allusion to the 'I and You' teachings of the theologian Martin Buber (1923), who influenced both Sachs' poetry (Fritsch-Vivié 1993: 79–80) and Celan's (Felstiner 1995: 140–1), not to mention Baron-Cohen's thinking on empathy (Baron-Cohen 2011: 5). The final line also recalls Celan's use of '*Meingedicht*', suggesting both 'my poem' and a poem that lies (as in '*Meineid*', 'deception') in his poem '*Weggebeizt*' (Celan 1982: 27); see Section 3.2 later. Ausländer's poem appears to express the immanence of God in nature, a suggestion borne out by further study of Brunner's philosophy (e.g. 1968) and his concern for the 'eternal essence' (in the words of Bernard's 'Preface' to Brunner 1968: 14) that underlies everything physical in the world.

The point about such further reading is not that it is necessary to the translation of this poem: the style of the poem provides enough clues to the poetics, in its narrower sense of the system linking the textual detail to the thoughts and attitudes behind them and the effects upon the reader. The further reading comes about *as a result* of translational poetics, of the need to translate, and alters the cognitive context of the translator, thus affecting her or his understanding of this poem, and of other poems by Ausländer, such as

'*Schnee*', 'Snow' (Ausländer 1982: 61; Boase-Beier and Vivis 1995: 39), with its apparent contrasts between the white snow and the black queen beyond the mountains. It helps shed light on expressions in that poem, such as 'At night // the white is black'. Further understanding of the poetry makes the individuality of a poet's thought clearer; thus the difference between, say, Ausländer's specific philosophy and Sachs' more eclectic view, concerned with Jewish mystical tradition and theology in general (cf. Holmqvist 1968: 33–4), becomes clearer. These differences are important, because there is a danger that Holocaust poets will otherwise be seen simply as poets who write about the Holocaust. A greater understanding of individual poets helps the translator to decide what background information the reader needs, as I shall show in Chapter 4.

Brunner's concern to show that anti-Semitism is simply a wrong way of thinking can now be seen to echo right through Ausländer's poetry. Her contrasts are not just about nature and the human, they are about right and wrong ways to think, and the dangers to which simplistic and unintegrated thinking can lead.

The need to uncover philosophical and other references and allusions in the work can also lead to further insights for the translator, not merely connected to the poet in question. Thus, for example, the study of Brunner's work to which a translation of Ausländer leads the translator also uncovers the fact that German '*nichts*' ('nothing') is derived from '*nicht ichts*' ('not something'), because this fact is discussed by Brunner (1968: 60). This, in turn, suggests that the odd lines '*vernichtet // ichten*' in Celan's '*Einmal*' (1982: 103), 'Once', which Hamburger, who translates 'annihilated // ied' (Hamburger 2007: 307) comments on in his 'Introduction' (Hamburger 2007: 33), do indeed have a connection with the Middle High German '*iht*' ('anything'), in spite of Hamburger's stating that Celan himself said '*ichten*' was formed from '*ich*' ('I'). In any case, translators should be wary of taking original poets at their word. And there is never any reason in poetry, and least of all in Celan's poetry, to assume that one meaning rules out another, as the case of '*mein*', mentioned earlier, exemplifies.

The poem '*Einmal*' (Celan 1982: 103), 'Once', in which the word '*ichten*' occurs, begins with a description of washing:

Einmal,
da hörte ich ihn,
da wusch er die Welt

This is translated by Hamburger (2007: 307) as:

Once,
I heard him,
he was washing the world

The presumed Indo-Germanic word for 'to wash', *'neigu', gives us 'neige', 'snow' in French, and gave us 'nix', 'snow' in Latin. Neither 'snow' nor the word for 'washing', though they are related, is, in fact, related to German 'nichts', 'nothing'. But they sound as though they are, especially given that Latin 'nix', 'snow' and German 'nix', the colloquial form of 'nichts', are homonyms. Celan's use of a non-existent verb 'ichten' is thus the positive of an imagined verb 'nichten', 'to negate' (and of 'vernichten', 'to destroy', the word that occurs in the previous line of the poem) and it is also, by its connection to 'nichts', at least in what we reconstruct as Celan's mind, as well as in that of any one (such as the translator) who follows up the etymologies, related to washing, that is, to purifying, which is the subject of the first stanza, given above. Washing is both to cleanse and to destroy evidence, and the concept of washing embodies Celan's sense of the contraries always at work in all our actions and thoughts, and, this poem suggests, in God's.

Brunner's point in his discussion of 'nicht ichts' is, in fact, that we can only conceive of the absolute in a relative sense: nothing is the absence of something, it 'inherits thing-hood from the counterfactual space' in which the thing exists (Fauconnier and Turner 2002: 241), and abstract concepts are perceived through the things they affect. This is a philosophy we can find at the heart of many of Ausländer's poems, such as her poems about time, like 'Am Ende der Zeit' (Ausländer 1978: 104) (see Section 2.2).

Such understanding, which comes about as a result of reading for translation, may be one reason for translating Holocaust poetry, as, indeed, Felstiner suggests (1995: xi). Also for Edwin Robertson, translating Bonhoeffer's work is necessary because this is 'the real heart of Bonhoeffer's thinking' (Robertson 2003: 12). Robertson describes how the work of translating the poetry led to BBC radio programmes in the 1960s produced by poet Terence Tiller, also a translator, and it is quite likely (though I have no evidence for this at present) that Tiller's own poetry (see e.g. Tiller 1968) was influenced by Bonhoeffer's. Certainly Robertson's theological thought was influenced by translating him (Robertson 2003: 10).

Bonhoeffer is best known for his poem 'Von guten Machten' (Bonhoeffer and Bonhoeffer 1947: 32–3), translated by Robertson as 'By Kindly Powers Surrounded' (2003: 104–5). But he wrote other poems, many about his experiences in prison in 1943–1945. 'Wer bin ich?' (Bonhoeffer and Bonhoeffer 1947: 16) appears in Schiff's anthology in a translation by Reginald Fuller, 'Who am I?' (1995: 182–3). The original version has a final rhyming couplet:

Wer	bin	ich?	Einsames	Fragen		treibt	mit	mir	Spott.
who	am	I	lonely	questioning	plays	with	me	mockery

Wer	ich	auch	bin. Du	kennst	mich,	Dein	bin	ich, o	Gott.
who	I	also	am you	know	me	yours	am	I o	God

Robertson, whose main concern is to understand the poetry as a representation of Bonhoeffer's thinking, avoids this rhyme in his translation (Robertson 2003: 39), and, in general, tends to miss its poetic qualities, perhaps considering them less important, as poetic embellishment. Fuller translates in an uncontroversial and rather conventional way:

Who am I? They mock me, these lonely questions of mine.
Whoever I am, Thou knowest, O God, I am Thine!

But Bonhoeffer was a highly unconventional man. The fact that he opposed Hitler is on its own enough to draw this conclusion: most people connected with the state churches did and said nothing to oppose the Nazis, and many seem to have been empty-headed enough even to actively embrace the Nazi German-Christian 'blend of neopagan and Christian beliefs' (von Kellenbach 2013: 40), or at least to keep silent about it. The Confessing Church, to which Bonhoeffer belonged, was formed when Nazi law dictated that persons of Jewish extraction were to be dismissed from church office; a 'very small minority' (von Kellenbach 2013: 42) of members of the Confessing Church, like Bonhoeffer, spoke out (see also Gordon 1997: 32–44).

One of the problems of reading the poetry of a religious poet like Bonhoeffer uncritically is that its Christian message can seem to be separate from its poetics. But it was not separate; when we read a poem such as 'Wer bin ich?' in order to translate it, the confrontation with what it might be in another language should signal the need to consider its poetics, including how the context in which it was written led Bonhoeffer to write in the way he did. 'Spott', 'mockery', then comes to seem an important word, especially when rhymed with 'Gott'. Not reading it for translation might well lead the translator either to opt for ending the poem with a conventional rhyme, or, being unable to find a suitable rhyme, to leave it out altogether. Reading for translation will not see these as the only options, because considering the linguistic possibilities of rhyme in English leads the translator to think about the opposition of mockery and God in Bonhoeffer's belief, and given the political context. For Bonhoeffer the Nazi German-Christian blended religion was itself a mockery, and so was the German-Christian designation 'gottgläubig', 'believing in God', the term used on official forms, and which meant believing in a Nazi God, or possibly that the Führer was God. Furthermore, the repeated question 'Who am I?' that mocks the speaker must be seen in relation to the Confessing Church's belief that its development from Judaism was important (as, of course, it was in a negative sense for the Nazis; cf. Gordon 1997: 38–41), whatever the established churches may have said. I would therefore prefer to translate more freely in order to give a hint of both the opposition and the question of origin (for naming in the Judeo-Christian tradition is to create):

Who am I? Lonely questioning plays its mocking game.
Whoever I am. Lord I am yours: you know my name.

Reading for translation is an active form of reading that builds cognitive contexts during reading and continues beyond the process of translation. This is why an important reason to translate Holocaust poetry is to get to the heart of the thinking that informed it. The Holocaust not only caused the deaths of many millions of people, and destroyed whole communities, but it also threatened to obscure the thoughts of its poets, including their poetic responses to the thinkers who came before them, and their influences on those who followed. Translation is an attempt to undo such obscuring. For Holocaust poetry this is especially true, because of the historical circumstances and their profound effects upon its poetics.

3.2 Translating to engage the reader

The Holocaust as a subject is only part of what characterizes Holocaust poetry. As I noted in Section 1.1, what makes it not merely poetry *about* the Holocaust is its poetic expression, especially in later poetry, of the changes the Holocaust has caused to our ways of thinking, of understanding and of representing the world, and its call to the reader to reflect on these changes. Translating it thus involves not only analytical comparative reading but also writing that embodies a mind-style appropriate to the post-Holocaust mind, and that enables engagement and creative reading (Attridge 2004: 79–83) by new readers to an extent that will produce cognitive effects as their mental schemata adapt in response to their reading.

In Section 3.1 some of the textual and contextual features were discussed that make up a poetics of Holocaust poetry when read from the point of view of its translation, that is, as translational poetics. While reading for translation brings its own gains in enhancing the translator's cognitive context, such cognitive effects and changes are unlikely to be the main or the only reason translators translate Holocaust poetry. It is worth considering here the other reasons. These are to some extent identical to the reasons for writing the original poetry: commemoration, bearing witness, giving voice to those who were silenced by the Holocaust. But a further reason for translating it relates to what is specific to poetry, as opposed to other forms of commemoration, or bearing witness or giving voice. This is the peculiar ability of poetry to reflect and embody contradiction. In Section 1.1, the tension present in all thinking about the Holocaust in the context of Adorno's 'negative dialectics' (see Buck-Moss 1977) was discussed. For Friedländer (1988: 287), it is a tension between a lack of closure, or meaning, or understanding – a sense of ineffability, the negative effect of which might be avoidance of thinking about the unbearable – on the one hand, and, on the other, our need to find meaning in events. This tension is reflected in Holocaust poetry in the struggle with older poetic certainties that leads both to a questioning of those earlier certainties and to the search for new ways of expressing and embodying life after the Holocaust, as we saw in the case of Ausländer's '*Biographische Notiz*' (2012: 145–6), 'Biographical Note', discussed in Section 2.2.

In Friedländer's statement that this tension is inevitable because we 'are dealing with an event which tests our traditional conceptual and representational categories' (Friedländer 1992: 2–3), we see that understanding and representation are connected. Descriptions such as 'traumatic realism' (Rothberg 2000) or 'awkward poetics' (Rowland 2005) are attempts to capture the way literature responds to this tension. Holocaust poetry written in English, such as that Rowland considers, embodies aspects of the tension. But it is unthinkable that we could try to understand it without knowing the work of those poets writing both in the presence of the events of the Holocaust and afterwards. Knowing this poetry requires translation.

The discussion about understanding and representation thus both provides an important reason for translating Holocaust poetry and supplies a crucial aspect of the context in which it is translated. The translator needs to be aware of the views of a critic like Steiner (1985: 180–93), who points to the power of indirection. Steiner regards Celan's poetry, with its language taken 'to the precise edge of the unsayable' (Steiner 2011: 198), as the best example of how to represent the Holocaust poetically.

Celan is, in fact, the Holocaust poet about whom most criticism has been written, and no Celan translator can be unaware of it. But the translator needs to read criticism critically. Englund (2012: 12), writing on the relationship between Celan's poetry and music, describes it as poetry in which 'meaning is constantly threatened but never completely abandoned', but Celan himself, who rejected any suggestion of hermeticism (cf. Hamburger 2007: 410–13), said that his poetry could best be understood by reading about Jewish mysticism (Felstiner 1995: 153). Though one must not take such comments entirely at face value either, Celan does seem here to be pointing to something that is in a sense the opposite of how Englund reads him. Rather than threatening but not abandoning meaning, perhaps we should see him as initiating but never pre-determining meaning. In his 'Foreword' to the 1960 book on the Kabbalah by Gershom Scholem, the writer whose work influenced Celan, as well as Benjamin and Sachs, editor Bernard McGinn notes that Rabbi Mendel of

Rymanow had said that the revelation on Mount Sinai only mentioned the first letter of the first commandment, leaving the rest to interpretation. Scholem agreed: this is 'to hear next to nothing, it is the preparation for all audible language, but in itself conveys no determinate, specific meaning' (McGinn 1996: xiv). This view of religious communication, that gives no definitive meaning but allows meaning to unfold, seems to come extremely close to Celan's idea of poetic communication as evidenced by the poems themselves, and this mystical element, which allows for the reader's interpretation and is exactly the opposite of the aestheticizing poetry Adorno feared, explains Steiner's approval. A translator needs to bear in mind these views because they are at the heart of why we translate Holocaust poetry.

Understanding such debates is also important to how we translate. Poetry represents the tension between the impossibility of finding a fixed meaning and our need to try to do so (cf. Danesi 2004: 9) by pointing the reader in certain directions, for example by foregrounding rhyme (as in Bonhoeffer's poem 'Who am I?', discussed in Section 3.1), while at the same time allowing freedom of interpretation. The critic William Empson said 'the machinations of ambiguity are at the very roots of poetry' and that poetry thus allowed 'room for alternative reactions' (Empson 1930: 1), and this is a view of poetry that persists in the most recent studies: poetry is not something that merely tells us things but is 'an incitement to world-changing reflection' (Jones 2012: 12).

Such considerations are also important to what we choose to translate. The simplest and most straightforward way in which rethinking is encouraged in the reader is through poems that deal directly with the Holocaust events and draw the reader straight into the world of the Holocaust, and these, as discussed in Chapter 1, make up a large proportion of those Holocaust poems that have already been translated. They include poems such as Mitchell's translations of Pagis' poems, for example 'Written in Pencil in a Sealed Railway-Car' (Mitchell 1981: 23), mentioned in Section 1.4, which ends in mid-sentence, so that the reader is made to feel an immediate sense of a life broken off. Ország-Land's translation of András Mezei's 'Gustav!' (Ország-Land 2010: 39), which recounts, in six short lines, the experience of coming face-to-face with one's neighbour in a firing squad, and is discussed in Section 1.3, works in a similar way. Such poems use simple language and little metaphor; their translation is generally straightforward. Their effect on the reader is in the momentary glimpse of a situation in which one could imagine oneself as victim, and it is important that they are translated.

Others, also mentioned in Section 1.3, need to be translated because they can help the readers rethink their cognitive models of the Holocaust by presenting the point of view of victims less often associated with the extermination policies of the Nazis: Romani poet Papusza's poem 'Tears of

Blood' or Sarcq's 'The Rag' (see *The Hypertexts*; http://www.thehypertexts. com; Sarcq 1995) are both rarely anthologized. When readers have a cognitive schema of the Holocaust that includes these other victims, poems such as von Törne's '*Rauch*' (1981: 164), become easier to understand. Otherwise, this poem, which asks 'Where have they gone, the tinkers and musicians?', could be read simply as a lament for the passing of a way of life that included itinerants, perhaps recalling the speaker's childhood. But clues in the poem such as 'Without trace // smoke in the clouds' and the title itself, 'Smoke', will call to mind the context of the Holocaust and the extermination of much of the Sinti population of Germany, if that is part of the reader's cognitive schema.

Yet other poems help us rethink the extent to which we trust accounts of the Holocaust. They might be views of what poetry can do, as in Ausländer's 'Biographical Note', discussed in Section 2.2, or models of the world as clear-cut, as in her poem 'As If', discussed in Section 3.1, or what we read in reports, as in von Törne's 'While Reading the Paper', discussed in Section 1.6.

For the translator, however important it is to translate poems that describe or conjure up single events from inside the camp or ghetto or cattle-truck and help the reader take on a new perspective in much the same way as do the many photographs that have been preserved from the time and can be found in books such as Gilbert's *Atlas of the Holocaust* (2009), the most challenging poetry expresses exactly what cannot be conveyed by photographs or such straightforward descriptive poems. In particular, rendering in another language reflections on the situation of those who lived after the Holocaust with the knowledge of what had happened – the thinking of the post-Holocaust mind – brings particular challenges for translators whose aim is to ensure the engagement of their readers.

These less well-known and less-anthologized poems are often less easy to categorize definitively as Holocaust poems. In von Törne's 'While Reading the Paper', for example, the image of 'yellow patches', which the speaker's sister sewed on her dolls, seems at first, like the smoke in the poem about tinkers and musicians, an intrusion into a poem not otherwise clearly about the Holocaust. But the intrusion of the image serves to locate the poem as a Holocaust poem for the reader.

Let us look again at the original German poem, '*Beim Lesen der Zeitung*' (von Törne 1981: 56), and consider further questions about how it might be translated in order to ensure that its translation allows a rethinking of the reader's cognitive models, as the original does. As we saw in Section 1.6, one of the ways in which the original expresses uncertainty about the truth of what we read in the newspaper is by leaving out the auxiliary after the phrase '*nichts gewußt*', thus leading the reader to consider what it might have been. The first two lines of the poem form one sentence, and are given here again with a gloss:

Ich	lese	in	der	Zeitung,	daß	die	Mörder
I	read(pr)	in	the	newspaper	that	the	murderers

Von	Mord	und	Totschlag	nichts	gewußt.
of	murder	and	manslaughter	nothing	known

As I explained in Section 1.6, there are several possible interpretations of the German sentence, depending on how one fills the gap after '*nichts gewußt*'. But there is a problem for the translator: though in German the auxiliary in reported thought or speech, which would normally appear after '*gewußt*' in the second line, expresses acceptance (if indicative) or scepticism (if subjunctive), English does not make this distinction, and so does not as a matter of course express the speaker's attitude. This means that the gap after the past participle '*gewußt*' in the original cannot simply be reproduced in English translation. The gap in the German version prevents the reader from regarding the phrase '*nichts gewußt*', which would normally come at the end of a sentence such as '*Wir haben nichts gewußt*', 'We didn't know anything', or might even be said as a short form on its own, as providing closure. Because in the sentence it depends on the complementizer '*daß*', 'that', it cannot normally end this sentence, which would require a finite verb form – an auxiliary – and it is this that is missing. A gap is an obvious way of engaging the reader: it begs to be filled. So what is the translator to do? One possibility is the suggested English translation (Boase-Beier 2006: 126) in the book that first discusses this poem. The translation there keeps the uncertainty by leaving out the verb completely:

Butchers ignorant of slaughter
- so at least the papers say.

The first line here is not clearly a representation of the thoughts of the newspaper reader; if the reader were agreeing with the newspaper account, one would expect the reader's thoughts to be represented as 'The butchers were ignorant of the slaughter'. So the first line is a more neutral echoing of what is read in the newspaper, and suggests a headline or sub-heading. However, in the first two lines of the German poem there are further implicatures (implications assumed to be intended; see Section 1.5). The clearest of these is implied by the fact that the auxiliary is absent: it sounds as though the reader of the newspaper is echoing the phrase '*nichts gewußt*', and therefore, whatever position the paper takes, has satisfactorily explained to herself or himself that the Germans who, after the war, as is well-documented (see e.g. Lifton 1986: 222, 489; Sereny 1995: 370–407), maintained they had not known of the atrocities being perpetrated, are to be believed. This additional implicature only becomes clear (to the reading translator) when the German poem is compared with its imagined English translation. How does one say '*nichts gewußt*' in English? What would English speakers say if they wanted to indicate ignorance of events about which they might reasonably be expected to have known? And, above all, how would the media characterize this common response in such a way that it could become a cliché? Clearly not in the way the above translation suggests. So it needs to be rethought. One possibility would be to quote the phrase 'didn't know', which is a possible echo of what people might say because it can also be used in the first person singular or plural. So the translation of the quoted two lines might instead be:

> Butchers 'didn't know' of slaughter
> So at least the papers say.

By keeping a phrase that might be spoken, the newspaper thus merely echoes what the butchers said, and remains neutral, leaving the forming of an opinion to the reader. In this case, the reader of the paper in the text world of the poem is the first-person narrator, who will probably be identified by the reader of the poem as the poet himself, because many of von Törne's poems can be read as explicitly autobiographical. If it is indeed the case, as the philosopher Dennett (1988: 185) maintains, that we can only process five or six levels of belief about the minds of others, the German poem will already demand a great deal of engagement on the part of the reader to work out who believes what. The translation is obviously about the situation in Germany, so the English reader will be likely to experience a further layer of reporting – by the translator on the original poem – and so it will become potentially more complex. But also, if we accept what Herman (2006: 373) says about narrative embedding, it will have more cognitive effects because it allows the reader to reconsider and develop his or her theories about the way other people's minds work. Furthermore, keeping the speaking voice of the original subjects (the 'butchers'), as the new translation does, not only allows the English poem to offer an equivalent in English to what they (and many others) said, but also allows the English version to be a possible reflection of what an English speaker might actually have said, and an English newspaper quoted. In terms of the possibility of taking multiple perspectives when reading, the addition of the translator's voice implied in the English words spoken (which clearly would have been German and so are being reported) allows for a further layer and a further perspective. Far from limiting empathy with the victims of the Holocaust, as statements about the supposed resistance of poetry, including Holocaust poetry, to translation (e.g. Langer 1995: 553) might lead one to expect, a translation that keeps both the voice of the murderers and the uncertainty of response in those reading the reports allows the reader to take each perspective in turn: that of those perceived (by the newspaper) as butchers, who 'didn't know'; the newspaper reporter who, in contrasting 'butchers' with the phrase 'didn't know', is being ironical; the reader of the paper, who comments on the irony in the phrase 'so at least the papers say' and so presumably shares, but is wary of, the ironical perspective; and the translator, who puts the whole into English.

Other examples of poetry that confronts and represents the post-Holocaust mind also pose interesting challenges when translating to engage the reader. Particularly those poets writing some years after the Holocaust wrote about living with the knowledge of its events and with the grief and trauma of loss. Their reactions to the Holocaust vary, and the translator, if aiming to preserve the individual stylistic characteristics of the poets, needs to be aware of this. We recall Caruth's definition of trauma, given in Section 1.5, as the later response to something not fully assimilated at the time (Caruth 1995: 4). Certainly the post-Holocaust mind, as we see it expressed through the mind-style of many Holocaust poets, can show elements of trauma. But trauma is also experienced differently by each individual (Caruth 1995: 4–5). Sachs, in particular, writes in response to the way acute distress about the Holocaust, by those directly suffering physical pain and by those affected by loss, upheaval or exile, becomes internalized, but it is, of course, her own view of that internalization. Consider her poem '*Sie schreien nicht mehr*' (Sachs 1971: 28), 'They no Longer Weep and Wail'. In this poem Sachs uses obvious Holocaust images – '*schreien*' ('to scream', 'cry' or 'wail'), '*Wunde*' ('wound') – as well as less obvious ones such as '*weh tun*' ('to hurt') and '*geisterhaft*' ('like ghosts, in a ghostly manner'). The poem is particularly interesting because it re-enacts the process by which physical wounds, or the memory of them, becomes internalized, resulting in psychological trauma. Sachs herself, at the time she wrote the poem, was suffering from clinical paranoia, which required her to stay for long periods of time in mental hospitals (cf. Fioretos 2011: 229–38). It is possible, according to Fioretos (2011: 234), to link the state of paranoia with a mystic state in which, working through pain, one reaches a higher understanding. And, indeed, a similar view of trauma and the sublime, in which suffering becomes 'an uncanny source of elation or ecstasy' (sometimes referred to as 'negative sublimity'), has been suggested by some scholars (see discussion by LaCapra 2001: 22–4). Though it is unclear whether Sachs would today be diagnosed as suffering from Post-traumatic Stress Disorder, it is possible that her paranoia, whatever its exact sources, gave her better access to, or at least a stronger inclination towards, the Jewish and Christian mysticism that influenced much of her poetry, and also gave her an insight into the way the trauma of Holocaust survivors develops (see Krystal 1995 for an enlightening discussion of the characteristics of trauma). The poem has only six lines and the middle two illustrate this process clearly:

Einer	steigt	auf	die	Wunden	des	Andern
one	climbs	onto	the	wounds	of-the	other

aber	es	sind	nur	Wolken
but	it	are	only	clouds

The first of these lines suggests an image from the gas chambers, as critics have pointed out (see e.g. Martin 2011: 124), where people scrambled over one another in a futile attempt to escape. But the verb '*steigen*', 'to climb', 'to rise', 'to step', also suggests the rising of smoke, and is the verb used by Celan in '*Todesfuge*' (1952: 38) '*dann steigt ihr als Rauch in die Luft*', 'then up you'll go as smoke in the air'. The verb is foregrounded because of its assonance with the words '*schreien*' ('cry'), '*einer*' ('one') and '*geisterhaft*' ('ghostly'). Thus the scrambling over bodies already anticipates, in both the word used and the image it conjures up, what is to happen to the bodies later. But of particular significance seems to be the word '*Wolken*', 'clouds'. It comes after the same number of syllables in the line as '*Wunden*' in the previous line and the phrase '*aber es sind nur*', which precedes it, makes a clear contrast: the wounds are now only clouds. The line that follows the two given goes on to say that these are clouds on which 'they' (the anonymous characters in the poem) now step, and the verb used here, '*treten*', has many connotations in German, for example, to step closer to something, to step too close to someone, to tread on someone's toes. It is important that the translation keeps the imagery that suggests the Holocaust as well as the change from the actual events to their internalization, from wounds to clouds:

> They no longer weep and wail
> when the pain comes
> One treads on the wounds of the other
> but it's only clouds
> they step on now
> that drip, like ghosts –

What I have done in this translation is to keep the Old Testament reference of the first line, which echoes the lamentation, in Jeremiah 9 (*New King James Bible* 1982: 10), 'I will take up a weeping and wailing'. The line is ambiguous in German: perhaps people will no longer weep and wail because they are saved, as the Christian New Testament, in Revelation 21, suggests: 'there shall be no more death, nor sorrow, nor crying. There shall be no more pain' (*New King James Bible* 1982: 10). But perhaps they have stopped weeping and wailing because they are dead, or because they are mentally dulled (in a state of paranoia or trauma or in the semi-conscious state of '*Muselmänner*' (literally 'muslims') to which many concentration camp inmates were reduced; cf. Weinberg 2013: 71), and, therefore, unable to react. The preservation of the position of 'wounds' and 'clouds' in the two central lines is crucial, because it foregrounds the fact that the former have become the latter. Sachs said, according to a number of sources (e.g. Fritsch-Vivié 1993: 99; Holmqvist 1968: 29): 'My metaphors are my wounds'. In English, as in German, this phrase – itself a metaphor – is ambiguous. It could mean 'My metaphors are not merely metaphors but are painful, like wounds' or 'My metaphors are the only expression of my wounds, you won't see physical wounds'. If we understand the metaphor as a blend, it means both these things, because there is a blended wound-metaphor space in which both concepts combine. And indeed, Sachs almost certainly meant both these things: wounds become metaphors and then the metaphors are painful. For the clouds drip in a ghostly manner: the parallelism of 'step' and 'drip' echoes the parallelism of '*treten*' and '*tropfen*' in the original poem, and suggests that the drips from the clouds occur (as though from a wound) when one steps on them. The repeated sounds of 'wounds – clouds' and 'step – drip' are thus also important, in iconically suggesting traumatic thinking, with its involuntary flashbacks and repetitive dreams (see e.g. Caruth 1995: 151–7). Indeed, '*geisterhaft*' in itself suggests the mental, rather than the physical: '*Geist*' is not only 'ghost' but also 'mind' in German. This late poem by Sachs (it was one of her last, published posthumously by her friends the Holmqvists), in contrast to her earlier ones, describes mental trauma rather than physical torture, and avoids the typical Holocaust imagery of her earlier poetry, such as her most famous poem '*O Die Schornsteine*', 'O The Chimneys', published in 1947 (Sachs 1988: 8). For the translator concerned about engaging the reader, her later poetry, probably influenced by news from Germany in the 1960s, the Frankfurt Auschwitz trials of 1963 to 1965 and the increasing public concern for the trauma of survivors, as well as her own situation and mental health, will demand particularly close attention to stylistic detail.

   Poems by Celan, such as '*Totenhemd*' (1968: 51), 'Winding Sheet', also suggest the way the post-Holocaust mind can, if traumatized, dwell on the Holocaust, unable to stop the recurring images. In this poem of three stanzas, after the image in the first stanza of 'That which you wove' with the suggestion that it might offer comfort ('When in the dark I waken the screams // it wafts above them') and, in the second stanza, that it might help one be free of guilt

('Who I am forgives // the one I once was'), the final stanza begins with a sudden menacing image:

Aber	der	Haldengott	
but	the	rubble-heap-god	

rührt	seine	dumpfeste	Trommel
hits	his	dullest	drum

(But the god of rubble-heaps strikes his dullest drum)

The image of a god of rubble-heaps, recalling the '*Trümmerhaufen*' of Germany in the aftermath of war and Allied bombing, and the '*Trümmerfrauen*' who worked at clearing them up, suggests, with its reference to a drum, the repetitive sounds or feelings of traumatic memory. But beyond this image, the language itself is full of significance. '*Halde*' is another word for '*Trümmerhaufen*' and '*Trümmer*' derives from '*Trumm*' ('piece'), which is originally from Old High German '*drum*', a word which, like the Old English 'thrum', means a 'small fragment'. '*Trümmer*', a word that is only present in the synonymity of '*Trümmerhaufen*' to '*Halde*', thus recalls the English word 'drum' for '*Trommel*', via its homophony with the Old High German word. And the Old High German '*drum*' and the Old English 'thrum' have given us the modern technical word 'thrum' in English: the end of a warp thread. 'Warp' derives from the Old English '*weorpan*', which led to '*werfen*' in German, a word that appears in the second stanza, and 'weapon' in English, and is related to the Indo-Germanic *'*uen*', which gave the German '*Wunde*' and the English 'wound'. Furthermore, because the first line (in its English translation) is 'That which you wove', the warp-end 'thrum' that echoes through '*Trommel*' and '*Trümmer*' ties together the images of weaving and drumming. For more discussion of the dense web of words in this poem, see Boase-Beier (2013), and see also Box 5, where some of these connections are represented.

The two lines are straightforward to translate:

But the god of the rubbleheaps
strikes his dullest drum

The problem is to weave into the poem various words that are etymologically linked, as well as clues to words that are etymologically linked but not actually present, and to words that sound as though they are etymologically linked but are not. I thus translated the first stanza with a repetitive pattern of alliterated words: 'wove', 'wear', 'waken', 'wafts':

That which you wove of lightest yarn
I wear to honour stone.
When in the dark I waken
the screams, it wafts above them.

Box 5 One thread in '*Totenhemd*'

Was Du aus Leichtem **wobst**

...

Aber der **Haldengott**
rührt seine dumpfeste **Trommel**

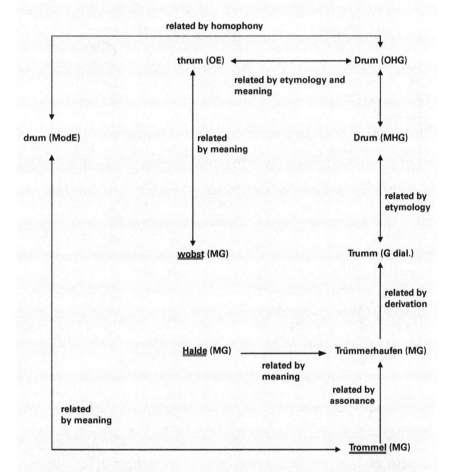

OE – Old English; ModE – Modern English; OHG – Old High German; MHG – Middle High German; MG – Modern German; G dial. – German dialect

Direction of arrows does not signal historical or other linguistic process but one possible way the translator might trace meanings and forms.

It is important that the readers of the English version should be able to use their existing knowledge of etymology, or be prompted to enhance their existing knowledge, in order to find out that 'waft', in spite of its similarity to 'weft' (a word which does not actually occur in the poem but is both related by etymology to 'weave' and suggested semantically by 'weave') is not actually related to it, but merely sounds as though it is. Celan's use of language was dense and obsessive, and there is an obsessive feel about the representation of memory in the poem for this reason. Words that merely suggest others to the obsessed mind are more indicative of such obsession than words that really relate to one another. But knowing, sensing or discovering the difference in order to experience traumatized thinking demands a great deal of engagement on the part of the reader and will not be possible unless the translator recreates at least some of these possibilities of engagement.

The nocturnal screaming, suggesting the recurring nightmares that are a common symptom of trauma (see e.g. Caruth 1995: 151–7), adds to the context within which the poem will be read, but, for the translator, the important thing is to ensure the reader 'becomes affectively implicated' (LaCapra 1998: 40), to some extent living through the process while trying to understand it, but remaining aware that he or she is not actually living through it. Both affective implication and critical distance depend on the dense web of obsessive imagery and language repetition, and this is why these poetic qualities of the original are crucial to the translated poem if it is to achieve its effects.

Trauma, as this poem suggests, often involves guilt (see also LaCapra 1998: 40–1); in Celan's case, his sense of guilt at his own survival when his parents had been killed is well documented (cf. Felstiner 1995: 26). Guilt is a feature of a great deal of the poetry written about the Holocaust, and not only by those with a direct experience of it, such as Celan. The younger von Törne, who started writing poetry in the 1950s, felt guilt not as a survivor but as the son of a (probable) perpetrator, an *SS-Standartenführer* (equivalent to a colonel; Hilberg 1985: 335). In her book on the guilt of perpetrators, von Kellenbach argues that guilt can be a positive force for good. It can be a way of avoiding the escapism of 'closure' on the past and an antidote to the self-centredness of the vast majority of the Nazi perpetrators tried after 1945 (Kellenbach 2013: 9). Most of them refused to step outside self-focus, thus avoiding recognition of what they had done, and also remained caught in the ideology that 'supplants personal moral agency and blocks the perception of the humanity, value and personal identity of victims' (Kellenbach 2013: 16). The failure to feel empathy for their victims, encouraged and enforced by Nazi ideology, thus not only made the murders and torture of the Holocaust possible but also later made it impossible to achieve any sort of 'moral transformation' (Kellenbach 2013: 21). If we take this view together with LaCapra's observation that perpetrators are also traumatized (LaCapra 1998: 41), as indeed is often attested in documents from the time (see Poliakov 1956: 130), it becomes clear that guilt can either contribute to avoidance of empathy or it can be a force for good, or, at least, for recognition and reparation. Von Törne, of course, had no objective reason to feel guilt: it was not his fault that his father was a Nazi, and he was only eleven years old when the war ended. Perhaps this is why the guilt his poems reflect is all the more striking: it is an imaginative guilt that expresses the adult's sorrow for the unthinking actions of a child, as though the child might have known what was really happening. In his poetry we see an important aspect of the post-Holocaust mind: not only what comes after – our ways of thinking or writing – are changed, but also the way we view retrospectively what was done or written before. In this way the poem 'While Reading the Paper' (given in full in the original earlier) not only makes the reader think about different levels of knowledge, but, in its final two lines, also creates a powerful sense of a blended world, in which the narrator looks back on his childhood. These two lines, in my translation, read:

> And I watched my sister with her dolls
> sewing yellow patches on in play

The reader, who in the first two lines experienced the speaker in the text world reading the paper and thinking about what it said, now observes the child, as she was in the embedded sub-world of the past (for the present tense of the first two lines has now become the past tense). The reader of the translation, like the reader of the original poem, and like the reader of the paper looking back, fuses the knowledge of what happened with the sewing-on of yellow patches, making them into a representation of the yellow stars the Jews were forced to wear. But, of course, the little girl did not know that, just as the reader of the paper did not know it at the time he watched his sister. The sense of guilt felt now arises from one's innocence then.

This blend of the innocent and the guilty is common to both Celan's and von Törne's poetry, and needs to be conveyed in translation. It is seen also in von Törne's autobiographical poem '*Gedanken im Mai*' (von Törne 1981: 168), 'Thoughts in May', which begins (in my translation): 'I speak of myself: Volker von Törne'. The title recalls the title of the German protest song, '*Die Gedanken sind frei*', written in the sixteenth century, and, according to Nader (who cites Breur 1997: 150), a song regularly sung in camps to keep inmates' spirits up (Nader 2007: 16). Of course, the point of the protest song is that, though one's body might be imprisoned, one's mind remains free. But the irony of von Törne's poem is that the post-Holocaust mind is not free. The poem continues with a series of repetitions with the same syntactic structure – '*Und ich trank die Milch … Und ich trug das Kleid … Und ich las die Bücher … Und ich hörte die Reden ... Und ich nannte ... Und ich betete ...*'. The poem, like Sachs' 'They no Longer Weep and Wail' and Celan's 'Winding Sheet', iconically enacts the repetitive nature of feelings of traumatic guilt: the corresponding English phrases would be: 'And I drank the milk ... and I wore the dress ... and I read the books ... and I heard the speeches ... and I called ... and I prayed...'. The litany of acts that have been (albeit unknowingly) committed culminates in the phrase '*Und schuldig war ich*', that is, literally 'And guilty was I'. The syntactic order is reversed here, and so the phrase is foregrounded. It echoes a famous poem '*Schuld*', 'Guilt', by Albrecht Haushofer, a Nazi sympathizer who realized his mistake and was executed for his involvement in the 1944 plot to assassinate Hitler; the poem was written shortly before his execution. It includes the line '*Doch schuldig bin ich*' (Haushofer 2012: 45).

In the translation of von Törne's poem, the change in order from '*Und ich trank ... und ich nannte*' to '*Und schuldig war ich*' needs to be honoured, to preserve the foregrounding effect. It is unlikely that knowledge of Haushofer's poem (or even of the famous protest song '*Die Gedanken sind frei*') will form part of the English reader's cognitive context. But the foregrounding of '*Und schuldig war ich*' is important. The phrase cannot, of course, be simply reversed in English, as in the literal translation given earlier. I therefore translate this phrase as: 'And mine was the guilt'. But the sentence does not end there. It goes on: 'For the death of every person, breathing in innocence // Beneath the gallows-branches // Of sweet-smelling limes.' In the original German 'breathing in innocence' is '*ahnungslos atmend*'. This participial phrase is ambiguous: it could be that others breathed in innocence or that the speaker did. The act of breathing (whether by the others or oneself) is contrasted with the cessation of breathing in those for whom the branches had really been used as gallows. And its participial form means it possibly refers to the past, and possibly to the present. There is a triple source of guilt: the speaker breathed in innocence (now felt to be tainted, to be ignorance rather than innocence) while others were murdered; the victims were unaware ('*ahnungslos*') about their fate; the speaker still breathes, though the branches of the lime were used as gallows. The juxtaposition of apparently innocent nature in the typical cliché of the 'sweet-smelling limes', as used in popular poems such as Otto Erich Hartleben's '*Süß duftende Lindenblüte*' (1906: 203) and given that the lime is traditionally a holy tree (Biedermann 1996: 208), with their use as gallows, is striking, and horrible. It seems crucial, therefore, to keep the close relationship that the compound 'gallows-branches' gives in English, as well as to preserve the various ambiguities made possible by the participial form of '*ahnungslos atmend*'.

What is important for the translator is to make sure that, as in the original poem, the reader is not merely told the poet feels guilty, but also himself or herself feels it, and is made to think through the ambiguities of guilt and responsibility: this is to read creatively. In fact, the poet von Törne, whose name opens the poem, is no more guilty than the reader and this fact also increases the degree of identification possible.

Holocaust memory is, of course, expressed not only in poems that reflect trauma or guilt, but also in poems of grief, especially in Celan's poetry: '*Heimkehr*' (Celan 1980: 94), 'Homecoming', and '*Espenbaum*' (Celan 1952: 15), 'Aspen Tree', both mentioned briefly in Section 1.5, are poems that create impossible worlds. Both poems also achieve cognitive effects by ambiguity. In '*Heimkehr*', ambiguity is on the one hand iconic in that it reflects, and activates in the reader, the sense that language hides potentially sinister meanings that can be exploited by the unscrupulous, and on the other it also serves of itself to engage the reader. The poem was written in 1959 (Celan 1980: 94) at a time when Celan had known for many years of the death of his parents, and had written many poems that spoke of his mother, or addressed her, as this poem appears to. It begins:

Schneefall,	dichter	und	dichter
snowfall	thicker	and	thicker

taubenfarben
dove-coloured

(Snowfall, thicker and thicker, dove-coloured)

The poem uses both images and words ambiguously. Lexical elements such as '*dichter*' ('thicker', and, as a noun, 'poet'), '*taub(en)-*' (as a noun: 'dove'; as an adjective: 'deaf') in these lines are ambiguous for reasons of etymology ('*dichter*') or because of (apparently non-etymological) homonymy ('*taub(en)-*'). The reader's interpretation may privilege one meaning over the other, but it is likely that the variety of possible meanings, which might indeed be contradictory, would be considered. Images themselves are also likely to be contradictory: the snow, which features in this poem, both covers and conceals, but also eventually melts to reveal. It might seem a contrast, in its pure whiteness, to the darkness, the night, and the colour black, which also feature in Celan's poems, as indeed they do in Ausländer's and Sachs'. But, in fact, snow 'hurts the eyes' later in the quoted poem, and is not pure white in Ausländer's poem 'Snow', where it 'glitters in every colour' (Boase-Beier and Vivis 1995: 39). Such images carry contradiction within themselves because there is, as in one of Sachs' poems '*kein reines Weiß auf Erden*' 'no pure white on earth' ('*Der Schlafwandler*' 1961: 66, 'The Sleep-Walker'). Thus, conceptual metaphors, while keeping their more conventional meanings, also take on the connotations of the post-Holocaust world and its inherent contradictions.

There are many words in the poem 'Heimkehr', from which the lines are quoted, that echo words coined or misused by the Nazis, for example 'gelagert', 'Heimkehr', 'heimgeholt'. 'Gelagert', 'layered', suggests 'Lager' or 'Konzentrationslager', 'concentration camp'; 'Heimkehr', 'homecoming' and 'heimgeholt', 'brought home', suggest the expression 'heimgeführt ins Reich' said of 'resettlers and refugees being led back home' (Klemperer 2000: 239) or 'heimfinden', 'to find one's way home', used for the 'glorification of blood' (Klemperer 2000: 264) in describing an annexed country such as Austria as having found its way home to its rightful place (minus its Jews and other undesirables). Other words carry connotations of the numbing caused by grief: 'Taube' can mean 'deaf', and later in the poem there are the words 'verloren', 'lost', and 'Stumme', 'silence'. The translator will have difficulty in preserving the double meanings of words such as 'Heim' or 'Lager', distorted by the Nazis, because these are words probably unknown to an English-speaking audience. In my translation I therefore opted to translate 'gelagert', layered, as 'piled up', to suggest the piles of belongings and also the bodies in the camps, and I translated 'Pflock', a word that also occurs in the poem and means 'post' or 'pole', as 'stake' in contrast to Hamburger's 'post' (2007: 125), in order to suggest stronger connotations of violence, since a stake is the post to which a sacrificial victim is tied for burning, or, more generally, a site of execution.

We saw in Section 2.1 that the reader is able to interpret 'Aspen Tree', the translation of Celan's 'Espenbaum' (1952: 15), on the basis of the conceptual metaphor PEOPLE ARE PLANTS. But the translator also needs to ensure that the reader can experience the grief expressed in the original. Written in the form of a Romanian folk-poem or doină, which often expresses grief at someone's death, it uses a sort of pathetic fallacy, so called by Ruskin because it was only a mind 'unhinged by grief' or other strong emotion that could imagine that nature could respond to the feelings of a human being (Ruskin 1863: 16). In the doină, nature serves as 'witness to personal despair' (Felstiner 1995: 49). I have discussed this poem and its translation at length elsewhere (see Boase-Beier 2011b), but it is worth mentioning here that the sense of grief is strengthened because all the comparisons in the poem are negated: they suggest nature does not echo what happened to the mother, and thus fails to be a mirror of the speaker's grief. The negative contrasts, in which the mother and nature behave differently, thus signal the failure of a blend of mother and nature that would, in the usual way doină and other poems of lament work, or indeed in pathetic fallacy as Ruskin described it, result in a personified mother-nature blend. If nature is personified because it is blended with the mother, then the mother lives on in nature, and there is closure that eventually brings grief to an end. But it does not happen here, and the failed blend is signalled even more clearly in the final stanza:

Oaken door, who pulled you off your hinges.
My gentle mother cannot come in.

Here the mother remains outside the unhinged world of the poem. And there is a further contrast in the action of pulling a door off its hinges, and the gentleness of the mother. It seemed important, therefore, to use the verb 'pulled' in my translation for what is in German closer to 'lifted' in '*hob dich aus den Angeln*', because the contrast is clear in the German: the expression '*die Welt aus den Angeln heben*', literally 'to lift the world off its hinges', means to cause chaos, to overturn the accepted order of things. The image of being unhinged is used in English to mean mad, or, as in Ruskin's expression, quoted earlier, at the mercy of an overwhelming emotion, and bears some similarity to the German '*aus den Angeln heben*'. Indeed, it relies on the same conceptual metaphor: LIFE IS A BUILDING (Kövecses 2002: 109). The problem is that 'lifted', the nearest equivalent, while it keeps the conceptual metaphor, reduces the strength of the action. It is important that the reader should be able, in the translation as in the original, both to experience the weight of the speaker's grief and to share in the sense of a catastrophe of world-changing dimensions.

Sometimes feelings are expressed less strongly: as regret rather than grief. Both feelings involve a counterfactual world in which what is lost (a person, a way of life, a future) is blended with the current situation. We see this very clearly in Wind's 'The Blessing' (1996: 24), which begins 'They could have said / stay'. In her book *Regret*, Landman argues for a more positive view of regret, as a feeling that can lead to change (Landman 1993: 16). In translating the poem into German, Gabriel (2004: 65) has, in fact, acted on this more positive aspect. By envisaging a world in which the Jews had not been persecuted or transported or murdered, the poem suggests a possible future after those events, and the translation in German helps make German readers aware of the blend of negative and positive feelings associated with such a world.

Poems of regret could be seen as part of a reconciliatory tendency among some Holocaust poets, where dismay about past suffering is linked with hope for the future. Sachs has often been viewed in this way, and, though it is true, as we have seen, that her later poetry shows the influence of mystical thinking, probably in part because of her reading in the 1950s of kabbalistic works such as the *Book of Zohar* (Scholem 1935), the Medieval work by Rabbi Moses de Leon, often assumed to have been written in the early second century, as well as the works of Old Testament translator and Hasidic scholar Martin Buber (cf. Fritsch-Vivié 1993: 98–9), her poetry is not on the whole poetry of hope and reconciliation. It is perhaps better described as a poetry of search in the mystical tradition: that is, based on the predominantly Christian notion of finding God (cf. Dan 2007: 10). Holmqvist, the editor of much of Sachs' poetry, calls it poetry of '*Sehnsucht*', that is, 'longing' (Holmqvist 1968: 9–10). The search, for Sachs, is partly a search for words that have, as Celan put it, quoting Adorno (Englund 2012: 8), a 'strong tendency to fall silent' (Felstiner 1995: 409). She also expressed her admiration for philosopher Simone Weil, and what Sachs called '*das Nichts lieben*' (Fritsch-Vivié 1993: 97), 'loving the nothing'.

Reading Buber, with his focus on the power of language in creation (cf. Fritsch-Vivié 1993: 98–9; Buber and Rosenzweig 1994: 27–39), would have made Sachs aware of the importance of language in poetry. The kabbalistic focus on the 'nonsemantic' aspects (Dan 2007: 66) of language has influenced not only earlier poets and philosophers but also cognitive poetics scholars like Tsur (see e.g. 2008). According to Sachs' biographer, the word and the identification with the word was for Sachs '*der Wesenskern des Judentums*' (Fritsch-Vivié 1993: 99), 'the constitutive kernel of Judaism'.

It is thus not surprising that many Jewish poets like Sachs or Celan felt poetry had a duty to use the creative power of language to oppose manipulation. But also for von Törne the reader needs to be alerted to the way language can be used by the unscrupulous to mean whatever they want. The lack of fixed meaning in poetry is the best way to illustrate this. Translating, because it always confronts the lexicalized word or phrase with something similar but differently expressed in another language, is a particularly appropriate way to grasp the unfixedness of meaning. For this reason, a foregrounding of the act of translation in the presentation of translated Holocaust poetry is important. I shall return to this point in Chapter 4.

Von Törne's rich use of stock phrases, as illustrated in the poems already discussed, serves not only to question their use and to recall that 'German speech under Nazism had become ossified with clichés, unexamined definitions and left-over words' (Steiner 1985: 45), but also to address the reader in terms that are familiar, so the translator faces a triply difficult task: to produce a phrase recognizable enough to draw the reader in, to make it enough of a cliché, even in English, to trigger an ironical response, and to do all this not only in a reading context in which the exact form of Nazi manipulation of language is unlikely to be known and has to be constructed by the reader, but also in poems that refer to German society twenty-five years after the Holocaust, and often do not refer directly to the Holocaust itself. I mentioned this problem in Section 2.1 in relation to '*deutsch sprechen*', 'to speak German' (or, as the dictionary would have it, 'to speak English'; Terrell et al. 1991: 163). Other poems juxtapose popular German products and their designations with National Socialist thinking, for example, in the poem '*Bleibende Werte*' (von Törne 1981: 50), 'Enduring Values': '*Mohrenköpfe.*

Dr Goebbels'. 'Mohrenköpfe' are a sort of chocolate-covered marshmallow but the term literally means 'heads of blackamoors'. Many poems have no obvious references to the Holocaust; it is only their co-occurrence with examples such as those mentioned that is likely to make it very difficult for the reader not to read references to a violent past into descriptions of the unsatisfactory situation for German workers at the time von Törne was writing. The reader is thus placed in the position of experiencing the post-Holocaust mind directly. Consider the poem 'Akkord' (von Törne 1981: 193), 'Piecework Agreement', which consists of a list of idioms for self-sacrifice and for inaction:

Trag deine Haut
Zu Markte. Laß
Dir das Fell
Über die Ohren
Ziehen. Halt
Die Knochen
Hin. Bleib auf
Dem Teppich. Sieh
In die Röhre. Reiß
Deine Tage herunter
Bis du genug
Hast und
Abkratzt

'Laß Dir das Fell über die Ohren ziehen', for example, means something like 'let yourself be tricked' but literally says 'allow your skin (fur) to be pulled over your ears'; 'halt die Knochen hin' means 'offer yourself up for sacrifice' but literally says 'hold out your bones'. The particularly graphic nature of the idioms von Törne uses to suggest the supposed agreement of workers to be exploited makes the reader think of expressions that, in the inconceivable world of the Holocaust with its cruelty and slave labour, or the dead world of unthinking acceptance of repression of any sort, might not only be manipulative, but might also take on their literal meaning. This is a fear also expressed in the poems of more recent German poets. In a poem about gardening by Sarah Kirsch, for example, 'graben', 'to dig', suggests a 'grave', 'Grab', and 'Gras' 'grass', suggests 'Sarg', 'coffin' (see Mulford and Vivis 1995: 22–3). Such poems raise questions especially about how to translate post-Holocaust poetry so that the reader experiences the post-Holocaust mind. The context in which the poems are presented in the originals suggests the persistence of Germany's past in its present. How they are read will depend to a large extent on the context in which the translations are presented, a point to which I will return in Chapter 4.

For a translator who wants the reader to be aware of the possible literal meanings of the idioms in the poem '*Akkord*', there is no point translating with a near equivalent: 'Let them pull the wool over your eyes' does not have the same connotations. Of course, 'to pull the wool over someone's eyes' possibly did originally mean literally to skin someone, as does 'to fleece someone'. But it could equally well be seen as a reference to putting up a blanket to hide things, because 'wool' in English is usually seen as a woven substance rather than the skin of an animal. Dictionaries of idioms give the origin as to pull a wig over someone's eyes (see e.g. Rees 1991: 270), which is certainly possible, if not entirely convincing. Thus it would be better, along the lines suggested by Berman (2012: 250–1), to keep the idiom as it is, or nearly so, and allow the reader to work out that it has the possible connotations of being literal. In order to indicate that it is, in fact, an idiom in German – for the irony depends upon this fact – such phrases need to be brought into line with English ones somewhat, thus creating a blend of English and German. 'Stick your neck out' is actually more suggestive than the German idiom of 'offering yourself for sacrifice or execution', but again can be adapted to make it more so. Thus one might translate the two idioms as follows:

> … Let them
> Pull your skin
> Over your
> Eyes. Stretch
> Out your
> Neck. …

The need to transform and reclaim language in cases such as this is signalled by using common idioms within poems, where they are automatically foregrounded, and this allows their negative connotations to be felt by the reader. Here the need for transformation is an implicature of language with negative overtones, but language can also be invested with new connotations. The obverse of putting degraded language on display for the reader's ironic contemplation is to already suggest the way forward to a new language. Von Törne rarely does this, undoubtedly because he saw, in the repressions of both the Democratic West and the Communist East Germany, the part of Germany where he was born but later did not live, many echoes of the dictatorship under which he was born. For Sachs, though, and also for Ausländer, examples of a language that is seen as having negative connotations are balanced by a 'faith in the creative and transformative power of language' (Bower 2000: 125). Bower uses the example of Ausländer's transformation of '*Volk*', 'people', a neutral word (though often, in German Romanticism, with connotations similar to the English 'folk' as in 'folk song') that was used by the Nazis to mean the people of pure German blood, and is used ironically by von Törne in

'Thoughts in May': 'as already the people were rising up against my people', *'mein Volk'* (von Törne 1981: 168). Ausländer, in the poem *'Lassen uns nicht'* (Ausländer 2012: 104), 'Not Let Ourselves', uses *'Mein Volk'* to mean the Jews of the world with whom she identifies, and then transforms the word: *'Mein Sandvolk // mein Grasvolk'*, 'my sand-people // my grass-people'.

Such examples suggest that a new way of writing poetry after the Holocaust was possible which not only reflected the events and expressed the problems of representation, but also, particularly under the influence of mystical thought in the poems of Ausländer and Sachs, hinted at the possibility of recovery. Where such hope is expressed in the poems, it is often very oblique, but these hints and suggestions need to be preserved in translation.

Celan also hints at the power of language to heal. The poem *'Weggebeizt'* (Celan 1982: 27), 'Cauterized', mentioned in Section 1.5, begins:

Weggebeizt	vom	
etched-away	by-the	
Strahlenwind	deiner	Sprache
ray-wind	of-your	language
das bunte	Gerede	des An-
the colourful	talk	of-the on-
erlebten –	das	hundert-
experienced	the	hundred
züngige	Mein-	
tongued	my	
gedicht,	das	Genicht
poem	the	not-poem

(Etched away by the ray-wind of your language, the colourful talk of the vicariously experienced, the hundred-tongued my-poem, the *Genicht*)

There are several translations of this poem (Hamburger 2007: 267; Felstiner 2001: 247; Gillespie 2013: 109) and they are all very different, just as interpretations of the poem also vary greatly (see e.g. Felstiner 1995: 218; Pöggeler 1994: 105–6; Neumann 1968: 80–1). The first word, which means worn away by a caustic substance or by wind or some other form of geological erosion, has generally been translated as 'etched away', but the rest of the first stanza, especially the word *'Meingedicht'*, is difficult. *'Meingedicht'* could mean 'my poem' but also, as in *'Meineid'*, 'perjury', it could suggest a false or lying poem. *'Meineid'* is formed from *'Eid'* 'oath' and an obsolete adjective **maina*, 'false'. *'Genicht'* is a word coined by Celan, and appears to be a portmanteau or blend of *'Gedicht'* 'poem' and *'nicht'* 'not'. *'Meingedicht, das*

Genicht' is translated as 'pseudo-poem, the noem' by Hamburger; 'My-poem, the Lie-noem' by Felstiner; and 'lie-poem, the noem' by Gillespie.

My translation of these lines is:

Cauterized by
the ray-wind of your words
the colourful talk of bought
experience – the hundred-
tongued my-
poem, the lie-poem.

I consider it important to keep the meaning of 'my' in '*Meingedicht*' because of Celan's belief that poetry was communication, a poem was always aimed at someone else. The contrast here seems to be between the words of the other, the '*Du*' of the poem, which have healing power, and a poem that without communication remains both false and self-referential, as is the thoughtless language that Celan elsewhere called '*Geschwätz*', or 'babble', a word used by Benjamin, and also by philosopher Martin Heidegger, whose thinking exerted a huge influence on Celan's poetry but whose early Nazi sympathies made the relationship of poet and philosopher extremely complicated (see Felstiner 1995: 144; Lyon 2006). '*Beize*' is also the substance put on wounds to burn excess tissue away and thereby to heal. The poem thus reflects the Nazis' 'killing to heal' doctrine, whereby, in their depraved world, undesirable people and communities were excised to heal the body of the '*Volk*' (cf. Lifton 1986: 15–16). And it also suggests the actual use of caustic substances, especially at Auschwitz, in experiments on inmates to attempt to sterilize them, as became known after the Nuremberg doctors' trials of 1946–7 (cf. Mitscherlich and Mielke 1995). But the poem subverts this scenario, for here the caustic substance does indeed heal, or at least has the potential to heal, the wound: at the end of the poem there 'waits, a breath-crystal, // your undeniable // witness'. I use 'cauterized' for '*weggebeizt*' because wounds are cauterized, and because the image of cauterizing in order to heal and revitalize the '*Volk*' was so often used by the Nazis (cf. Lifton 1986: 496). It is also one of the roots, via Greek '*kaustos*', 'burnt', of the word 'Holocaust'. Language, Celan is saying, in contrast to the Nazis' degenerate semi-medical worldview, can actually heal, because it can uncover the distortions it has suffered and so survive. So it is important that the language of the translation bears all traces possible of that language which it is poetically to subvert.

Simply writing in German, but a German transformed so that it is neither the German of the Nazis nor a German that behaves as though nothing had happened, is in a sense an act of hope. Not to consider the stylistic detail of the language in translating it would therefore be a betrayal.

4

Translation and understanding

4.1 Translated Holocaust poetry and the education of the reader

At various public readings of translated Holocaust poetry, I have been struck by the appreciation and absorption of the audience. And yet, most Holocaust poetry is not enjoyable in the same sense as nature poetry or poetry about relationships might be. It refers to events that most of the audience have fortunately not experienced, and it describes states of mind that are not easy to contemplate: terror, grief, trauma, sadness, regret. It is also not easy or accessible poetry, because it is translated from other languages and has its source in other cultural and historical contexts. The poetic traditions it alludes to and calls into question are also largely unknown to the audience. So what is it that the audience gets out of hearing the poetry? And could there be lessons here for the future publication of translated Holocaust poetry?

There is, of course, an intense interest in the Holocaust, even among those too young to remember the events or their immediate aftermath. This is partly because it is a period of history not too far removed from our own, in a geographical context not too distant from England. There is, inevitably, an element of voyeurism in our fascination with the Holocaust. We cannot help but be drawn to the dreadfulness of it because we want to know and understand. But poetry does not provide details of horrible events, on the whole, so this is not the main reason for its resonance with readers and listeners.

When questioned, audiences speak of the 'shock of recognition' that comes with the realization that they could have been involved in these events, and of the fact that the poetry makes you think.[2] The person who used these words was unconsciously echoing Hughes, who spoke of the power of Pilinszky's poetry in gathering 'the sense of Cosmic hopelessness into a familiar, intimate shock' (Hughes 1989: 16). And people frequently say they 'enjoyed' the reading. Though the word 'enjoyment' always makes one a little uneasy in this context, I think it is valid. The enjoyment comes from cognitive effects: from the discovery of new poets, from unexpected insights, from these 'shocks of recognition', an acknowledgement of shared humanity, and from the effort of thinking and rethinking one's cognitive models, of feeling oneself accessing new ways of looking at the world.

The translation of Holocaust poetry into English has up to now been a rather unambitious undertaking. As we have seen, there are many victims that it fails to bring to our attention, it fails to bring any but the best-known poets into English, and sometimes it fails to encourage questioning of the reader's cognitive models in the way the original poetry did. This is rarely the fault of the translators themselves, but rather of the way the poetry is chosen, presented and published. Of course, the anthologies and single collections of translated Holocaust poetry, the individual translated poems in journals and books, and in scholarly studies, have all played an enormously important part in making the poetry available to the English-speaking world. But we need to do far more.

There are two things to take into account here in deciding what needs to be done, and how. The first is the special nature of poetry and its place in thinking about the Holocaust. As I hope to have demonstrated, poetry is neither historical documentation nor a mere cry of anguish; one only needs to read what poets themselves claim for poetry to understand at least what its aspirations are. Geoffrey Hill said it was 'the atonement of aesthetics with rectitude of judgment' (Hill 2004: 472), Seamus Heaney spoke of the way a poem 'enters our field of vision and animates our physical and intelligent being' (Heaney 1995: 15) and for Adrienne Rich, when we read it 'we are, to an almost physical degree, touched and moved' (Rich 2007: 32).

The second thing to be taken into account is that translation is neither a necessary but obscuring evil nor simply a transparent way of conveying what some foreign poet said. This has also been said and demonstrated many times by translators such as Scott (2012), Jones (2011) or Grossman (2010: 91–119). But, though I am less pessimistic than Venuti (2008) about the level of understanding of translation, there is clearly more to be done, so that the way we see translation can change. However, my main concern in this book is not the status of translation *per se* but the way readers, including scholars of the Holocaust and of Holocaust poetry, understand translation and how our understanding affects the way we read.

To think about both the nature of poetry and the nature of translated poetry, and their consequences, we need to go back to the question of understanding and meaning, and the way meanings both persist and change. When I talk to people about my work, or give public readings of translated Holocaust poetry,

I am often asked, 'Why do you work on Holocaust poetry?' What people mean is, 'Why do *you* work on Holocaust poetry?' (Since you are not Jewish, or gay, or Romani, not the child of survivors or perpetrators: this is what the questioners imply.)

So it seems worth tracing, for a moment, my personal reasons for this work, in the hope that they will shed light both on why we might want to understand more about the translation of Holocaust poetry, and on what we might want to change.

I have several times, when answering these questions, traced the origin of my interest in translated Holocaust poetry to an incident that happened when I was three years old. It had nothing to do with poetry or translation, on the face of it, but everything to do with understanding. My father was reading the paper and my brother and I were playing (though not with dolls). He put the paper down and said, in a sort of despairing voice that I have never forgotten, 'They did such terrible things to the Jews'. There was only one thing we children wanted to know at the time: who or what were the Jews? Later I wanted to know who 'they' were, who had done the terrible things, whether they were different from 'us', and whether they did these things only to the Jews. And later still, I wondered what my father, on that day in 1957, had been reading. And yet later, what does poetry say and do that carries on where the newspaper left off? And still later, how does translated poetry help us understand more? It simply could not be the case that the process of translation didn't matter, that it just gave us some sort of sense of the original and that was all. Frustratingly, this appeared to be the common view.

Part of the source of the multiple failures of translated Holocaust poetry to reach its full potential is that the view that translation doesn't matter ignores not only the nature of translation but also the nature of poetry. I hope that the discussion in Chapters 2 and 3 has demonstrated some of the ways in which translation is already inscribed in the original poetry and some of the ways in which the process of translation gives us insights into the poems that we would not otherwise have. So it seems that an important place to start in trying to do more would be to raise awareness of the fact that readers of Holocaust poetry are reading translations, with all that this entails.

We could start by thinking of the main areas in which translated Holocaust poetry could become more ambitious:

(i) It could be presented in such a way that readers are encouraged to see they are reading poetry in translation and consider the role of the translator and the translator's choices

(ii) There could be more emphasis on the later, less explicit poems of those Holocaust poets who are known in English translation, because those poems embody and express the effects of the Holocaust on the minds and on the writing of these poets.

(iii) The translation and presentation of Holocaust poetry could draw the reader's attention to the importance of language and style and thus awaken the reader's multilingual sensibilities.

(iv) There could be more support for the reader in terms of historical and geographical background, to aid context-building.

(v) There could be more translations of poets who are less well known.

(vi) There could be more translations of poets writing in other languages than the most common ones such as German, French and Hungarian, and those who were victims for other reasons than being Jewish, or who wrote about those other victims.

(vii) Festivals could feature translated Holocaust poetry, and criticism, reviews and scholarly writing on Holocaust literature, including, and especially, poetry, could pay more attention to the role of translation.

(viii) Translators themselves could engage more with translation theory; they could read more of the books other translators and scholars write, and reflect, publically and in introductions and prefaces, on the links between theory and practice.

This list makes it clear that I am not suggesting translators alone can change the rather unsatisfactory situation of translated Holocaust poetry, nor that scholars can in isolation alter the lack of concern for translation as a major element in understanding Holocaust literature. It is useful at this point to consider the translation of Holocaust poetry in terms of the 'networks of people and texts' (Jones 2011: 13) involved, as mentioned in Section 3.1. In using Actor Network Theory, Jones draws upon studies such as Even-Zohar (2012), a study which, in its original 1978 version, contributed to the polysystem view of literary translation. This is the view, discussed in Section 2.1, that translated literature as a whole needs to be seen in relation to the 'co-systems' of the target and source literature (Even-Zohar 2012: 163). Jones is less interested in the norms that may arise from the demands of literary systems themselves than Even-Zohar, or than Toury (1995), another of the original proponents of the polysystem view, and more interested in the various individual actors in the system and the factors that influence decisions about what and how to translate. Poetry translation, in Jones' view, is a 'personal, interpersonal and poetic action within a complex real-life context' (Jones 2011: 24). That context, Jones goes on to explain, in line with cognitive poetic views of literature, involves both 'the inner worlds of thought and feeling, and the outer worlds of interacting and doing' (Jones 2011: 24). A translator interacts not only with the text and all the factors that influence the text but also with the target audience including reviewers and other readers. All these 'other subjects, human-made artefacts and physical objects' (Jones 2011: 27) form the basis for the system of networks that describe the context of translating poetry.

Such a view might have several consequences for what and how we translate and the way we present it. In what follows, when I discuss its presentation, I am assuming the poetry is published in printed books, but, in fact, e-books offer many of the same possibilities, and in some cases more.

I have already suggested in Chapter 2 that the readers' awareness that they are reading a translation can and should profoundly affect the way they engage with the poem. Point (i) on the list suggests that this awareness should be supported. As readers, our emphasis is then able to shift from seeing the poetry as a conveyor of historical information, or as a reaction to historical events, to reading it as a representation of an act of communication by a poet, and then by a translator willing to engage with that poet. This does not mean that its role as a conveyor of history or a reaction, or a preserver of memory, is shut out, but merely that the reader is able to take a view that is less narrow: the poet and the translator are saying something to me and I need to think how I feel about it. Because translation, clearly presented as such, foregrounds the translator's reading of and engagement with the original poem, it can help shift focus from the original poem as an account of events to its relation to how we think and speak about the events. What the translator has done is to give an account of that particular poet's way of poetically transforming events.

There are several ways in which readers can be made aware that they are reading such accounts, that is, encouraged to read the translation as a translation. It is already common for some publishers of translated poetry to feature the name of the translator prominently on the cover of the book, but not all do this; see the website of CEATL (European Council of Literary Translators' Associations; www.ceatl.eu), for examples. Where it happens, it shows the reader that this is, for example, Dove bringing us Steinherr (2010), or Hamburger bringing us Celan (2007). If someone else has written an introduction to the translated poetry, this helps to underline the importance of the work as a work of translation. If George Szirtes is commenting on Francis Jones' translation of Radnóti (Jones 2000), we want to know what he says. Introductions by other poets and scholars, translators' prefaces, notes and biographies all serve to draw the reader's attention to the translator as the author of the translated work. This has been noted many times before, most famously, perhaps, by Venuti (see 2008: 1–34). However, my argument in favour of such visibility is not only that it helps counteract the invisibility that so angers Venuti. It is important not only in order to foreground translation and to support the translator's rights, but also because such visibility is absolutely necessary in order to read the text consciously as a translation, and to be able to think through the consequences of this fact for the Holocaust poetry we are reading. We need to know how the translator has seen the task, his or her reasons, perspective, and approach. All this will help widen the focus from the poem as representation of Holocaust events – crucial though that is – to the way the poem makes us reflect on those events and the sort of changes we are prepared to make in our own perceptions as a result.

Later poetry, as suggested in point (ii), is important partly because the change of emphasis that can come about for the reader in consciously contemplating what it means to read these poems in translation has a parallel in the way individual Holocaust poets themselves developed. We have seen that there was a gradual but noticeable movement away from early attempts to document, recount, or imagine events (as in Sachs' '*O die Schornsteine*' [1988: 8], 'O The Chimneys', or Celan's '*Todesfuge*' [1952: 37–9], 'Death Fugue'), towards a later concern with how we write, how we think and speak, what we reject as ways of writing, thinking and speaking and what we embrace (as in Sachs' '*Sie schreien nicht mehr*' [1971: 28], 'They no Longer Weep and Wail', or Celan's '*Weggebeizt*' [1982: 27], 'Cauterized').

We can see how this poetic development is cut off in a poet like Meerbaum-Eisinger, whose poetry showed such promise. Like almost all Holocaust poets, Meerbaum-Eisinger was a translator. Her slim *œuvre* includes translations of major Yiddish poet Itzik Manger, of Paul Verlaine from French, of Romanian poet Discipol Mihnea (Meerbaum-Eisinger 2013: 72–8). Because the ability to cross languages, or rather the inability *not* to do so, is inscribed in the work of these poets, a poetic development that increasingly considers questions of language and representation was inevitable. We would have seen it in Meerbaum-Eisinger, had she survived, just as we would have seen it in all those other Holocaust poets who did not survive, and whose poetry therefore represents an early stage in their poetic development. All the more reason why poets such as Meerbaum-Eisinger should be translated more, as well as all those others, like Itzhak Katzenelson, who lived in the Warsaw ghetto and died in Auschwitz, or anarchist and pacifist playwright and poet Erich Mühsam, who was murdered in Oranienburg Concentration Camp in 1934 (as documented already in the anonymous 1936 English Publication *The Yellow Spot*). If we cannot change the fact that their poetry never had the chance to develop and reflect the post-Holocaust situation and their own poetic engagement with it, at least we can create new contexts and dialogues for our engagement with their early poetry, written in direct response to the catastrophic events. Some poets like Radnóti or Szlengel already had a highly developed poetics by the time they were killed, because they had already been writing poetry for many years before they were overtaken by the events of the Holocaust.

Nevertheless, even though their poetry might have been more mature than that of less experienced poets, their deaths in the Holocaust meant it could not engage with the post-Holocaust world, which had such profound effects on questions of representation and aesthetics. In the case of poets such as Celan or Sachs who did survive long enough both to develop poetically and to respond to the post-Holocaust world, it is all the more frustrating that it is their earlier, more explicit, poetry that is better known in translation.

Greater availability of their later work in English translation would, therefore, be a good thing. This later poetry gives us access to what I have been calling 'the post-Holocaust mind', and it also helps us understand the poets' own stories. Stories are not just sequences that we construct when we read novels or poems; we also create stories of people's lives and development. When I said just now that 'we would have' seen Meerbaum-Eisinger's development into a poet who reflected on the Holocaust in her poetics, I was telling a counterfactual story in analogy to the development of those poets who survived. It is arguable that our need to understand how people dealt afterwards with their role in the Holocaust, whatever it might have been, is as great as our need to understand how the Holocaust came about, and what actual events were involved. As von Kellenbach (2013: 21) puts it: we need 'stories that express the circuitous and complicated processes of moral transformation and ideological disentanglement' that happen after the Holocaust. As Turner (1996) says, stories are not just something that happens in literature; they are how we think. The danger of excessive anthologizing is that it can erase the story of a poet's development. For this reason, the recent appearance of Hamburger's translation of Sachs' *Glowing Enigmas* (Hamburger 2013) is particularly welcome as it draws together later poetry that had already appeared in translation, but not as a complete collection.

The later development of those poets who began writing during the Holocaust often happened alongside their work as translators and the growing understanding that brought them, as shown in Chapter 3, about the nature of representation. Sachs' work, as is well known (cf. Fioretos 2011: 27–134), showed very clearly the influence of her translations of Swedish Modernist poets such as Erik Lindegren (who in 1937 had translated T. S. Eliot), Gunnar Ekelöf und Johannes Edfelt. She had published the anthology *Von Welle und Granit*, (*Of Waves and Granite*) in East Berlin in 1947, and her own poetry from this time on had taken on the experiments with rhyme, metre and punctuation, the undermining of conventional imagery and the questioning of faith, that were to be found in the work she had translated. The development from her earlier poetry, about flowers and deer, music-boxes and heroic battles, to even the early Holocaust poems such as '*O die Schornsteine*', is quite astonishing. Though her earlier poetry is competent, it is extremely conventional (see Fioretos 2011: 34). After 1947 she rejected all her earlier work. I would argue that her development from then on, towards more oblique, less explicit poetry, was not only influenced by the Swedish Modernist poets she continued to translate, but also by the act of translation itself. The realization that other languages say things differently, and that the German language could be stretched, altered and renewed, was an important insight.

I suggest in (iii) that the encouraging of exactly this insight could usefully inform the way translated poetry is presented to the reader. That is, the sort of awareness Sachs gained about the multilingual possibilities of poetry, and about the engagement required of the translator, are insights that are also invaluable to both the general reader and the analytical reader of translated poetry, as discussed in Chapter 2.

So how might such multilingual sensibility and awareness be supported? When considering how published translations might have a less monolingual focus, it is worth returning to the question recently posed by Scott (2012: 1), and mentioned in Section 1.6, as to whether translated poetry is aimed at those who can read the original, or those who cannot. Scott says it must be for the former, because this is the only way to avoid the translation appearing to be merely making an inaccessible source text somehow visible to an ignorant reader, thereby distracting from the real 'business' of translation, which is to focus on 'readerly consciousness' (Scott 2012: 1–3). I agree with Scott that the concern of translation studies should not be a completed text in a target language that can almost be read as though no translation had happened, though I disagree that this is, in fact, the current concern of all translation studies scholars, or even most of them. The very basis of the translational poetics I elaborate here (see Section 3.1) is that it concerns the potential for translation in the source text. However, we must distinguish between different readers, as I demonstrated in Chapters 2 and 3: there will be readers who do not know the source text and there will be others (including translators and translation scholars) who do. Reading translation as translation will always entail a concern with language itself and with the possibility of what Scott calls the source text's 'textual self-regeneration' (Scott 2012: 4). For Scott, there is another consequence of the focus on the source and the reader: in what seems direct opposition to Venuti (2008: 83–124), the personal experience of alterity is more important than putting oneself in the other's shoes, personal experience being, in this case, the 'transformation of other into self' (Scott 2012: 4). But, especially with Holocaust poetry, there are different considerations: the concern of a translator must in part be empathetic, that is, you transform yourself into the other, imaginatively, while being aware that you are not the other (cf. Laub 1992: 66; LaCapra 2001: 47). As a translator, my aims are thus very different from Scott's: though I am also concerned with how we read and though I would also argue that absorbing and appropriating the original text as its translator is one way of ensuring its necessary transformation, I maintain that the reader must be transformed, too.

This is not only true of the translator as reader; it also applies to the reader of the translation. Instead of saying of the 'monoglot reader' (Scott 2012: 13) that the translation is not meant for him or her, one might try to *transform* the reader into a multilingual reader, or at least a reader of multilingual sensibility. This is what I described in Section 2.1, and it is what is meant by point (iii). Let us consider some of the ways in which this transformation of the reader's mental models towards multilingualism might be encouraged.

I considered in Section 3.1 how the translator's engagement with the translation of Ausländer leads, in turn, via Brunner's philosophy (see 1968), to a concern, when translating Celan's '*Einmal*' (1982: 103) with the origins of '*neige*' in French (from *'*neigu', Indo-Germanic for to wash, via '*nix*', 'snow' in Latin) and how it might relate, or appear to relate, to German '*nichts*', 'nothing'. The etymological dictionary (e.g. Duden 2007) suggests it does not, and yet this fact does not prevent it from appearing to. But what does this observation have to do with how translated poetry might be presented for the general reader? Linguistic questions are of great interest to readers if skilfully presented; this is shown by the popularity of scholarly but accessible linguistics books such as Steven Pinker's *The Blank Slate* (2003) or David Crystal's *Spell It Out* (2013). As I suggested in Chapters 2 and 3, appearance, connotation, folk etymology and sound similarity were as important for Celan as actual etymology, as indeed they are for many writers, and for all translators. In the case of Holocaust poetry, this is more important than ever, because of what such elements at the edges of lexical form and meaning suggest about the potential for language to be misused or manipulated. Such issues give fascinating insights into poetry in general and Holocaust poetry in particular, and can be included in brief notes for the reader. The translator's insight that foregrounding of apparent etymology leads to a deeper understanding of the cross-linguistic elements of poems will add context for the reader. To see how this might work, consider another Celan poem, '*Bei Wein und Verlorenheit*' (Celan 1980: 15), 'As Wine and Lostness':

Bei	Wein	und	Verlorenheit,	bei
by	wine	and	lost-ness	by
beider	Neige:			
of-both	decline			
ich	ritt	durch	den	Schnee
I	rode	through	the	snow

(As wine and lostness, as both declined, I rode through the snow)

'*Neige*' ('decline, ending', a noun), like *'*neigu'. 'to wash', does not relate etymologically to '*nichts*' ('nothing'), and neither German word relates to German

'Schnee' or English 'snow' or to French 'neige', but they look as though they do. German 'Neige' and 'Schnee' are thus not related and neither are German 'Neige' and French 'neige'. The relation (of similarity) is activated by the proximity of the German word 'Neige' in line two of the poem to the implied French word 'neige' that we see if we read German 'Schnee' in line three multilingually. This is a similar case to that of 'Halde' and 'Trommel', discussed in Section 3.2, and Ausländer's use of 'Nachtigallensang', discussed in Section 2.2. There is no reason why such interesting connections, which give insight into the multilingual background of the poetry, could not be made available to readers of Celan or Ausländer. For such phenomena are not just linguistic games, but a reflection of the way the mind works. Argentinian Jewish poet Alejandra Pizarnik described it as a process by which the mind 'veers off' into a 'curious Boschensian kitchen' where there is 'a simmering of language'.[3] In Holocaust poetry, such veering off can take one into dark or obsessive thoughts. In this sense, cross-linguistic slippage is not simply a reflection of a multilingual background, but it is also iconic of the mind's ability to see connections, or inability not to see them. Helping a reader of the translated versions to think about such links, by noting the etymological and other connections, gives a better sense of the mind-style of the poems. Reading translated poetry together with its original, as a further way of gaining a greater sense of the importance of language, can be a possibility open to the reader of the translations simply by putting in a few pointers to cross-linguistic similarities and differences. Reading thus supported approaches the comparative reading described in Chapter 2. There is no reason why comparative reading should not be possible for the general reader. One of the arguments for bilingual presentation of poetry translation is that it allows the two texts to be read together, and even readers who are not fully competent in the source language will still be able to experience the shape of the original and see its layout and punctuation, and its repetitions. I argued in Chapter 2 that reading a poem as a translation is a comparative mode of reading: it does not necessarily involve an actual comparison, but only the knowledge that such a comparison is possible. It puts the reader in the position of the multilingual thinker. If there is further textual apparatus to support such a way of thinking, reading can approach the analytical reading of the scholar that I outlined in Section 2.2. As an example, consider Jones' translation of Radnóti's poem 'Forced March' (Jones 2000: 67), which describes the poet's forced participation in a march from Bor in Eastern Serbia to the west through Hungary towards Germany, as the war was approaching its end.

Here are the first three lines:

It's a fool who, fallen to earth,   gets up and trudges on,
flexes his ankle and knee,   a single walking pain,
but still, as if lifted by wings,   sets off again on his way.

It is natural to read this poem, in this publication, as a translation from Hungarian, as the original is given on the facing page, and the context of the march itself is explained in Jones' 'Translator's Preface and Notes'. For a Hungarian speaker, a comparative reading of the poem might involve consideration of the word 'fool' as a translation of the Hungarian '*bolond*', and possible alternatives and their connotations. For a reader who does not speak Hungarian, reading it as a translation might involve the following questions:

Does the alliteration of 'fool', 'fallen', 'flexes' represent similar alliteration in the original, or is it perhaps an echo of assonance in the original? Is there a difference? Is the contrast of 'fallen to earth' and 'lifted by wings', so suggestive of angels, equally suggested by the Hungarian? Does the Hungarian word rendered by 'fallen' also have connotations of moral and spiritual decline? What do the gaps in the lines suggest and are their connotations different in the original? Does it, for example, relate to a particular tradition in Hungarian poetry?

I am not suggesting that any sort of answers – for there are several in each case – should be provided. Indeed, an informal survey[4] of preferences with respect to notes in translated poetry suggests that, while background information is appreciated, anything that closes off interpretation would be resisted by a majority of readers. The readers surveyed were specialists in translation and therefore can be taken as a model to which general readers can aspire if presentation helps them to do so. In the case of 'Forced March', some contextual detail about the march itself is provided, and about Radnóti. A facsimile, within the book, of the original manuscript found on the poet's exhumed body indicates that the gaps in the lines were there in the handwritten version. This background provides sufficient context for the sort of questions suggested to be thought about, and enables the reader to see that these are questions that might warrant further investigation.

As the discussion in Chapter 2 suggested, this sort of concern with poetic form and style, though possible in a monolingual presentation, especially for trained poetry readers, is made more likely by a bilingual presentation with its foregrounding of language and of the physical shape of the poem.

As a further example, consider the poem 'Below' by Celan, which first appeared in English in a monolingual edition in the *Penguin Modern European Poets* series (Hamburger and Middleton 1972: 47). The first line reads:

Led home into oblivion

To the monolingual reader not concerned with translation, the opening of the poem will relate to the title of the previous poem, 'Homecoming'. One might also ask how 'led home' relates to Hamburger's 'fetched home' in the previous poem on the facing page, just as the monolingual reader of the original (Celan 1980: 94–5), where these two poems are also on opposite pages, would have seen a connection between '*heimgeführt*' and '*heimgekehrt*'. But reading the poems in this way in the monolingual English version is extraordinarily difficult; they feel oddly disjointed, as though connected only by meaning. Hamburger's introduction will certainly provide some insights, but the whole book appears somewhat obscure. In the 2007 bilingual Hamburger book (first published in this form in 1988), the intervening German poems make the semantic link between 'led home' and 'fetched home' weaker, and the links one sees on the page are more likely to be between English and German. The confrontation of the English with the German leads even the monolingual reader to '*Schnee*' as the original of 'snow' and '*Heim*' as the original of 'home'. One can also see words in the German of '*Heimkehr*' that appear to alliterate: '*schliefst*', '*Schlitten*', and one recalls such German words as '*Heimat*'.

The reader of the original German monolingual book would, of course, not have had poems in another language interspersed with the German ones. So why does the reading of the English monolingual book feel so disjointed? I suspect the answer is simply that Celan's heavy use of repetition, both within and across the two poems, foregrounds the language and distracts from an attempt to understand based solely on semantics. '*Heimgeführt ins Vergessen*', the original of the line above, picks up '*des Verlorenen*' in '*Heimkehr*' on the opposite page, '*angelagert*' picks up '*gelagert*' and so on. In the English versions the translations are, respectively, 'led home into oblivion' and 'the lost'; 'heaped up' and 'stacked'. The connections are semantic and so there is less foregrounding of repetition. The bilingual presentation supplements the repetition, because of the closeness of German and English, and because the comparison provides an enhanced stylistic cohesion.

What the bilingual presentation does is to foreground linguistic repetition and draw the reader to form rather than semantics. They are exactly the same translated poems as in the monolingual English publication, and yet the former appears immeasurably richer.

Such examples suggest some general characteristics of reading translated poetry in the knowledge that it is translated: a focus on language, a separation of language from reference, a sense of the importance of style and the effects of sound. Recall that Tsur spoke of a disruption of 'the automatic transition from the *signifiant* to the *signifié*' (Tsur 2008: 5; see Section 1.3). He describes this process of disruption as a focus on the 'non-speech mode of processing acoustic signals' that is normally 'shut out from consciousness' (Tsur 2008: 9) when we are listening to meaningful speech. It is not that a bilingual presentation of poems prevents our reading them as semantically meaningful: it is simply that our focus changes. And by changing our focus when reading Holocaust poetry, we are led to a consideration of its multilingual origins. A bilingual presentation of translation is not one aimed at a bilingual reader; it is a way of presenting translation that makes of the reader a bilingual (or multilingual) reader. It becomes impossible for the reader not to consider the act of translation.

Point (iv) in the list is based on the assumption that it is very difficult for readers to read poetry as translated poetry, or indeed as poetry at all, if their cognitive context is insufficient to allow them to enter the text world of the poem. English readers on the whole will know what the Holocaust was, but public events, such as those mentioned at the start of this chapter, suggest that that knowledge is sketchy. Poetry books do not need to become historical or academic works in order to provide the necessary context. Indeed, the whole point is that they are not, and that cognitive context can be built by the reader in engaging with the poetry. Some starting points are needed, however. Readers need to know when and where the events took place, what they were and who the victims and perpetrators were. An introduction, possibly with the addition of maps, can be useful. Brief notes on relevant geographical locations, such as Ukraine, the Bukovina, Czernowitz, are helpful in the case of the many poets from this region, such as Ausländer, Celan, Pagis or Meerbaum-Eisinger.

We might consider again Ausländer's '*Biographische Notiz*' (2012: 145–6), 'Biographical Note', discussed in Section 2.2, in terms of how it could be presented as a translation. The landscape the poet reflects on is contextualized for the German reader of the original by the first stanza, which reads:

Ich	rede		
I	speak		

von	der	brennenden	Nacht
of	the	burning	night

die	gelöscht	hat	
which	extinguished	has	

der	Pruth		
the	Pruth		

(I speak of the burning night which put out the Pruth)

Many, perhaps most, German readers will, in fact, not know exactly where the River Pruth runs. It is in an area far from Germany, in what is now (at the time of writing) part of Ukraine. But it will be clear it is a body of water, or it could not extinguish a fire. The fact that it is grammatically masculine in German strongly suggests a river. In the context of Ausländer's other poems, and the title of this poem, it is easy enough to work out that it must be the river that runs through the area in which she was born.

For the English reader it is more difficult. There is no gender to give a clue, unless one is a speaker of German and the poem is presented bilingually.

It is likely to designate something that contains water, such as a river, a lake or a large pond, or it might even be the name of the local fire brigade. The question is how much this lack of background matters to a reading of the poem, that is, to what extent the reader's cognitive context can be built without knowing exactly what the Pruth is. This seems particularly relevant if we see the cognitive context that is constructed as a 'cognitive map' (Ryan 2003), which, once in place, serves to help organize what we imagine to be happening in the text, and, in this case, in later poems by Ausländer and possibly also those of other Czernowitz poets. Given the contrast between the burning and the extinguishing, the suggestion of the saving power of nature, which is carried over but negated in the weeping willows, blood-beeches and the silenced song of the nightingale in the next stanza (see Section 2.2), it seems important that the reader should be able to imagine a river as part of her or his cognitive map, and that she or he can imagine it was actually, in what can be assumed to be a real historical event, used to put out burning buildings. This allows the reader to think about who set the buildings on fire, and thus to consider whether those who did so might also be the agents of 'silenced' in the following stanza, which is expressed as a past participle and so is the result of an action.

So where should the necessary background information (assuming a printed book) appear? One possibility is in footnotes or endnotes. Very few books of translated Holocaust poetry use footnotes, but some, such as Kaufman's 1986 translation of Abba Kovner, or Feldmann and Swann's 1992 translation of Primo Levi, do use endnotes; others, for example Jones' 2000 translation of Radnóti, include background notes in the preface. I am not aware of any large surveys that have been done to determine how much background information readers like and how they prefer it to be presented, and indeed, a survey of this type would hardly be helpful if what it elicited were unconsidered responses that reflected the *status quo*. The small informal survey I mentioned earlier, as well as anecdotal information from public readings, suggests that footnotes are seen to distract the reader, to interrupt reading, to adversely affect the appearance of the poem on the page, and to risk providing information that the reader would rather work out or be able to keep vague. The answer, therefore, might be to provide notes at the front or back of the book. A few dates, historical events and a map would be sufficient.

Such information seems important if we consider the process of building a context dynamically when reading a poem. In Ausländer's poem '*Biographische Notiz*', the speaker '*ich*', who opens the poem, in saying 'I speak of', is, as it were, inviting the reader into the world of his or her memory, not into the region of the river Pruth itself. The title of the poem will encourage the reader to identify '*ich*' with Ausländer (cf. Semino 1997: 38), especially if information about the actual poet's background is available in the book. The reader's existing schemata need to be sufficient to allow the poem to fit in, and to interact with it. If the poem is too inaccessible in that its link to the real world is too hard to make (see Semino's discussion of Ryan's (1991) accessibility conditions for more on this: Semino 1997: 81–3), then reading the poem is unlikely to be a particularly interesting experience. What the presentation of information in the text thus needs to do is to find a balance between too little information, which would render poems rather meaningless, or too much information, which would not allow the reader's imagination free rein, and, in Relevance-Theory terms, would not allow enough cognitive effects on the reader for the reading to seem worthwhile. It is also important to distinguish between information that provides historical and geographical context for the poem and information that provides details of translation problems. Participants in the small survey mentioned earlier were not only more likely to read analytically than the general reader, but also far more likely to read with a multilingual sensibility. If the aim is to encourage reading that is enhanced in both respects, readers need sufficient background, but they do not need to be told what the differences between source text and translated text are. It is up to the readers to find out.

If one motivation for translating Holocaust poetry is to gain a better understanding of the wider picture, including the effects of the Holocaust on literature in its aftermath, it suggests that the reader should also have access to such an increased understanding. Providing background on poems is, therefore, not merely something that allows greater accessibility, but it also contributes in itself to the wider picture of the Holocaust. However, if the only poets who are translated are the well-known ones such as Ausländer, Sachs and Celan, the sense that arises for the reader is that only those poets who were both directly affected and who survived have something to say about the Holocaust. Thus, though translators and publishers may provide background for the poetry and render it accessible enough for imaginative engagement to take place, they may still present a distorted picture.

Points (v) and (vi) suggest ways to counteract this: by translating lesser known poets, especially by focusing on those languages less often translated, as well as on poets who became Nazi victims for reasons that are, in general, less well known.

Because the effects of the Holocaust on literature can be seen particularly in the case of German, since German had to respond to being both the language of the perpetrator and the language of many of the victims, it would be good to see more English translations of later German-language poets, such as von Törne or Steinherr, who engage with the Holocaust. These poets are particularly easy for English readers today to relate to, and the amount of additional background needed to ensure accessibility is less extensive. Von Törne writes about places such as Masurien (1981: 154), or Wannsee

(1981: 147) or persons such as Karl Heinz Pawla (1981: 123), where some background would be needed, but he also mentions many places, products and people likely to be even more familiar to the English reader now than when the poems were published in 1981: Hannover, Dr Oetker, Goebbels (von Törne 1981: 195, 50).

Where non-German Holocaust poets have been translated into English, this has to a large extent been because of the efforts of a fairly small number of translators: we have already seen how Hughes helped Pilinszky to become known to English readers (Hughes 2006). He was helped in his efforts by Daniel Weissbort, who both encouraged Hughes and anthologized poets such as Pilinszky and Ficowski (see Weissbort 1991). But many poets who are still virtually unknown here are worth translating. As we have seen, many poets did not survive the Holocaust, and their work is, perhaps understandably, little known, unless, like Radnóti, they were already established before the war. But other poets who survived, and whose poetry shows the influence of the Holocaust, are nevertheless little known in English translation. Examples are Nathan Zach (originally from Berlin, but writing in Hebrew), or Leopold Staff (writing in Polish) or Edvard Kocbek (writing in Slovenian). There are a few translations by these poets in Weissbort's 1991 anthology *The Poetry of Survival*, and a few translated collections (e.g. Everwine's recently re-issued 1977 translation of Zach; see Everwine 2011), but very little otherwise. Other poets of the Holocaust have simply been overshadowed as poets because they are best known as writers in other genres. Katsetnik 135633 (Yehiel De-Nur), born in Poland but writing in Hebrew, is famous for the semi-factual novel *House of Dolls* (Kohn 1955), but his poetry, apart from two translations by Antony Rudolf in the anthology *Voices of Conscience* (1995), edited by Hume Cronyn et al. is virtually unknown here. Others poets are known only to specialists: Rachel Korn, who was born in East Galicia and wrote in Yiddish, has been translated (e.g. by Levitan 1985), but does not appear to be known to English readers.

Even Meerbaum-Eisinger, whose work has been published in several editions in Germany (most recently in 2013) and has been set to music, has rarely appeared in English translation; Silverblatt and Silverblatt (2008), which I mentioned in Section 1.5, is an exception. Though multiple translations of the same poet, such as Celan or Sachs, do have a central role to play in ensuring that translated Holocaust poetry is read as translation, it might nevertheless make sense to use limited resources on publishing translations by poets less well known.

Point (vi) suggests that, in addition to translating less well-known poets in general, it is also important that there should be translations from languages that less often serve as sources of Holocaust poetry: Slovene, as in the case of Kocbek, or Norwegian, as in the case of Gunvor Hofmo (e.g. 1946), or Dutch, as in the case of Jacques Presser (see 1969). Of course, discussions around the effects of the Holocaust on literature are especially well known in Germany; as we have seen, Germany had to confront its past manipulation of language and literature more obviously than did other countries. But there was collaboration and compromise in other countries, too, perhaps most famously by the French Vichy government, but also by the governments of Croatia, Norway and other countries. The response of poetry is interesting here, too, and further publications of relevant poets in English translation, properly contextualized, are desirable.

While the preponderance of German-Jewish poets as well as poets of Jewish origin from other countries means that their translation has been attempted by many poet-translators able and willing to consider the poet's Jewish background, such as Hamburger, Felstiner or Szirtes, there has been little translation of poets who were victims of the Nazis for other reasons than their Jewish background, as noted in Chapter 1. It is a great pity that there appears to be no available poetry by victims of the 'Euthanasia' campaign (see Section 1.3), or their families. One can only hope that in future some will come to light, and will be translated. The same applies to those persecuted for their Roma or Sinti origins; little of their poetry is known, so little has been translated. There may be poetry written by Jews of North Africa, many of whom were incarcerated in labour camps there (see Satloff 2006: 17–21). This would be an interesting and worthwhile translation project, not least because a better understanding of the interaction of Jews and Arabs at this time can help work against prejudice about Muslim-Jewish relations. Indeed, this was partly Satloff's aim, and his research has since inspired work in interfaith understanding (see e.g. the Faith Matters website, http://faith-matters.org).

Point (vii) suggests, as does Jones' study of translation within the framework of Actor Network Theory (Jones 2011: 13), that translation alone, however good it is, and however much it aims to engage the reader and encourage creative reading, cannot ensure that Holocaust poetry in a greater range and variety than is today the case will be translated into English and find an audience able to engage with it. Other persons besides the translator have roles to play in the production of a translation, in particular the publisher and the editor, who will usually be involved in the design and layout of books, and in decisions about the sort of background material discussed under point (iv). Publishers are also concerned with marketing and promotion, and the role of organizers of launches, festivals and other promotion events should also not be ignored. All too often, at these events, the role of the translator is downplayed: he or she is a sort of adjunct to the original poet, translating and acting as intermediary between the real poet on stage and an audience of listeners who rarely speak the source language. But this need not be so. Some festivals such as Lancaster Litfest events (see their website litfest.org),

and tours such as those organized by Arc Publications (www.arcpublications.
co.uk), do consciously foreground discussion of translation, almost always
attracting very good audiences.

One of the problems with the view that the translator is merely a
go-between for a foreign poet, who needs to be present at public events, is
that this means dead poets do not stand much chance, unless they are already
famous. It might be feared that a relatively unknown poet, such as Katzenelson
or Meerbaum-Eisinger, who cannot appear personally, and of whom there are
no recordings or films, and few images, might be less interesting to audiences
used to celebrity writers. But events at which specifically translated poetry is
read by the translator suggest this is not the case, as long as the audience
knows what to expect; figures supplied by Arc Publications show audience
sizes at least as large as for original poetry (except where original poets are
reading at prize events, or have achieved celebrity status).

As Hamburger says rather wryly (1969: 2), more people make a living from
writing about poetry than from writing poetry itself. One consequence of this
is that a poet may become known through criticism for a particular theme,
view, belief, attitude or way of writing, which then in turn affects the way her
or his poetry is read. Though it may be the case that general readers do not
read works by poetry scholars and critics, nevertheless public perception, and
therefore reading, is inevitably shaped by such views, so criticism matters, as
the case of Sachs illustrates.

After initially being ignored, at least in West Germany, in the years after
the war – in fact, her work was translated into Swedish and Norwegian
before it appeared in West Germany (cf. Martin 2011: 33–4) – Sachs was
later described by critics, journalists, academics and fellow poets as a poet
of reconciliation (e.g. Jens 1968; Hamm 1991) upon her receipt of a number
of German literary prizes and, in 1966, the Nobel Prize for Literature. Recent
critics, notably Martin (2011) have argued that critical reception read into
her work what was required by history and a need to come to terms with
the past, particularly in Germany. The view of Sachs as a poet who never
expresses anger or hate, and who trusts in a future of reconciliation, who is
'*nahezu abwesend*' ('almost absent') from her works, was probably to a large
extent determined by her fragile appearance. The foregoing description that
suggests a lack of poetic presence in her work comes from the 1991 review
by Hamm in *Die Zeit*, and he describes the young Sachs in a photograph
as an '*auffallend schönes Mädchen*' (a 'strikingly beautiful girl') and uses
adjectives such as '*zierlich*', '*schmal*', both words indicating delicateness
of build, to describe her as a 75-year-old woman receiving the Nobel Prize
for Literature (Hamm 1991: 76). The need to make connections between
literary work and physical attributes, particularly in the case of women, by

German (usually male) critics has been noted elsewhere, for example in the case of Austrian poet Ingeborg Bachmann (Schardt 1994) or German-Romanian writer Herta Müller (Braun 2013). It is interesting in the case of Sachs because it suggests that her work was read with less regard to its actual poetic style than as a symbol of what the public needed, helped by what the poet's appearance suggested, and the desire of male critics to show themselves to be empathetic and chivalrous.

The public perception in Germany of Sachs as a poet of reconciliation may well have influenced what has been anthologized in English, and what was translated: as noted earlier, though most of her work has appeared in translated collections, much of her latest poetry, posthumously published, for example that in '*Teile dich Nacht*' (Sachs 1971), 'Night, Divide', in many ways the most interesting (because it is the culmination of an increasing tendency to spareness of form and a corresponding compression of meaning), has not yet appeared in English translation.

A perception of a poet as anonymous, and absent from her work, has several consequences. For one thing, it relegates her poetry to the level of outpourings of grief and expressions of suffering that could have been written by anyone. It also foregrounds the Holocaust as the topic at the expense of the question of how to represent it. And it reduces translation to a somewhat mechanical rendering of content rather than an attempt to recreate a particular voice and style and a particular response to the Holocaust.

What this brief excursus into Sachs' reception suggests is that the way we write about Holocaust poets will affect the way they are read and the way they are read in their original language will affect what is translated and how it is translated. But the original reception also affects our view of translation. If Holocaust poetry is treated as either documentation or an involuntary outpouring of feeling, then translation will have a different task from that which will fall to it if Holocaust poetry is regarded as a dialectical treatment of what is possible and what has changed. In the latter case, the focus of the translator will be on the language and its physical features, on the poetics that inform the poetry (and the poetry it is writing against) and on the effects on the reader.

Point (viii) suggests that translation practice need not happen independently of translation theory. Studies such as Chesterman's *Memes of Translation* (1997) have shown that there are recurring themes in theoretical approaches and descriptions, but that these themes are always affected by the historical, political and cultural situation at any particular time. Theories, in turn, and especially views on the nature of translation itself, also affect how poems are translated. Yet the translation of Holocaust poetry has not, up to now, explicitly engaged with translation theory. As I showed in Chapter 2, some experienced translators such as Felstiner and Hamburger talk in detail about their translations of Holocaust poetry, but very few mention theoretical discussions. Some translators might be wary of theories because they feel they are prescriptive. But this is a misunderstanding; most translation theories, in spite of what one or two scholars such as Newmark (1980) have said, do not try to tell translators how to translate. Theories and views that do suggest ways to translate (including the view in this book) are not meant to be exclusive: they are just ways of seeing things. Knowing about them is useful precisely because they show that people see things differently. If currently available translations of Holocaust poetry rarely appear to engage with translation theory, the converse is also true: translation theory has, with a few exceptions (e.g. Boase-Beier 2004, 2006, 2011b; Kuhiwczak 2007), not engaged with the questions that the translation of Holocaust poetry throws up.

This seems odd, given that views of translation that are current or beginning to be explored in the second decade of the twenty-first century have absorbed influences from discussions about the multiculturalism of society, from developments in other areas of academic study such as postcolonialism, poststructuralism, philosophy and cognitive studies (including cognitive linguistics and cognitive poetics). Translation could best be characterized today as an activity that is seen by scholars not only as resting on a number of theoretical underpinnings (see Fawcett and Guadarrama Garcia 2010), and involving a number of agents (Jones 2011) but also as including a number of practices. We thus need to think of the term 'translation' as what Tymoczko (2007: 85) calls, borrowing from Wittgenstein, a 'cluster concept'. Now that it is an established discipline, it should be particularly open to exploring interactions with various other areas.

The insights that engagement with the translation of Holocaust poetry might bring to translation theory would include the need for more studies of the effects of such factors as truth, memory, witness and historical background on the translation of fictional texts, including poetry, and the question of debates on aesthetics (such as that surrounding Adorno's comments) and how and to what extent they might impact on translation today. They would include considerations such as those discussed in this section about presentation and reception (cf. also Iser 2004: 9–10) and their effects on the cognitive context of the reader of translated poetry. They would include the particular multilingual basis of Holocaust poetry, and the way this affects both translation practice and translation theory. And they would include the poetic engagement of Holocaust poets with questions of language and communication in the philosophies of Benjamin, Buber, Scholem, Levinas and others, and how this might influence our thinking about translation.

4.2 The afterlife of Holocaust poetry

According to Benjamin (1972: 10), the '*Überleben*' of a text, which Rendall translates as '"afterlife" or "survival"' (Benjamin 2012: 76), is not what actually comes after it but is an inherent quality of the text that allows it to be translated. It could be argued that this is a quality of poetry itself, because of its openness to different interpretations, even by the same reader, because it is frequently re-read and because it has the potential to change the way our minds work. Adrienne Rich expresses its power thus: when we read poetry, 'imagination's roads open before us, giving the lie to that slammed and bolted door, that razor-wired fence, that brute dictum "There is no alternative"' (Rich 2007: 38, 32). Poetry, in this view, provides an alternative world and so its survival is ensured in our changed ways of thinking. But Benjamin linked the afterlife of writing specifically to translation (cf. also Attridge 2004: 75). In this final section, I would like to consider exactly what the nature of that afterlife might be, given all that has been said in the previous chapters. One of Ausländer's poems reads, in translation (Boase-Beier and Vivis 1995: 83):

> When I go away
> from our forgetful earth
> will you speak my words
> a while for me?

Translation is one of the ways – indeed, the main way – in which the words of a Holocaust poet can be spoken for the poet after the poet has gone. But what does it mean to speak their words, and what effects do these re-spoken words have? According to Toury (1995: 23–39), translated texts become part of the target culture and the overall target literary system; Even-Zohar says they constitute 'a most active system within it' (Even-Zohar 2012: 163). One way we see that this is the case is by the influence of the poetry on other literature in the target system. These influences are generally quite hard to pin down, but poets are aware of them: Robin Milner-Gulland, for example, in his 'Introduction' to the *Selected Poems* of Yevtushenko which he co-translated in 1962 with Peter Levi, considers that 'the impact of such writers was considerable' (Milner-Gulland and Levi 2008: 13). Milner-Gulland describes that influence as the revival of a view that poetry was a 'popular, and populist, activity' (Milner-Gulland and Levi 2008: 13). It was partly in recognition of these influences that Hughes and Weissbort established *Modern Poetry in Translation* (see Hughes 2006: 204), a journal which is still continuing to bring new translated poetry to an English readership. Once such influences occur, the original poet has entered the literary system of English, because his or her work is present in that of the receiving system, and readers are affected by it, whether they know it or not.

But when Holocaust poetry is translated into English and enters the literary system of English, it is in danger of being read as English poetry, a problem common to all translated texts, of any genre (cf. Venuti 2008: 1–13). With Holocaust poetry, because of our knowledge of its historical and geographical background, this is perhaps less of a problem than the opposite: an equally unthinking assumption that what we are reading is the original poetry, that its re-creation in English has changed nothing, or only changed it for the worse, as many of the views quoted in this book suggest. Accepting and thinking about the role of translation in this poetry can and does, as we saw in Chapter 2, lead to a deeper engagement with it. I would argue also that, in order to understand the transformation that is necessary if it is to live on, we need to consider the special status of translated poetry within what we see as the system of English poetry, or of Holocaust poetry or of Holocaust writing. How broadly or narrowly one defines the part of the system being looked at is a matter of choice and interest, for a literary system is a cognitive entity: it is a way of organizing our views of literature (cf. Even-Zohar 1990). Holocaust poetry's role in commemoration makes it a special case; Hoffman (2004: 199; and see also Franklin 2011: 233–4) argues that children of Holocaust survivors eventually need to turn away from the Holocaust as a defining aspect of their lives. But at the same time she says that the most important thing is to be listened to, to have one's suffering honoured and respected: only then is a traumatic state of mind avoided (Hoffman 2004: 47–57). Holocaust poetry has the potential to be translated in such a way that it enables listening by future readers distant in time and place from the events of the Holocaust. In this case, if the text lives on, it allows a turning away that is not abandonment but the certainty that responses to the Holocaust have become integrated into our ways of thinking. The post-Holocaust mind does not need to be marked only by trauma. It is worth considering what this means for the translator and for the reader of translation.

The overall picture of translated Holocaust poetry that has emerged in the course of this book is one of a hitherto little understood and rarely discussed aspect of Holocaust writing. The view presented in Chapter 3, that reading Holocaust poetry for translation is always a comparative reading that already takes into account the multilingual and multicultural nature of the text, and thus enables the translator to ensure that the reader can engage in a similarly comparative way with the translation, will only be of use if, in keeping with Jones' view of the 'web' (Jones 2011: 51) of translation, the production and reception of the translated poetry are suitably supported; the previous section outlines some of the ways this might happen. Jones' (2011) investigation of poetry translating is mainly based on case studies of the translation of Bosnian poetry where, it could be argued, some of the issues (the European context, a background of conflict) are similar to those involved in Holocaust poetry. In such cases, Actor Network Theory (defined in Section 3.1), upon which Jones partly bases his explanatory model, is particularly helpful because the translation is dependent upon other webs that existed in the events themselves that gave rise to the original poetry. In the case of Holocaust poetry, this is suggested by views such as that of Rothberg, who calls the Holocaust an '"interdisciplinary" project' (Rothberg 2000: 3).

The background from which the original Holocaust poetry emerged needs to be taken into account by the translator. That is, seeing the translation of Holocaust poems as an action that takes place as part of a larger network of interacting factors is not merely a description. It has practical consequences for the translator. There were many different groups of people who participated, willingly or unwillingly, before, at the time and later, in the Holocaust. The most obvious ones are perpetrators, victims and bystanders. There are also the many who helped Jewish and other victims of Nazi terror, and their families. There are survivors. There are the families of all these people. All of these had a direct involvement. There were also many who went before: the thinkers and, especially, the deficient thinkers who here, as in every catastrophe of human design, exert evil influence, propagate misunderstanding, spread habits of indifference or turn whatever talents they possess to stifling thinking in others. Then, afterwards, there are historians of the Holocaust, academics who write about its literature, teachers who teach it and students who learn about it. There are those who write books about the Holocaust, those who publish them and those who read them. Into this network of human actors and non-human factors fit the translators of poetry, eye-witness accounts, survivor testimony, diaries and memoirs, and their readers. These people – the writers, teachers, translators, learners and readers – are those who keep alive the memory of the Holocaust, who try to learn from it what lessons they can and to enable others to learn them. If our work is to be a source of education for ourselves and others, translators of Holocaust poetry need to know what happened before the poems they are translating were written, what history of choice lies behind a word or phrase or pattern in the text, what other choices might have been made by the writer, what literary traditions and cultural and historical influences belong to the writer's wider cognitive context. Seen from this perspective, the translator has a particular role as a communicator of what someone else has written with all that it carries of its context, to people other than those originally addressed, with all that can be guessed or assumed or known of their context. It is for this reason that it does not, to me, make sense to say translation is this or that, window, mirror, copy, equivalent, bridge, enabler of reading, without taking into account that translation is always a translation of *something*, and so its particular purpose and nature are determined in part by what it is a translation of. Translating poetry that has such a deep connection with the events and actors that informed it implies a particular commitment for the translator, including the commitment to understand as much as is possible about those events and actors and to enable a similar search for understanding to be possible for the reader. The need to know as much as possible about the Holocaust in order to know how to translate and present its poetry for new readers leads me to concur with Rothberg that it is important to go back to what writers were saying in the immediate aftermath of the Holocaust. His reasons, as literary and critical theorist, for doing this are to see such discussions in their proper historical context and with their proper 'historical legacies' (Rothberg 2009: 22). My reasons, as a translation studies scholar, but more particularly as a translator, are to know more about the context in which poems were written because that context formed part of the cognitive context of the poet, and so influenced the poetics. It is thus important, in my view, not only to follow research paths the poetry suggests, into its etymology or its link to Jewish mysticism, for example, or the events of the Holocaust itself, but also to trace the discourse it formed part of at the time of writing. It is extremely enlightening to read early reports such as *The Yellow Spot*, published in London in 1936 by 'a group of investigators', containing extracts from Nazi documents, facsimiles from German newspapers, early photos of concentration camps and the unbearably innocent hopes of the then Bishop of Durham, who ends his 'Introduction', after noting his admiration for Germany's intellectual achievements and his abhorrence of the present 'barbarities', especially the persecution of the Jews, with the words 'The publication of this book will, I think, hasten the return of sanity by making yet more vocal and insistent the protest of the civilised conscience' (1936: 8). Early documentations after the war such as *The Black Book* (1946), by 'The Jewish Black Book Committee', which included the World Jewish Congress and other Jewish groups, though disdained by Arendt in a review from the same year (cf. Arendt 1994: 197–205) as 'submerged in a chaos of details' and unable to 'make clear the nature of the facts', are also important, as are the reactions to them. There were many academic works that tried to gain a greater overview of events and provide explanations, such as Weinreich's 1946 book *Hitler's Professors* (Weinreich 1999), reviewed by Arendt in the same article, or Poliakov's *Harvest of Hate* (1956). There are popular histories, such as Lord Russell of Liverpool's angry 1954 book *The Scourge of the Swastika*. With its 'ruffians', 'scoundrels', 'frenzied marionettes' and 'murderous medicos' (Russell 2002: 21, 189, 203, 219), it now seems quaint, but both the book and the accusations of anti-Germanism it provoked at the time (see Horne's 'Introduction', 2002: vii–x) are interesting for the insight they give into the political situation in England as more became known about the Holocaust. There are also early discussions of Holocaust literature, such as Halperin's *Messengers from the Dead* (1960), as well as those early works of literature themselves, for example Frankl's 1959 memoir *Man's Search for Meaning* (Frankl 2004) or Groll's 1946 German anthology of poetry from the Nazi years and some of the other poetry I have discussed in this book. There are, of course, many other works needed for historical context such as contemporary reports and biographies, and ideological or medical documents. But it is the views of those trying to understand the unfolding catastrophe as it happened, and to understand, as reports and trials brought its effects into public view in the immediate aftermath, what it meant for literature, for historiography, for the law, that provide the most interesting and useful context for the translator trying to understand the development of Holocaust poetry from the documentary early poetry, such as that in the 1945 French collection of Buchenwald poetry published as *Der gefesselte Wald* (Kirsten and Seeman 2012), *The Chained Forest*, to the later poetry of Sachs and its poetics of trauma or the poetry of a younger poet such as von Törne, and his explorations of guilt and knowledge.

As I have been arguing throughout this book, Holocaust poetry cannot be defined simply by the events it deals with or the symbols it uses. The later poetry in particular needs to be defined by a Holocaust poetics that is largely a poetics of contradiction, contrast, ambiguity and fragmentation; this is a poetics that embodies the post-Holocaust mind and is crucial to the survival of the poetry. Different poets have different poetic systems and different concerns. We have seen that the translation of Celan needs to take etymology into account more than, say, the poetry of von Törne. Translators of any Holocaust poet need to be aware of how their poetics integrates and responds to the historical and political situation, their religious and cultural background, their personal circumstances. As Celan's poem '*Mit wechselndem Schlüssel*' (1982: 36), in my translation 'With Changing Keys' reads:

With changing keys
you open the house up, where
the snow of the unspoken blows.

Since so much of Holocaust poetics lies exactly in what is unspoken, the search for what lies behind the poetics, and needs to be brought into the translation, is different in each case. Translators will also, as I suggested in Section 3.2, translate for different reasons, including enhancing knowledge of the Holocaust and of the philosophies, histories, languages and cultures that influenced it, commemorating those killed, bearing witness to events, giving voice in particular to the poetic voices that were silenced, acting against what Arendt calls 'the strange interdependence of thoughtlessness and evil' (Arendt 2006: 288). A translator might hope it will serve some of the same purpose that all education about the Holocaust serves: to 'motivate us not only to concentrate on our own suffering, but be open and especially sensitive' to the suffering of others (Grunwald-Spier 2010: 81, quoting Holocaust survivor, academic and teacher Irena Veisaite). This can also be part of its legacy. But it can only hope to do any of these things if it is translated in full awareness of its context.

The close reading and thinking that is required of the translator will, by virtue of its necessary focus on the poem itself, be in a good position to mitigate against the misuse of poetry for political ends. We saw in Section 4.1, in the somewhat unlikely case of Sachs, how a Holocaust poet's work was made to serve political purposes. The misuse of Sachs' poetry to serve an argument about Jewish-German reconciliation in the 1960s was perhaps not especially grave, but it was a good example of unthinking reception, of the forming of public opinion based on superficiality rather than a reading of the work. Obviously, careful critics, such as Martin (2011) and some of those she cites, are not led into misusing poetry in this way. A translator of Sachs' work, bound to engage closely with the text, to focus on language and style rather than the poet's appearance, is likely to read the work properly, and to experience the development of Sachs' voice and poetics. Indeed, translating a poem *precludes* a facile reading of it as an expression of a convenient political view.

Translating also precludes the avoidance of thinking Arendt criticized, which in a writer can amount to what Semprun, reflecting upon his life in Buchenwald and his later attempts to represent it in literature, calls 'an alibi. Or a sign of laziness'. By this he means the view that there are things that cannot be spoken about because they are 'ineffable' (Semprun 1997: 13). Poetry allows everything to be said, and the translator is driven not only to find out what that is, but also to act upon it.

Semprun is struck by the personal note in Celan's poem '*Todtnauberg*' (1975: 255–6), as conveyed through Hamburger's translation (2007: 334–7), about his meeting with Heidegger and his frustrated hope for a word from the philosopher on the question of guilt and responsibility (Semprun 1997: 288–91). In expressing individual experience, poetry is an act of defiance against the depersonalization of the Holocaust, which turned human beings into an inhuman 'question' not requiring empathy (see Lifton 1986 or Rothberg 2009: 44–7; see also Section 1.3). Nader in his book *Traumatic Verses* argues that those poems, in particular, that were written in concentration camps 'counter the Nazis' intentions to eradicate traces of their victims' (Nader 2007: 2). He uses satirist and political poet Karl Schnog's poem '*Jedem das Seine*' (Nader 2007: 143–4), 'To Each His Own', to illustrate the poet's ironical engagement with the saying written on the gate of Buchenwald. One of the most important aspects of the translator's task is to preserve such acts of defiance as part of the response to the Holocaust.

In order to do this, it is important to think about the irony, and how one might translate it. One could argue that Schnog, by being ironical about the phrase on the gate, is personalizing what is a completely impersonal saying. It has the form of an idiom, and, indeed, is a common saying in German, as in English, like *'Arbeit macht frei'* ('Work brings freedom'), which was written on the gate of Auschwitz, and also on the gates of Dachau and Sachsenhausen, both of which (as well as Buchenwald) Schnog survived. Such statements aim at the status of universal truths and add to the necessary depersonalization of those who pass through the gate (see Rosenbaum 1998: 208–14, in discussion with philosopher Berel Lang). The irony already inherent in 'his own' (that is, what the Nazis decided was an inmate's due) and 'freedom' (usually death) in these signs is taken over and made personal in Schnog's poem. Part of the problem of translating such a poem is that perhaps there *is* no irony in the original. Though I described these phrases in Section 2.1 as ironical, because in general I would bow to the opinion of those who, like Primo Levi, have been there (Levi 2005: 8; cf. also Lang's view, Rosenbaum 1998: 215), I am nevertheless not convinced that this is quite right. Reading accounts of the establishment of Dachau, the first concentration camp, where the phrase *'Arbeit macht frei'* first appeared, in contemporary works, such as some of those just mentioned, and also later ones, such as Harding (2013), it seems as though the phrase may have been meant seriously. Possibly deriving originally from a novel by the unfortunate nineteenth-century linguist Lorenz Diefenbach (1873), and a phrase in common currency the Nazis must have approved of, it seems likely it was not ironical in exactly the same way that the Nazis were not being ironical when they called themselves a master race. The irony arises from the contrast of the slogans on the gates with the reality as inmates knew it then and as we know it now, and as the German people at the time the first camps were established would have known, had they chosen to.

If this is the case, then Schnog's turning round of the irony: *'Und Ihr? Ihr bekommt dann das Eure!'* ('And you? Then you'll get yours!') might risk dignifying it with a meaning it did not have. The translation by Nader (2007: 144), which begins 'Their lordships have a good sense of humour', thus failing to capture the always ironic sense of the German *'wirklich Humor haben'*, which is said when someone is being deadly serious, but ridiculous, may thus paradoxically come closer, if not to Schnog's poem, then to the very lack of irony in the original slogan on the gate. The irony of Nader's English version is almost all in the reading.

These are the sort of considerations that must go through the mind of the translator. In this sense, to the extent that Lang, who spoke of 'the art of evil', is right to see Nazi evil as a systematic 'overall design' with its own stylistic qualities and its own set of choices (Rosenbaum 1998: 214–16), the writing of poetry is a conscious attempt to counteract the choices that resulted in that artistic design. Poetically representing the individual is thus a way of positively counteracting the evil of intentional depersonalization. Translating poems such as Mezei's 'Gustav!' (see Section 1.3), and many of the others in that book (Ország-Land 2010) that personalize experience, as well as those in '*Der gefesselte Wald*' (Kirsten and Seeman 2012), or in Nader's book *Traumatic Verses* (2007), serves to ensure the survival of the poetic individuality of characters, voices and poets.

The conscious decision to translate such poems thus requires what Lang elsewhere describes as 'moral as well as aesthetic justification' (Lang 1988: 4). Communicating in itself is a moral decision (cf. Levinas 1990: 108). There is a moral accountability in translating Holocaust poetry, in deciding what and how to translate, just as there is in writing it, and the moral and aesthetic aspects are, as Lang notes, closely linked (Levinas 1990: 108). The translator has a moral responsibility to get the poetics right and, if the survival of the poem is to be ensured, not to treat it as though its aesthetic aspects did not matter.

The focus on Holocaust poetics, in turn, leads the translator to question what it is that translating the poetry of the Holocaust changes. Beyond bearing witness or allowing silenced voices to speak, important as these are in themselves, its importance for the translator lies less in what it tells us about the Holocaust than in what it tells us about ourselves, how it changes our cognitive models: such changes are also an aspect of the afterlife of the poems.

I have been arguing that such cognitive changes come about for the translator because of the particular engagement with the poetics of the original works, and all that informed them, that is needed in order to read them for translation, as illustrated in Section 3.1. This engagement on the translator's part is necessary so that the reader can be similarly engaged, as I suggested in Section 3.2.

How, then, can we describe the effects upon the reader of translated Holocaust poetry in terms of an integration of the post-Holocaust mind into the way the reader sees the world? What does translation, aided by some of the suggestions in the previous section, which will help the reader read the translated poem for what it is – a communication in poetic form of a poetic response to the Holocaust – aim to do to the reader? What is specific to the way reading Holocaust poetry affects the mind of the reader?

Oatley (2011: 100–1) argues, in much the same way that Richards once argued (Richards 1960: 43), that reading literature can change the reader in quite significant ways, because of the trust and engagement needed. Oatley makes the point that one of the reasons we are suspicious of acknowledging the educating and self-educating nature of literature is that it did not help prevent the German nation from embracing Nazism. But this was possible because 'the Nazis replaced the idea of self-betterment through education and reading by practices designed to induce as many as possible into willing conformity, and to coerce the unwilling remainder by justified fear' (Oatley 2011: 164).

What literature can do, in Oatley's view, is help us enter the minds of others, explore our relationships, rethink our mental models of social structures and group dynamics, and engage with ourselves and our own thoughts. These four cognitive effects of literature can be seen clearly when we consider the reading of Holocaust poetry. It can enable us to feel, as closely as it is possible to feel when we were not actually there, what it means to be in the position, say, of the speaker in Mezei's poem 'Gustav!', who spots his neighbour in the group of executioners and wants to die quickly. It can help us enter the post-Holocaust mind and its obsessions, as we meet it in a poem like Celan's 'Totenhemd'. It can help us think through our relationships: what would we have done if we had been the neighbour in Mezei's poem or what will we do if we encounter someone whose thinking is marked by trauma? It can help us think through social structures as they operate in other, less sinister, forms of bureaucracy, as we experience the different voices of Celan's 'Todesfuge', and it can help us question our own guilt as we read von Törne's 'Gedanken im Mai'. But reading Holocaust poetry in translation can do even more, and the cognitive changes it can bring about in the reader's mind are part, and indeed the main part, of what constitutes its afterlife.

I would suggest that there are six main ways in which reading translated Holocaust poetry – if it is translated and supported along the lines I outlined in Section 4.1 – can affect readers' minds that differ from, or are more specific than, Oatley's four general effects.

(i) When we read translated Holocaust poetry, we gain an enhanced understanding of remembrance. Rosen in his 'Introduction' to a book of essays to honour Holocaust survivor and writer Elie Wiesel, calls this 'bestowing memory on a generation that was not there' (Rosen 2006: xvii). Here he specifically mentions Wiesel's fiction, agreeing with one of the other contributors (Hartman 2006: 113) about its 'morality' as an act of remembrance. Poetry is by nature fictional, and Gubar's book on Holocaust poetry suggests remembrance is also central here; its role is 'conveying the dead past of a foreign place into the living present' of the mind of the reader (Gubar 2003: 246). W. H. Auden in 1940 made the now overused remark that poetry 'makes nothing happen' (Auden 1976: 246), but the case of Yevtushenko's poem 'Babiy Yar' suggests otherwise. Yevtushenko wrote the poem in 1961, after visiting Babiy Yar, the ravine outside Kiev (then in the USSR) where between 100,000 and 200,000 people had been murdered by the Nazis in 1941. They were mainly Jews, but included Roma people, hospital patients, prisoners of war, priests and many others. When his poem appeared, it was a great relief to many in Russia and Ukraine that someone had spoken out; the Russian authorities eventually allowed a memorial many years later (Petrowskaja 2011). The poem was translated very soon after publication into about seventy languages; Celan translated it into German; Shostakovich based his Thirteenth Symphony on it (Schiff 1995: 92). Its effects would clearly have been greatly reduced without translation and without translators to do the conveying of the past and the foreign place. But it is not simply that translation makes such remembrance possible; translated Holocaust poetry, by being translated, makes the reader reflect on the distance it has travelled, on the roles and reasons of those involved in ensuring such remembrance, since the translator is unlikely to have been the person who experienced the events or feelings the poem recalls. When reading the translation of Yevtushenko's 'Babiy Yar', the English reader, like the original reader, will interpret 'hated // by every anti-semite // as if I were a Jew' (Milner-Gulland and Levi 2008: 83–4) to mean that the speaker, and by extension the poet, is not Jewish. But what of the translators? The speaker in the poem says the reason for his empathy is 'I am a Russian', but every reader today will be aware that that is not sufficient reason. Presumably, the poet was expressing what he felt *should* be what it means to be Russian; he was consciously calling upon fellow Russians to reject anti-Semitism and to commemorate the massacre at Babiy Yar. It is possible that translator Levi's Jewish antecedents made him particularly interested in Yevtushenko, who had become famous for this poem, and its rejection of anti-Semitism, some years before. The point is not to find answers to these questions, but to ask them.

Both Hoffman (2004: 161) and Lifton (1986: ix) note that Hitler said 'Who now remembers the Armenians?' The suggestion is that, if we had done so, the Holocaust might have been less likely to happen. We cannot know, but thinking about remembrance, who we remember, why we remember and what we need to remember, can have consequences for the reader's mental models. This is where poetry that remembers those outside the poet's own religious, ethnic or national group, such as the (as yet unpublished) poems by Muslim writer, translator and interfaith worker Raficq Abdulla about Buchenwald, is especially important.

(ii) Reading translated Holocaust poetry encourages an enhanced ability to empathize. All poetry (and literature) in general encourages empathy, but the characteristics of Holocaust poetry, as discussed in Section 1.3 (cf. Gubar 2003: 243), particularly demand empathetic involvement. Such poetry allows us, as readers, to enter a blended world, in which we see things through our own eyes as well as those of the individuals inhabiting the (usually historically and geographically remote) world of the poem. That blended 'if I were you' world is important because it is the way readers relate the insights gained from reading the poem to their own cognitive schemata, in order to feel empathy. As I noted in Section 1.3, empathy is not without its dangers, quite apart from 'facile "identification"' (Hoffman 2004: 171). Stonebridge (2011: 5), for example, discussing Martha Gellhorn's report on the Eichmann trial, notes that empathy cannot be the basis for justice. Gellhorn (1962) had stated that because the Arabs in Palestine could not feel empathy with what the Jews had suffered, it was in turn hard to feel empathy for them. Stonebridge then asks 'on what grounds does lacking empathy disqualify one from the entitlement to justice' (Stonebridge 2011: 5). Stonebridge is right to ask this; imputing lack of humanity to someone cannot be a reason to treat them without humanity: this is exactly the reasoning Lang (in his discussion with Rosenbaum 1998: 214) attributes to the Nazis. Another danger is that empathy can cloud judgement, whether of witness statements (see Clendinnen 1999: 20), poems (see Hamburger 1986: 10) or, indeed, translations.

But in Baron-Cohen's terms, empathy is not merely identification: it is always accompanied by our own response. There is an element of reflection and self-awareness, for we have to identify what the other feels and respond in a way that is 'appropriate' (Baron-Cohen 2011: 11). Thus empathy allows us insights into ourselves. Reading a translated poem such as 'Gustav!' might make us ask whose position we are taking, and so make us aware of what I have heard Rabbi Lionel Blue (on the radio) memorably call 'the Nazi in me'. You cannot oppose evil to humanity, warns Semprun, because evil is part of humanity (Semprun 1997: 88). Rothberg (2009: 79) makes a similar point in discussing Aimé Césaire's *Discourse on Colonialism* (2000). Césaire, originally writing in 1955, argues that the other evils we commit suggest the presence inside society of exactly what drove Nazism (cf. also Bauman and Donskis 2013: 7–9).

It is for this reason that Rothberg (2009; cf. also Hoffman 2004: 216) has argued against the 'uniqueness' view of the Holocaust, and in favour of the need to learn lessons from it. What reading translated Holocaust poetry can suggest to us is the need to examine our own prejudices and fears, including those that relate to how and with whom we empathize.

Translated Holocaust poetry by its very nature makes us feel empathy at several removes: we realize that not only do we not share the suffering of the Buchenwald poet who writes 'No pity rises in us // Where to find tears // On this hill // In this time?' (Kirsten and Seeman 2012: 83), but we do not even share the language in which it is expressed. For it was never expressed by the poet like this. Though this is a poem called 'Autumn in Buchenwald', it is my translation of a poem written in German by Kirsten and Seeman, which was a translation of a poem written in French by Verdet, itself a translation (as far as I can reconstruct) from a German manuscript of Buchenwald poet Hackel. But the empathy the English reader feels with the speaker's despair at the inability to feel empathy is nevertheless real. This fact reminds us that empathy is not dependent on immediacy: the sufferings of others can be spoken by intermediaries. One of the reasons I would not want to speak of the translator as a 'secondary witness' (cf. Davies 2014; Weissman 2004) is that re-telling does not create distance. As I suggested in Section 2.1, adding the voices of others authenticates feelings by acknowledging them. And the fact that empathy is, indeed, felt at several removes should give us further cause to reflect on its nature. It is the reflection, rather than the feeling, that marks the particularly important nature of the cognitive effects of Holocaust poetry, and it is that reflection that translation, with its obvious emphasis on what can and cannot be said, and on what the translator chooses to convey, can enhance.

(iii) Reading Holocaust poetry has special cognitive effects because it foregrounds the question of language, and makes us think through the relationship of language and thought. According to Jakobson, language is the 'overcoming of isolation in space and time' (Jakobson 1985: 101). That is, just as Celan said about poetry, language serves communication and makes it possible. We cannot, if we are reading Holocaust poetry in translation, ignore the fact that it is communicating, and that it is able to cross space and time. This much is obvious, but the increased foregrounding of language leads the reader to consider language and its relation to thought. According to Adrienne Rich, there is a distinction 'between those for whom language has metaphoric density and those for whom it is merely formulaic' (Rich 2007: 33). If we see language as having 'metaphoric density', then it is able to evoke what is not there, and to create imaginary worlds. The opposite of this – language as merely formulaic – is exactly what we have seen as characteristic not only of Nazi thought but also of all those who unquestioningly accepted Nazi thought, and it is satirized in poetry such as von Törne's, and also in Celan's, where the slipperiness of language is both thematized and iconically represented in ambiguous words and expressions. Reading such poetry in translation calls attention to the distance between a word and what it represents, as Benjamin said (2012: 126). A focus on language, then, and its ability to communicate rather than merely mimic, enables the reader to think through her or his own attitudes to language. Why, for example, hold the view that 'Always there is the problem that much of the poetry is translated from other languages'? Why does Young (1993: 549), making this comment, see it as a problem, instead of something to be celebrated? What do the tired old metaphors (Young favours gaps and bridges) and clichés such as *'traduttore, traditore'* (Glowacka 2012: 75; 'translator, traitor') say about our inability to think through the relationships between languages and between words and what they represent?

(iv) Reading Holocaust poetry in the understanding that it has been trans-lated makes it unlikely that one will read it in a way that is attuned to content rather than poetics. For Rich, poetry of itself embodies 'an awareness, a resistance, that totalizing systems want to quell' (Rich 2007: 25). In this sense, it counteracts the tendency I mentioned earlier, and which Oatley comments on (2011: 164), to supplant self-education and replace it with conformity. If poetry is resistance, translated poetry is a double act of resistance, given that the Nazis tried through their '*Sprachregelung*' (see Section 2.1) to make the world not only uneducated but also linguistically aligned. But poetry is not only an act of resistance; it encourages us not only to think but also to think about thought, to think through what it means to resist stultification by totalitarian systems or through laziness. The analytical reading that translated Holocaust poetry demands does not allow the reader to be other than intellectually engaged, so it helps underline the importance of thinking. Many writers on the Holocaust have commented on the role of avoidance of thinking (see Section 1.3). Von Kellenbach (2013: 17) quotes from a letter written by Bonhoeffer from prison in 1942 (2010: 43): 'Stupidity is a more dangerous enemy to the good than malice'. Arendt (2006: xiv) spoke of a 'failure to think'. One might call this intentional stupidity; Midgley locates wickedness in negativity, an avoidance of thinking, a 'deliberate blindness' (Midgley 2001: 64–5). It is one thing to read 'While Reading the Paper' in German. But when we read it in translation, the distance between Holocaust facts and the newspaper's report is foregrounded by our hearing what was said in English. A lot more thought is needed to make sense of what was said, and what the attitudes of the report and the poem's narrator might be. It simply is not possible to think superficially.

(v) Translated Holocaust poetry can make us rethink our ideas about knowledge. For Rothberg (2000: 9), 'traumatic realism' mediates between an inability to know, understand and represent the Holocaust and the need to do so, because it has incorporated post-Holocaust knowing, understanding and representing; this is the contradiction that characterizes the post-Holocaust mind. When we read a poem such as Meerbaum-Eisinger's 'A Song for the Yellow Asters' in English, we are led to think about what she knew at the time, and how what we know now colours our view of the joy she expresses. To see 'star' in 'asters' is more difficult than to see '*Sterne*' in '*Astern*' (the dative form in the German title) and so the reader of the translation both has to work harder to do so and also is more likely to question the extent to which the stars are there in the poem or in the reader's own mind.

(vi) Finally, reading translated Holocaust poetry makes a confrontation with the nature and limits of communication inevitable. Not only are poetry and language communicative entities, but translation is itself an act of communication (cf. Venuti 2008: 276). And translated poetry is not simply an example of communication; it foregrounds the act of communication, especially if the reader reads the poem in the awareness that someone has translated it. It thus can make the reader think about the open-endedness of poetic communication, commented on by Iser (2004: 14) and Attridge (2004: 79–93) and also about the possibilities for misunderstanding and manipulation. Like reading original literature, it demands trust (cf. Oatley 2011: 100–10), but reading translation demands a greater trust: we have to trust the translator, too.

For the reader of translated Holocaust poetry, there are thus many new insights to be gained, and these are, in particular, insights into how we might incorporate the effects of the Holocaust into our cognitive schemata, how we might be encouraged to rethink, to question, to search. But this will only happen if translators, and their publishers, are prepared to be bold. We need to move on from a view that what we are translating and publishing are 'poems about the Holocaust'. They are poems that have the power to change the way we think, but they can only do this if the effects of translation are fully acknowledged.

Notes

1 Several talks and workshops looked at this poem in 2013. Participants were asked, on the basis of only a gloss, or a gloss and one translation, for points that might cause difficulty in translating the poem oneself. This line was invariably mentioned. That it is also the line in which particular deviation in the three existing translations can be noted is thus unlikely to be coincidence.

2 Informal questioning at several readings in 2013 and early 2014.

3 From Papers (CO 395) in Princeton University Library. Translation by Cecilia Rossi.

4 Sixteen members of the MA and PhD in Literary Translation at UEA in March 2014.

References

Aaron, F. W. (1990), *Bearing the Unbearable: Yiddish and Polish Poetry in the Ghettos and Concentration Camps*. Albany, NY: State University of New York Press.

Adorno, T. W. (1973), *Negative Dialektik; Jargon der Eigentlichkeit* (*Gesammelte Schriften* Vol. 6). Frankfurt am Main: Suhrkamp.

Adorno, T. W. (2003), *Kulturkritik und Gesellschaft* Vol. 1. Frankfurt am Main: Suhrkamp.

Alter, R. (1991), *Necessary Angels: Tradition and Modernity in Kafka, Benjamin, and Scholem*. Cambridge, MA: Harvard University Press.

Arc Publications.www.arcpublications.co.uk

Arendt, H. (1992), 'Introduction' to Walter Benjamin, in H. Arendt (ed.), *Illuminations*, trans. H. Zohn. London: Harper Collins, pp. 7–58.

Arendt, H. (1994), *Essays in Understanding 1930-1954*. New York: Schocken.

Arendt, H. (2006), *Eichmann in Jerusalem: A Report on the Banality of Evil*. London: Penguin.

Aristotle (1951), 'Poetics', trans. S. H. Butcher, in J. H. Smith and E. Winfield Parks (eds), *The Great Critics*. New York: Norton, pp. 28–61.

Attridge, D. (2004), *The Singularity of Literature*. London: Routledge.

Attridge, D. (2011), *Reading and Responsibility: Deconstruction's Traces*. Edinburgh: Edinburgh University Press.

Auden, W. H. (1976), *Collected Poems*, ed. E. Mendelson. London: Faber and Faber.

Ausländer, R. (1978), *Aschensommer: Ausgewählte Gedichte*. München: Deutscher Taschenbuch Verlag.

Ausländer, R. (1982), *Mutterland; Einverständnis: Gedichte*. Frankfurt am Main: S. Fischer Verlag.

Ausländer, R. (2008), *The Forbidden Tree: Englische Gedichte*. Frankfurt am Main: S. Fischer Verlag.

Ausländer, R. (2012), *Gedichte*, ed. H. Braun. Frankfurt am Main: S. Fischer Verlag.

Ausubel, N. and Ausubel, M. (eds) (1957), *A Treasury of Jewish Poetry*. New York: Crown.

Barnstone, W. (1993), *The Poetics of Translation: History, Theory, Practice*. New Haven, CT: Yale University Press.

Baron-Cohen, S. (2011), *Zero Degrees of Empathy*. London: Allen Lane.

Bauman, Z. (1989), *Modernity and the Holocaust*. Cambridge: Polity.

Bauman, Z. and Donskis, L. (2013), *Moral Blindness: The Loss of Sensitivity in Liquid Modernity*. Cambridge: Polity.

Bell, A. (trans.) (2003), *W.G. Sebald: The Natural History of Destruction*. London: Penguin.

Benjamin, W. (1966), *Versuche über Brecht*, ed. R. Tiedemann. Frankfurt am Main: Suhrkamp.

Benjamin, W. (1972), 'Die Aufgabe des Übersetzers', in T. Rexroth (ed.), *Walter Benjamin: Gesammelte Schriften* IV/I. Frankfurt am Main: Suhrkamp, pp. 9–21.

Benjamin, W. (1992a), 'Theses on the Philosophy of History', trans. H. Zohn, in H. Arendt (ed.), *Walter Benjamin: Illuminations*. London: Fontana, pp. 245–55.

Benjamin, W. (1992b), 'Über Sprache überhaupt und über die Sprache des Menschen', in R. Tiedemann (ed.), *Walter Benjamin: Sprache und Geschichte – Philosophische Essays*. Stuttgart: Reclam, pp. 30–49.

Benjamin, W. (2012), 'The Translator's Task', trans. S. Rendall, in L. Venuti (ed.), *The Translation Studies Reader* (3rd edn). London: Routledge, pp. 75–83.

Bennett, A. and Royle, N. (2004), *Introduction to Literature, Criticism and Theory* (3rd edn). Harlow: Pearson.

Berman, A. (2012), 'Translation and the Trials of the Foreign', trans. L. Venuti, in L. Venuti (ed.), *The Translation Studies Reader* (3rd edn). London: Routledge, pp. 240–53.

Bernard, W. (1968), 'Preface' to Constantine Brunner, *Science, Spirit, Superstition: A New Enquiry into Human Thought*, trans. A. Suhl. London: George Allen and Unwin.

Biedermann, H. (1996), *The Wordsworth Dictionary of Symbolism*, trans. J. Hulbert. Ware: Wordsworth.

Binding, K. and Hoche, A. (1920), *Die Freigabe der Vernichtung Lebensunwerten Lebens*. Holmen, WI: Policy Intersections Research Centre.

Boase-Beier, J. (2004), 'Knowing and Not Knowing: Style, Intention and the Translation of a Holocaust Poem'. *Language and Literature* 13(1): 25–35.

Boase-Beier, J. (2006), *Stylistic Approaches to Translation*. Manchester: St. Jerome Publishing.

Boase-Beier, J. (2009), 'Translating the Eye of the Poem'. *CTIS Occasional Papers* 4: 1–15.

Boase-Beier, J. (2010a), 'Translation and Timelessness'. *Journal of Literary Semantics* 38(2): 101–14.

Boase-Beier, J. (2010b), 'Who Needs Theory?', in A. Fawcett, K. Guadarrama Garcia and R. Hyde Parker (eds), *Translation: Theory and Practice in Dialogue*. London: Continuum, pp. 25–38.

Boase-Beier, J. (2011a), *A Critical Introduction to Translation Studies*. London: Continuum.

Boase-Beier, J. (2011b), 'Translating Celan's Poetics of Silence'. *Target* 23(2): 165–77.

Boase-Beier, J. (2013), 'Translating a Holocaust Poem with Jean Boase-Beier'. http://www.writerscentrenorwich.org.uk/searchresults-all/translatinga holocaustpoemwithjeanboasebeier.aspx.

Boase-Beier, J. (2014a), 'Using Translation to Read a Poem', in J. Boase-Beier, A. Fawcett and P. Wilson (eds), *Literary Translation: Redrawing the Boundaries*. London: Palgrave Macmillan, pp. 241–52.

Boase-Beier, J. (2014b), 'Bringing Home the Holocaust'. *Translation and Literature* 23: 222–34.

Boase-Beier, J. and Vivis, A. (trans.) (1995), *Rose Ausländer: Mother Tongue*. Todmorden: Arc Publications.

Boase-Beier, J. and Vivis, A. (trans.) (forthcoming), *Volker von Törne: Ice Age*. Todmorden: Arc Publications.

Bodensohn, F. (2014), *Literatur als Propagandainstrument des NS-Regimes: Verbreitung der Blut-und-Boden Ideologie aus Hitler's 'Mein Kampf' in der NS-Literatur.* Hamburg: Diplomica.

Boland, E. (trans.) (2004), *After Every War: Twentieth-Century Women Poets.* Princeton, NJ: Princeton University Press.

Bonhoeffer, D. (2010), *Letters and Papers from Prison*, eds. J. W. de Grunchy and V. Barnett, trans. B. Rumscheidt and M. Rumscheidt. Minneapolis, MN: Fortress Press.

Bonhoeffer, D. and Bonhoeffer, K. (1947), *Auf dem Wege zur Freiheit: Gedichte und Briefe aus der Haft*, ed. E. Bethge. Berlin: Haus und Schule.

Bosley, K. and Wandycz, K. (trans.) (1981), *Jerzy Ficowski: A Reading of Ashes.* London: Menard Press.

Bower, K. M. (2000), *Ethics and Remembrance in the Poetry of Nelly Sachs and Rose Ausländer.* Woodbridge: Camden House.

Braun, H. and Sprick, H. (eds) (1999), *'Mutterland Wort': Rose Ausländer 1901-1988.* Köln: Rose Ausländer Stiftung.

Braun, R. (2013), 'Famously Literary? The Nobel Prize and Herta Müller's Authorial Body', in B. Haines and L. Marven (eds), *Herta Müller.* Oxford: Oxford University Press.

Breur, D. (1997), *Ich lebe, weil du dich erinnerst: Frauen und Kinder in Ravensbrück*, trans. R. Leikes and D. Ondesluijs. Berlin: Nicolai.

Brodie, G. (2012), 'Theatre Translation for Performance: Conflict of Interest, Conflict of Cultures', in R. Wilson and B. Maher (eds), *Words, Images and Performances in Translation.* London: Continuum, pp. 63–81.

Brunner, C. (1919), *Der Judenhass und die Juden.* Berlin: Oesterheld und Co.

Brunner, C. (1968), *Science, Spirit, Superstition: A New Enquiry into Human Thought*, trans. A. Suhl. London: George Allen and Unwin.

Buber, M. (1923), *Ich und Du.* Berlin: Schocken.

Buber, M. and Rosenzweig, F. (1994), *Scripture and Translation*, trans. L. Rosenwald and E. Fox. Bloomington, IN: Indiana University Press.

Buck-Moss, S. (1977), *The Origin of Negative Dialectics: Theodor W. Adorno, Walter Benjamin and the Frankfurt Institute.* New York: The Free Press.

Burke, M. (2011), *Literary Reading, Cognition and Emotion: An Exploration of the Oceanic Mind.* London: Routledge.

Burleigh, M. (2002), *Death and Deliverance: Euthanasia in Germany 1900-1945.* London: Pan Macmillan.

Carson, C. (trans.) (2004), *The Inferno of Dante Alighieri.* London: Granta Books.

Carson, R. (1999), *Silent Spring.* London: Penguin.

Caruth, C. (ed.) (1995), *Trauma: Explorations in Memory.* Baltimore, MD: Johns Hopkins University Press.

Celan, P. (1952), *Mohn und Gedächtnis.* Stuttgart: Deutsche Verlags-Anstalt.

Celan, P. (1968), *Ausgewählte Gedichte; Zwei Reden.* Frankfurt am Main: Suhrkamp.

Celan, P. (1975), *Gedichte II.* Frankfurt am Main: Suhrkamp.

Celan, P. (1980), *Die Niemandsrose; Sprachgitter: Gedichte.* Frankfurt am Main: S. Fischer Verlag.

Celan, P. (1982), *Atemwende: Gedichte.* Frankfurt am Main: S. Fischer Verlag.

Celan, P. (1983), *Gesammelte Werke Bd III*, eds. B. Allemann, S. Reichert and R. Bücher. Frankfurt am Main: Suhrkamp.

Césaire, A. (2000), *Discourse on Colonialism*, trans. J. Pinkham. New York: Monthly Review.

Chalfen, I. (1979), *Paul Celan: Eine Biographie seiner Jugend*. Frankfurt am Main: Insel Verlag.

Chesterman, A. (1993), 'From "is" to "ought": Laws, Norms and Strategies in Translation Studies'. *Target* 5: 1–20.

Chesterman, A. (1997), *Memes of Translation*. Amsterdam: John Benjamins.

Chomsky, N. (2008), 'On Phases', in R. Freidin, C. P. Otero and M. L. Zubizaretta (eds), *Foundational Issues in Linguistic Theory: Essays in Honor of Jean-Roger Vergnaud*. Cambridge, MA: MIT Press, pp. 133–66.

Clark, B. (2014), 'Stylistics and Relevance Theory', in M. Burke (ed.), *The Routledge Handbook of Stylisitcs*. London: Routledge, pp. 155–74.

Clendinnen, I. (1999), *Reading the Holocaust*. Cambridge: Cambridge University Press.

Cole, T. (2000), *Selling the Holocaust*. New York: Routledge.

Comans, P. (trans.) (2009), *Abraham Sutzkever: Geh über Wörter wie über ein Minenfeld*. Frankfurt am Main: Campus Verlag.

Conrady, K.-O. (ed.) (1977), *Das große deutsche Gedichtbuch*. Kronberg: Athenäum.

Cook, G. (1994), *Discourse and Literature*. Oxford: Oxford University Press.

Cort, A. (2011), *Symbols, Meaning and the Sacred Quest: Spiritual Awakening in Jewish, Christian and Islamic Stories*. USA: Geo Cannon Books.

Cronyn, H., McKane, R. and Watts, S. (eds) (1995), *Voices of Conscience: Poetry from Oppression*. North Shields: Iron Press.

Crystal, D. (2003), *The Cambridge Encyclopedia of Language*. Cambridge: Cambridge University Press.

Crystal, D. (2013), *Spell it Out*. London: Profile Books.

Csokits, J. (1989), 'Janós Pilinszky's "Desert of Love": A Note', in D. Weissbort (ed.), *Translating Poetry: The Double Labyrinth*. London: Macmillan, pp. 9–15.

Culler, J. (1989), 'On the Negativity of Modern Poetry: Friedrich, Baudelaire, and the Critical Tradition', in S. Budick and W. Iser (eds), *Languages of the Unsayable: The Play of Negativity in Literature and Literary Theory*. New York: Columbia University Press, pp. 189–208.

Daive, J. (2009), *Under the Dome: Walks with Paul Celan*, trans. R. Waldrop-Anyart. Providence, RI: Burning Deck.

Dale, P. (trans.) (1996), *Dante: The Divine Comedy*. London: Anvil Press Poetry.

Damrosch, D. (2003), *What Is World Literature?* Princeton, NJ: Princeton University Press.

Dan, J. (2007), *Kabbalah: A Very Short Introduction*. Oxford: Oxford University Press.

Dancygier, B. (2012), *The Language of Stories: A Cognitive Approach*. Cambridge: Cambridge University Press.

Danesi, M. (2004), *Poetic Logic: The Role of Metaphor in Thought, Language and Culture*. Madison, WI: Atwood.

Davies, P. (2014), 'Translation and Holocaust Testimonies: A Matter for Holocaust Studies or Translation Studies?', in J. Boase-Beier, A. Fawcett and P. Wilson (eds), *Literary Translation: Re-Drawing the Boundaries*. London: Palgrave Macmillan, pp. 204–18.

Death, S. (trans.) (2011), *Steve Sem-Sandberg: The Emperor of Lies*. London: Faber and Faber.

Dennett, D. (1988), 'The Intentional Stance in Theory and Practice', in R. Byrne and A. Whiten (eds), *Machiavellian Intelligence: Social Expertise and the Evolution of Intellect in Monkeys, Apes and Humans*. Oxford: Clarendon, pp. 180–202.

Díaz-Diocaretz, M. (1985), *Translating Poetic Discourse: Questions on Feminist Strategies in Adrienne Rich*. Amsterdam: John Benjamins.

Diefenbach, L. (1873), *Arbeit macht frei*. Bremen: Verlag von J. Kühtmanns Buchhandlung.

Donahue, N. H. and Kirchner, D. (2005), *Flight of Fantasy: New Perspectives on Inner Emigration in German Literature 1933-1945*. Oxford: Berghahn Books.

Dove, R. (trans.) (2010), *Ludwig Steinherr: Before the Invention of Paradise*. Todmorden: Arc Publications.

Duden (2007), *Das Herkunftswörterbuch*. Mannheim: Dudenverlag.

Eichendorff, J. von (1988), *Gedichte*, ed. H. Schultz. Frankfurt am Main: Insel.

Ellis, S. (trans.) (1994), *Dante: Hell*. London: Chatto and Windus.

Emmott, C. (2002), '"Split Selves" in Fiction and in Medical "Life Stories": Cognitive Linguistic Theory and Narrative Practice', in E. Semino and J. Culpeper (eds), *Cognitive Stylistics: Language and Cognition in Text Analysis*. Amsterdam: John Benjamins, pp. 153–81.

Emmott, C., Sandford, A. and Morrow, L. (2006), 'Capturing the Attention of Readers? Stylistic and Psychological Perspectives on the Use and Effect of Text Fragmentation in Narratives'. *Journal of Literary Semantics* 35: 1–30.

Empson, W. (1930), *Seven Types of Ambiguity*. Harmondsworth: Penguin.

Englund, A. (2012), *Still Songs: Music in and Around the Poetry of Paul Celan*. Farnham: Ashgate.

Erk, D. (2012), *So viel Hitler war selten*. München: Heyne.

European Council of Literary Translators' Associations, www.ceatl.eu.

Evans, R. J. (2005), *The Third Reich in Power: How the Nazis Won Over the Hearts and Minds of a Nation*. London: Penguin.

Evans, S. E. (2010), *Hitler's Forgotten Victims: The Holocaust and the Disabled*. Stroud: The History Press.

Even-Zohar, I. (ed.) (1990), '*Polysystem Studies*'. Special Issue of *Poetics Today* 11(1).

Even-Zohar, I. (2012), 'The Position of Translated Literature within the Literary Polysystem', in L. Venuti (ed.), *The Translation Studies Reader* (3rd edn). London: Routledge, pp. 162–7.

Everwine, P. (trans.) (2011), *Nathan Zach: The Countries We Live In*. Portland, OR: Tavern Books.

Fairley, I. (trans.) (2001), *Paul Celan: Fathomsuns and Benighted - Fadensonnen und Eingedunkelt*. Manchester: Carcanet.

Fairley, I. (trans.) (2007), *Paul Celan: Snow Part - Schneepart and Other Poems (1968-1969)*. Manchester: Carcanet.

Faith Matters, http://faith-matters.org

Fauconnier, G. and Turner, M. (2002), *The Way We Think*. New York: Basic Books.

Fawcett, A. and Guadarrama Garcia, K. (2010), 'Introduction' to A. Fawcett, K. Guadarrama Garcia and R. Hyde Parker (eds), *Translation: Theory and Practice in Dialogue*. London: Continuum, pp. 1–22.

Feldman, R. and Swann, B. (trans.) (1992), *Primo Levi: Collected Poems*. London: Faber and Faber.

Felman, S. (1992a), 'Education and Crisis, or the Vicissitudes of Teaching', in S. Felman and D. Laub (eds), *Testimony: Crises of Witnessing in Literature, Psychoanalysis, and History*. London: Routledge, pp. 1–56.

Felman, S. (1992b), 'The Betrayal of the Witness: Camus' *The Fall*', in S. Felman and D. Laub (eds), *Testimony: Crises of Witnessing in Literature, Psychoanalysis, and History*. London: Routledge, pp. 165–203.

Felstiner, J. (1992), 'Translating Paul Celan's "Todesfuge": Rhythm and Repetition as Metaphor', in S. Friedländer (ed.), *Probing the Limits of Representation: Nazism and the 'Final Solution'*. Cambridge, MA: Harvard University Press, pp. 240–54.

Felstiner, J. (1995), *Paul Celan: Poet, Survivor, Jew*. New Haven, CT: Yale University Press.

Felstiner, J. (trans.) (2001), *Selected Poems and Prose of Paul Celan*. New York: Norton.

Ferrar, M. (2012), *A Foot in Both Camps*. LBLA Digital.

Ficowski, J. (trans.) (1956), *Piesni Papuszy (Papušakre Gila)*. Wrocław: Wydawnictwo Zaklad Im. Ossolinskich.

Fioretos, A. (1994), 'Preface' to A. Fioretos (ed.), *Word Traces: Readings of Paul Celan*. Baltimore, MD: Johns Hopkins University Press, pp. ix–xxii.

Fioretos, A. (2011), *Nelly Sachs: Flight and Metamorphosis*, trans. T. Tranæus. Stanford, CA: Stanford University Press.

Fischer, O. and Nänny, M. (eds) (2001), *The Motivated Sign*. Amsterdam: John Benjamins.

Florsheim, S. J. (ed.) (1989), *Ghosts of the Holocaust: An Anthology of Poetry by the Second Generation*. Detroit, MI: Wayne State University Press.

Fowler, R. (ed.) (1975), *Style and Structure in Literature: Essays in the New Stylistics*. Oxford: Blackwell.

Fowler, R. (1977), *Linguistics and the Novel*. London: Methuen.

Fowler, R. (1996), *Linguistic Criticism*. Oxford: Oxford University Press.

Frankel, E. and Teutsch, B. P. (1995), *The Encyclopedia of Jewish Symbols*. Lanham, MD: Rowman and Littlefield.

Frankl, V. E. (2004), *Man's Search for Meaning*. London: Rider.

Franklin, R. (2011), *A Thousand Darknesses: Lies and Truth in Holocaust Fiction*. Oxford: Oxford University Press.

Freeman, M. (2005), 'The Poem as a Complex Blend: Conceptual Mapping of Metaphor in Sylvia Plath's "The Applicant"'. *Language and Literature* 14(1): 25–44.

Friedlander, A. (1987), 'A Comment on: Alvin H. Rosenfeld, "Reflection on Isaac" and John Felstiner, "Paul Celan's 'Todesfuge'"'. *Holocaust and Genocide Studies* 2(1): 203–4.

Friedlander, H. (1995), *The Origins of Nazi Genocide: From Euthanasia to the Final Solution*. Chapel Hill, NC: The University of North Carolina Press.

Friedländer, S. (1988), 'Saul Friedländer' (contribution to discussion), in B. Lang (ed.), *Writing and the Holocaust*. New York: Holmes and Meier, pp. 287–9.

Friedländer, S. (ed.) (1992), *Probing the Limits of Representation: Nazism and the 'Final Solution'*. Cambridge, MA: Harvard University Press.

Friedrich, H. (2006), *Die Struktur der modernen Lyrik von der Mitte des neunzehnten bis zur Mitte des zwanzigsten Jahrhunderts*. Reinbeck: Rowohlt.

Fritsch-Vivié, G. (1993), *Nelly Sachs*. Hamburg: Rowohlt.

Fulbrook, M. (2012), *A Small Town near Auschwitz: Ordinary Nazis and the Holocaust*. Oxford: Oxford University Press.

Gabriel, M. (trans.) (2004), *Barbara Wind: Auf Asche Gehen: Gedichte zum Holocaust*. St. Ottilien: EOS.

Gaddis Rose, M. (1997), *Translation and Literary Criticism: Translation as Analysis*. Manchester: St. Jerome Publishing.

Garbe, D. (1999), *Zwischen Widerstand und Martyrium: Die Zeugen Jehovas im 'Dritten Reich'*. Munich: R. Oldenbourg Verlag.

Garvin, P. (trans. and ed.) (1964), *A Prague School Reader on Esthetics, Literary Structure, and Style*. Washington: Georgetown University Press.

Gavins, J. (2007), *Text World Theory: An Introduction*. Edinburgh: Edinburgh University Press.

Gellately, R. and Stoltzfus, N. (eds) (2001), *Social Outsiders in Nazi Germany*. Princeton, NJ: Princeton University Press.

Gellhaus, A. (ed.) (1997), *'Fremde Nähe': Celan als Übersetzer*. Marbach am Neckar: Deutsche Schillergesellschaft.

Gellhorn, M. (1962), 'Eichmann and the Private Conscience'. *Atlantic Monthly* 209(2): 52–9.

Gilbert, M. (2009), *The Routledge Atlas of the Holocaust* (4th edn). London: Routledge.

Gillespie, S. H. (trans.) (2013), *Corona: Selected Poems of Paul Celan*. New York: Station Hill.

Glowacka, D. (2012), *Disappearing Traces*. Seattle, WA: University of Washington Press.

Goldhagen, D. J. (1996), *Hitler's Willing Executioners: Ordinary Germans and the Holocaust*. London: Abacus.

Goldman, A. (2006), *Simulating Minds: The Philosophy, Psychology and Neuroscience of Mindreading*. Oxford: Oxford University Press.

Gömöri, G. and Gömöri, M. (eds) (2012), *I Lived on this Earth: Hungarian Poets of the Holocaust*. London: Alba Press.

Gordon, E. (1997), *And I Will Walk at Liberty: An Eye-Witness Account of the Church Struggle in Germany 1933-1937*. Bungay: Morrow and Co.

Gregor, N. (ed.) (2005), *Nazism, War and Genocide: New Perspectives on the History of the Third Reich*. Exeter: Exeter University Press.

Groll, G. (ed.) (1946), *De Profundis: Deutsche Lyrik in dieser Zeit*. München: Verlag Kurt Desch.

Grossman, E. (2010), *Why Translation Matters*. New Haven, CT: Yale University Press.

Grunwald-Spier, A. (2010), *The Other Schindlers: Why Some People Chose to Save Jews in the Holocaust*. Stroud: The History Press.

Gubar, S. (2003), *Poetry After Auschwitz: Remembering What One Never Knew*. Bloomington, IN: Indiana University Press.

Gutt, E.-A. (2000), *Translation and Relevance*. Manchester: St. Jerome Publishing.

Hall, G. (2009), 'Texts, Readers – and Real Readers'. *Language and Literature* 18(3): 333–9.

Halperin, I. (1960), *Messengers from the Dead: Literature of the Holocaust*. Philadelphia, PA: The Westminster Press.

Hamburger, M. (1969), *The Truth of Poetry: Tensions in Modern Poetry from Baudelaire to the 1960s*. London: Weidenfeld and Nicolson.

Hamburger, M. (1986), *After the Second Flood: Essays in Modern German Literature*. Manchester: Carcanet.

Hamburger, M. (trans.) (2007), *Poems of Paul Celan*. London: Anvil.

Hamburger, M. (trans.) (2013), *Nelly Sachs: Glowing Enigmas*. Portland, OR: Tavern Books.

Hamburger, M. and Middleton, C. (trans.) (1972), *Paul Celan: Selected Poems*. Harmondsworth: Penguin Books.

Hamburger, M., Mead, R., Mead, M. and Roloff, M. (trans.) (2011), *Nelly Sachs: Collected Poems 1944-1949*. Los Angeles, CA: Green Integer.

Hamm, P. (1991), 'Unser Gestirn ist vergraben im Staub'. *Die Zeit* 50: 76.

Harding, T. (2013), *Hanns and Rudolf: The German Jew and the Hunt for the Kommandant of Auschwitz*. London: William Heinemann.

Hartleben, O. E. (1906), *Meine Verse 1883-1904*. Berlin: Fischer.

Hartman, G. (2006), 'Elie Wiesel and the Morality of Fiction', in S. T. Katz and A. Rosen (eds), *Obliged by Memory*. New York: Syracuse University Press, pp. 107–16.

Haushofer, A. (2012), *Moabiter Sonette*. München: C.H. Beck.

Havránek, B. (1964), 'The Functional Differentiation of the Standard Language', in P. Garvin (trans. and ed.), *A Prague School Reader on Esthetics, Literary Structure, and Style*. Washington, DC: Georgetown University Press, pp. 3–16.

Heaney, S. (1995), *The Redress of Poetry*. London: Faber and Faber.

Herman, D. (ed.) (2003), *Narrative Theory and the Cognitive Sciences*. Stanford, CA: CSLI Publications.

Herman, D. (2006), 'Genette Meets Vygotsky: Narrative Embedding and Distributed Intelligence'. *Language and Literature* 15(4): 357–80.

Hermans, T. (1991), 'Translational Norms and Correct Translations', in K. van Leuven-Zwart and T. Naaijkens (eds), *Translation Studies: The State of the Art*. Amsterdam: Rodopi, pp. 155–70.

Hermans, T. (1999), *Translation in Systems: Descriptive and System-Oriented Approaches Explained*. Manchester: St. Jerome Publishing.

Hilberg, R. (1985), *The Destruction of the European Jews*. New York: Holmes and Meier.

Hill, G. (2004), 'Poetry as "Menace" and "Atonement"', in J. Cook (ed.), *Poetry in Theory: An Anthology 1900-2000*. Oxford: Blackwell, pp. 464–73.

Hoffman, E. (2004), *After Such Knowledge: A Meditation on the Aftermath of the Holocaust*. London: Vintage.

Hofmo, G. (1946), *Jag vil hjem til menneskene*. Oslo: Gyldendal.

Holmqvist, B. (ed.) (1968), *Das Buch der Nelly Sachs*. Frankfurt am Main: Suhrkamp.

Horne, A. (2002), 'Introduction' to Lord Russell of Liverpool, *The Scourge of the Swastika*. London: Frontline Books.

Howard, T. and Plebanek, B. (trans.) (2001), *Tadeusz Różewicz: Recycling*. Todmorden: Arc Publications.

Howe, I. and Greenberg, E. (eds) (1976), *A Treasury of Yiddish Poetry*. New York: Schocken.

Hughes, T. (1976), 'Introduction' to *Janós Pilinszky: Selected Poems*, trans. T. Hughes and J. Csokits. Manchester: Carcanet, pp. 7–14.

Hughes, T. (1989), 'Postscript to János Csokits' Note', in D. Weissbort (ed.), *Translating Poetry: The Double Labyrinth*. London: Macmillan, pp. 16–19.

Hughes, T. (1994), *Winter Pollen: Occasional Prose*, ed. W. Scammell. New York: Picador.

Hughes, T. (2006), *Selected Translations*, ed. D. Weissbort. London: Faber and Faber.

Hughes, T. and Csokits, J. (trans.) (1976), Janós Pilinszky: Selected Poems. Manchester: Carcanet.

The Hypertexts, *http://www.thehypertexts.com*.

Iser, W. (1971), 'Indeterminacy and the Reader's Response in Prose Fiction', in J. Hillis Miller (ed.), *Aspects of Narrative*. New York: Columbia University Press, pp. 1–45.

Iser, W. (1974), *The Implied Reader: Patterns of Communication in Prose Fiction from Bunyan to Beckett*. Baltimore, MD: Johns Hopkins University Press.

Iser, W. (2004), 'The Resurgence of the Aesthetic'. *Comparative Critical Studies* 1(1–2): 1–15.

Iser, W. (2006), *How to do Theory*. Oxford: Blackwell.

Jääskeläinen, R. (2000), 'Focus on Methodology in Think-Aloud Studies in Translating', in S. Tirkkonen-Condit and R. Jääskeläinen (eds), *Tapping and Mapping the Process of Translation and Interpreting: Outlooks on Empirical Research*. Amsterdam: John Benjamins, pp. 71–82.

Jakobson, R. (1960), 'Closing Statement: Linguistics and Poetics', in T. Sebeok (ed.), *Style and Language*. Cambridge, MA: MIT Press, pp. 350–77.

Jakobson, R. (1978), *Selected Writings V. On Verse, its Masters and Explorers*. The Hague: Mouton.

Jakobson, R. (1985), 'Language and Culture', in S. Rudy (ed.), *Selected Writings VII: Contributions to Comparative Mythology, Studies in Linguistics and Philology, 1972-1982*. Berlin: Mouton de Gruyter, pp. 101–12.

Jakobson, R. (2012), 'On Linguistic Aspects of Translation', in L. Venuti (ed.), *The Translation Studies Reader* (3rd edn). London: Routledge, pp. 126–39.

Jakobson, R. and Pomorska, K. (1983), *Dialogues*. Cambridge, MA: The MIT Press.

Jauss, H. R. (1982), *Toward an Aesthetics of Reception*, trans. T. Bahti. Minneapolis, MN: University of Minnesota Press.

Jens, W. (1968), 'Laudatio auf Nelly Sachs', in B. Holmqvist (ed.), *Das Buch der Nelly Sachs*. Frankfurt am Main: Suhrkamp, pp. 381–9.

Jewish Black Book Committee (1946), *The Black Book: The Nazi Crime Against the Jewish People*. New York: The Jewish Black Book Committee.

Johnson, M. (1987), *The Body in the Mind: The Bodily Basis of Meaning, Imagination and Reason*. Chicago, IL: Chicago University Press.

Jones, F. R. (trans.) (2000), *Miklós Radnóti: Camp Notebook*. Todmorden: Arc Publications.

Jones, F. R. (2011), *Poetry Translating as Expert Action*. Amsterdam: John Benjamins.

Jones, T. (2012), *Poetic Language: Theory and Practice from the Renaissance to the Present*. Edinburgh: Edinburgh University Press.

Joseph, B. (2000), '*What gives* with *es gibt*? Typological and Comparative Perspectives on Existentials in German, in Germanic, and in Indo-European' *American Journal of Germanic Linguistics and Literature* 12(2): 187–200.

Katz, D. (2004), *Words on Fire: The Unfinished Story of Yiddish*. New York: Basic Books.

Kaufman, S. (trans.) (1986), *Abba Kovner: My Little Sister and Selected Poems.* Cleveland, OH: Oberlin College.

Kaufman, S., Orchan, N., Hamburger, M., Mead, R., Mead, M. and Roloff, M. (trans.) (1971), *Abba Kovner and Nelly Sachs: Selected Poems.* London: Penguin.

Kellenbach, K. von (2013), *The Mark of Cain: Guilt and Denial in the Post-War Lives of Nazi Perpetrators.* Oxford: Oxford University Press.

Kershaw, I. (1983), *Popular Opinion and Political Dissent in the Third Reich: Bavaria 1933-45.* Oxford: Clarendon Press.

Kiedaisch, P. (1995), *Lyrik nach Auschwitz? Adorno und die Dichter.* Stuttgart: Reclam.

Kiparsky, P. (1973), 'The Role of Linguistics in a Theory of Poetry'. *Daedalus* 102: 231–44.

Kirkup, J. (1995), *Strange Attractors.* Salzburg: University of Salzburg Press.

Kirsten, W. (2012), 'Nachwort' to W. Kirsten and A. Seeman (trans. and eds), *Der gefesselte Wald: Gedichte aus Buchenwald.* Göttingen: Wallstein, pp. 165–71.

Kirsten, W. and Seeman, A. (trans. and eds) (2012), *Der gefesselte Wald: Gedichte aus Buchenwald.* Göttingen: Wallstein.

Klemperer, V. (2000), *The Language of the Third Reich*, trans. Martin Brady. London: Athlone Press.

Kohn, M. (trans.) (1955), *Katsetnik 135633: House of Dolls.* London: Simon and Schuster.

Kövecses, Z. (2002), *Metaphor: A Practical Introduction.* Oxford: Oxford University Press.

Kristeva, J. (1987), *Black Sun*, trans. L. Roudiez. New York: Columbia University Press.

Krystal, H. (1995), 'Trauma and Aging: A Thirty-Year Follow-Up', in C. Caruth (ed.), *Tauma: Explorations in Memory.* Baltimore, MD: Johns Hopkins University Press, pp. 76–99.

Kuhiwczak, P. (2007), 'The Grammar of Survival. How do we read Holocaust Testimonies?', in M. Salama-Carr (ed), *Translating and Interpreting Conflict.* Amsterdam: Rodopi, pp. 61–73.

Kuiken, D. (2008), 'A Theory of Expressive Reading', in S. Zygnier, M. Bortolussi, A. Chesnokova and J. Auracher (eds), *Directions in Empirical Literary Studies.* Amsterdam: Benjamins, pp. 49–68.

LaCapra, D. (1998), *History and Memory after Auschwitz.* London: Cornell University Press.

LaCapra, D. (2001), *Writing History, Writing Trauma.* Baltimore, MD: Johns Hopkins University Press.

Lakoff, G. and Johnson, M. (1980), *Metaphors We Live By.* Chicago, IL: University of Chicago Press.

Lakoff, G. and Turner, M. (1989), *More than Cool Reason: A Field Guide to Poetic Metaphor.* Chicago, IL: University of Chicago Press.

Lancaster Litfest, litfest.org.

Landman, J. (1993), *Regret: The Persistence of the Possible.* Oxford: Oxford University Press.

Lang, B. (ed.) (1988), *Writing and the Holocaust.* New York: Holmes and Meier.

Lang, B. (2000), *Holocaust Representation: Art Within the Limits of History and Ethics.* Baltimore, MD: Johns Hopkins University Press.

Langer, L. (1995), *Art from the Ashes: A Holocaust Anthology*. Oxford: Oxford University Press.

Lanzmann, C. (1995), 'The Obscenity of Understanding: An Evening with Claude Lanzmann', in C. Caruth (ed.), *Trauma: Explorations in Memory*. Baltimore, MD: The Johns Hopkins University Press, pp. 200–20.

Laub, D. (1992), 'Bearing Witness, or the Vicissitudes of Listening', in S. Felman and D. Laub (eds), *Testimony: Crises of Witnessing in Literature, Psychoanalysis and History*. London: Routledge, pp. 57–74.

Lawson, P. (ed.) (2001), *Passionate Renewal: Jewish Poetry in Britain Since 1945*. Nottingham: Five Leaves.

Leak, A. and Paizis, G. (eds) (2000), *The Holocaust and the Text: Speaking the Unspeakable*. London: Macmillan.

Leech, G. and Short, M. (2007), *Style in Fiction: A Linguistic Introduction to English Fictional Prose* (2nd edn). Harlow: Pearson.

Lefevère, A. (ed.) (1992), *Translation/History/Culture: A Sourcebook*. London: Routledge.

Lemon, L. T. and Reis, M. J. (trans.) (1965), *Russian Formalist Criticism: Four Essays*. Lincoln, NE: University of Nebraska Press.

Levi, P. (2005), *The Black Hole of Auschwitz*, trans. S. Wood. Cambridge: Polity.

Levi, P. (2013), *The Drowned and the Saved*, trans. R. Rosenthal. London: Abacus.

Levinas, E. (1990), *Nine Talmudic Readings*, trans. A. Aronowicz. Bloomington, IN: Indiana University Press.

Levitan, S. (trans.) (1985), *Rachel Korn: Paper Roses*. Ontario: Aya Press.

Lévy, I. J. (trans.) (2000), *And the World Stood Silent: Sephardic Poetry of the Holocaust*. Chicago, IL: University of Illinois Press.

Lewy, G. (2000), *The Nazi Persecution of the Gypsies*. Oxford: Oxford University Press.

Liberman, A. (1987), 'Roman Jakobson and his Contemporaries on Change in Language and Literature (the Teleological Criterion)', in K. Pomorska, E. Chodakowska, H. McLean and B. Vine (eds), *Language, Poetry and Poetics: The Generation of the 1890s – Jakobson, Trubetskoy, Majakovskij*. Berlin: Mouton de Gruyter, pp. 43–55.

Lifton, R. J. (1986), *The Nazi Doctors: Medical Killing and the Psychology of Genocide*. New York: Basic Books.

Lindeperg, S. (2011), '"Night and Fog": A History of Gazes', in G. Pollok and M. Silverman (eds), *Concentrationary Cinema: Aesthetics as Political Resistance in Alain Resnais's 'Night and Fog'*. New York: Berghahn Books, pp. 55–70.

Loewy, E. (1966), *Literatur unterm Hakenkreuz: Das Dritte Reich und seine Dichtung*. Frankfurt am Main: S. Fischer Verlag.

Lyon, J. K. (2006), *Paul Celan and Martin Heidegger: An Unresolved Conversation, 1951-1970*. Baltimore, MD: Johns Hopkins University Press.

Malmkjær, K. (2004), 'Translational Stylistics: Dulcken's Translations of Hans Christian Andersen'. *Language and Literature* 13(1): 13–24.

Malmkjær, K. (2005), *Linguistics and the Language of Translation*. Edinburgh: Edinburgh University Press.

Maršálek, H. (1977), *Mauthausen. Die Geschichte des Konzentrationslagers*, trans. G. Gaddi. Milan: La Pietra.

Martin, E. (2011), *Nelly Sachs: The Poetics of Silence and the Limits of Representation*. Berlin: de Gruyter.

Mayne, S. (trans.) (1981), *Burnt Pearls: Ghetto Poems of Abraham Sutzkever*. Oakville, Ontario: Mosaic Press.

McGinn, B. (1996), 'Foreword' to *Gershom Scholem: On the Kabbalah and Its Symbolism*, trans. R. Manheim. New York: Schocken, pp. vii–xviii.

Meerbaum-Eisinger, S. (2013), *'Du, weißt Du, wie ein Rabe schreit': Gedichte*. Aachen: Rimbaud.

Merkle, L. (2005), *Bairische Grammatik*. Munich: Allitera Verlag.

Miall, D. (2007), *Literary Reading: Empirical and Theoretical Studies*. New York: Peter Lang.

Miall, D. and Kuiken, D. (1994), 'Foregrounding, Defamiliarization and Affect: Response to Literary Stories'. *Poetics* 22: 389–407.

Midgley, M. (2001), *Wickedness: A Philosophical Essay*. London: Routledge.

Midgley, M. (2014), 'I Am More Than the Sum of My Parts'. *Times Higher Education*, 3 April: 47–9.

Milner-Gulland, R. and Levi, P. (trans.) (2008), *Yevgeny Yevtushenko: Selected Poems*. London: Penguin.

Mintz, A. (1996), *Hurban: Responses to Catastrophe in Hebrew Literature*. New York: Syracuse University Press.

Mitchell, S. (trans.) (1981), *Dan Pagis: Points of Departure*. Philadelphia, PA: The Jewish Publication Society of America.

Mithen, S. (1996), *The Prehistory of the Mind*. London: Phoenix.

Mitscherlich, A. and Mielke, F. (eds) (1995), *Medizin ohne Menschlichkeit: Dokumente des Nürnberger Ärzteprozesses*. Frankfurt am Main: S. Fischer Verlag.

Mukařovský, J. (1964), 'Standard Language and Poetic Language', in P. Garvin (trans. and ed.), *A Prague School Reader on Esthetics, Literary Structure, and Style*. Washington: Georgetown University Press, pp. 17–30.

Mulford, W. and Vivis, A. (trans.) (1995), *Sarah Kirsch: T*. London: Reality Street Editions.

Müller, F. (1979), *Eyewitness Auschwitz: Three Years in the Gas Chambers*, trans. S. Flatauer. Chicago, IL: Ivan R. Dee.

Munday, J. (2012), *Introducing Translation Studies: Theories and Applications* (3rd edn). London: Routledge.

Myers, D. G. (1999), 'Responsible for Every Single Pain: Holocaust Literature and the Ethics of Interpretation'. *Comparative Literature* 51(4): 266–88.

Nader, A. (2007), *Traumatic Verses: On Poetry in German from the Concentration Camps, 1933-1945*. New York: Camden House.

Nänny, M. and Fischer, O. (eds) (1999), *Form Miming Meaning*. Amsterdam: John Benjamins.

Neumann, P. (1968), *Zur Lyrik Paul Celans*. Göttingen: Vandenhoek and Ruprecht.

New King James Bible (1982), Nashville, TN: Thomas Nelson.

Newmark, P. (1980), 'What Translation Theory is About'. *Quinquereme* 3(1): 1–21.

Nida, E. (1964), *Toward a Science of Translating*. Leiden: E.J. Brill.

Oatley, K. (2011), *Such Stuff as Dreams: The Psychology of Fiction*. Chichester: Wiley-Blackwell.

Olschner, L. M. (1985), *Der feste Buchstab: Erläuterungen zu Paul Celans Gedichtübertragungen*. Göttingen: Vandenhoek and Ruprecht.

Ország-Land, T. (trans.) (2010), *András Mezei: Christmas in Auschwitz*. Middlesbrough: Smokestack Books.

Osers, E. (trans.) (1977), *Rose Ausländer: Selected Poems*. London: London Magazine Editions.

Ouhalla, J. (1994), *Introducing Transformational Grammar: From Rules to Principles*. London: Arnold.

Owen, W. (1990), 'Preface', in J. Stallworthy (ed.), *The Poems of Wilfred Owen*. London: Chatto and Windus, p. 192.

Palmer, A. (2004), *Fictional Minds*. Lincoln, NE: University of Nebraska Press.

Parks, T. (1998), *Translating Style*. London: Cassell.

Parks, T. (2007), *Translating Style* (2nd edn). Manchester: St. Jerome Publishing.

Peer, W. van (1986), *Stylistics and Psychology: Investigations of Foregrounding*. London: Croom Helm.

Pendas, D. O. (2006), *The Frankfurt Auschwitz Trial, 1963-1965: Genocide, History, and the Limits of the Law*. Cambridge: Cambridge University Press.

Petrowskaja, K. (2011), 'Spaziergang in Babij Jar'. *Frankfurter Allgemeine Sonntagszeitung*, 25 September: 31.

Pilkington, A. (2000), *Poetic Effects: A Relevance Theory Perspective*. Amsterdam: John Benjamins.

Pinker, S. (2003), *The Blank Slate*. London: Penguin.

Plath, S. (1981), *Collected Poems*. London: Faber and Faber.

Poe, E. A. (2008), *The Complete Poetry*. New York: New American Library.

Pöggeler, O. (1994), 'Mystical Elements in Heidegger's thought and Celan's Poetry', in A. Fioretos (ed.), *Word Traces: Readings of Paul Celan*. Baltimore, MD: Johns Hopkins University Press, pp. 75–109.

Poliakov, L. (1956), *Harvest of Hate*. London: Elek Books.

Popov, N. and McHugh, H. (trans.) (2000), *Paul Celan: Glottal Stop*. Middletown, CT: Wesleyan University Press.

Potter, R. (2012), *Modernist Literature*. Edinburgh: Edinburgh University Press.

Presser, J. (1969), *Orpheus en Ahasverus*. Amsterdam: Athenaeum-Polak and van Gennep.

Pym, A. (2010), *Exploring Translation Theories*. London: Routledge.

Rees, N. (1991), *Bloomsbury Dictionary of Phrase and Allusion*. London: Bloomsbury.

Rich, A. (2007), *Poetry and Commitment*. New York: W.W. Norton.

Richards, I. A. (1929), *Practical Criticism*. London: Routledge and Kegan Paul.

Richards, I. A. (1960), *Principles of Literary Criticism*. London: Routledge and Kegan Paul.

Riffaterre, M. (1959), 'Criteria for Style Analysis'. *Word* 15: 154–74.

Riffaterre, M. (1992), 'Transposing Presuppositions on the Semiotics of Literary Translation', in R. Schulte and J. Biguenet (eds), *Theories of Translation*. Chicago, IL: University of Chicago Press, pp. 204–17.

Robertson, E. (trans.) (2003), *Voices in the Night: The Prison Poems of Dietrich Bonhoeffer*. Bath: Eagle.

Ronen, R. (1994), *Possible Worlds in Literary Theory*. Cambridge: Cambridge University Press.

Rosen, A. (2005), *Sounds of Defiance: The Holocaust, Multilingualism and the Problem of English*. Lincoln, NE: University of Nebraska Press.

Rosen, A. (2006), 'Introduction' to S. T. Katz and A. Rosen (eds), *Obliged by Memory*. New York: Syracuse University Press, pp. xiii–xviii.

Rosen, A. (2010), *The Wonder of Their Voices: The 1946 Holocaust Interviews of David Boder*. Oxford: Oxford University Press.

Rosenbaum, R. (1998), *Explaining Hitler: The Search for the Origins of his Evil*. London: Macmillan.

Rosenfeld, A. (1980), *A Double Dying: Reflections on Holocaust Literature*. Bloomington, IN: Indiana University Press.

Rothberg, M. (2000), *Traumatic Realism: The Demands of Holocaust Representation*. Minneapolis, MN: University of Minnesota Press.

Rothberg, M. (2009), *Multidirectional Memory: Remembering the Holocaust in the Age of Decolonization*. Stanford, CA: Stanford University Press.

Rousset, D. (1946), *L'univers concentrationnaire*. Paris: Pavois.

Rowland, A. (2001), *Tony Harrison and the Holocaust*. Liverpool: Liverpool University Press.

Rowland, A. (2005), *Holocaust Poetry: Awkward Poetics in the Work of Sylvia Plath, Geoffrey Hill, Tony Harrison and Ted Hughes*. Edinburgh: Edinburgh University Press.

Ruskin, J. (1863), *Modern Painters*, Vol. III. New York: John Wiley.

Russell of Liverpool, Lord (2002), *The Scourge of the Swastika: A Short History of Nazi War Crimes*. London: Frontline Books.

Ryan, M. L. (1991), *Possible Worlds, Artificial Intelligence and Narrative Theory*. Bloomington, IN: Indiana University Press.

Ryan, M. L. (2003), 'Cognitive Maps and the Construction of Narrative Space', in D. Herman (ed.), *Narrative Theory and the Cognitive Sciences*. Stanford, CA: CSLI Publications, pp. 214–42.

Sachs, N. (trans.) (1947), *Von Welle und Granit*. Berlin: Aufbau Verlag.

Sachs, N. (1961), *Späte Gedichte*. Frankfurt am Main: Suhrkamp.

Sachs, N. (1971), *Teile dich Nacht: Die letzten Gedichte*. Frankfurt am Main: Suhrkamp.

Sachs, N. (1988), *Fahrt ins Staublose: Gedichte*. Frankfurt am Main: Suhrkamp.

Sacks, J. (2005), *To Heal a Fractured World: The Ethics of Responsibility*. London: Continuum.

Sarcq, A. (1995), *La Guenille*. Paris: Actes Sud.

Satloff, R. (2006), *Among the Righteous: Lost Stories from the Holocaust's Long Reach into Arab Lands*. New York: Public Affairs.

Saussure, F. de (1959), *Course in General Linguistics*, trans. W. Baskin. New York: The Philosophical Library.

Schardt, M. (ed.) (1994), *Über Ingeborg Bachmann II: Portraits, Aufsätze, Besprechungen 1952-1992*. Hamburg: Igel Verlag Literatur und Wissenschaft.

Schiavi, G. (1996), 'There is always a Teller in a Tale'. *Target* 8(1): 1–21.

Schiff, H. (ed.) (1995), *Holocaust Poetry*. New York: St. Martin's Press.

Schiff, H. (1995), 'Introduction' to *Holocaust Poetry*, ed. H. Schiff. New York: St. Martin's Press, pp. xiii–xxiv.

Schlant, E. (1999), *The Language of Silence: West German Literature and the Holocaust*. London: Routledge.

Schloss, E. and Kent, E. J. (1988), *Eva's Story*. London: Castle-Kent.

Scholem, G. (trans.) (1935), *Die Geheimnisse der Schöpfung. Ein Kapitel aus dem Sohar*. Berlin: Schocken Verlag.

Scholem, G. (1996), *On the Kabbalah and Its Symbolism*, trans. R. Manheim. New York: Schocken.

Schröder, J., Bonath, B., Salzmann, B., Wischinski, C. and Wittmann, A. (eds) (1995), *Die Stunde Null in der deutschen Literatur*. Stuttgart: Reclam.

Schwarz, J. (2013), 'The Holocaust and Postwar Yiddish literature', in A. Rosen (ed.), *Literature of the Holocaust*. Cambridge: Cambridge University Press, pp. 102–17.

Scott, C. (2000), *Translating Baudelaire*. Exeter: University of Exeter Press.

Scott, C. (2012), *Literary Translation and the Rediscovery of Reading*. Cambridge: Cambridge University Press.

Sebald, W. G. (1999), *Luftkrieg und Literatur*. Munich: Carl Hanser Verlag.

Seel, P. (1995), *I, Pierre Seel, Deported Homosexual*, trans. J. Neugroschel. New York: Basic Books.

Semino, E. (1997), *Language and World Creation in Poems and Other Texts*. London: Longman.

Semino, E. (2008), *Metaphor in Discourse*. Cambridge: Cambridge University Press.

Semino, E. and Culpeper, J. (eds) (2002), *Cognitive Stylistics: Language and Cognition in Text Analysis*. Amsterdam: John Benjamins.

Semprun, J. (1997), *Literature or Life*, trans. L. Coverdale. New York: Viking.

Sereny, G. (1995), *Albert Speer: His Battle with Truth*. New York: Alfred A. Knopf.

Sereny, G. (2001), *The Healing Wound: Experiences and Reflections, Germany 1938-2001*. New York: W.W. Norton.

Shklovsky, V. (1965), 'Art as Technique', in L. T. Lemon and M. J. Reis (trans. and eds), *Russian Formalist Criticism: Four Essays*. Lincoln, NE: University of Nebraska Press, pp. 3–24.

Short, M. (1996), *Exploring the Language of Poems, Plays and Prose*. London: Longman.

Silverblatt, I. and Silverblatt, H. (trans. and eds) (2008), *Selma Meerbaum-Eisinger: Harvest of Blossoms*. Evanston, IL: Northwestern University Press.

Simpson, P. (2004), *Stylistics: A Resource Book for Students*. London: Routledge.

Sklar, H. (2013), *The Art of Sympathy in Fiction: Forms of Ethical and Emotional Persuasion*. Amsterdam: John Benjamins.

Slobin, D. (2003), 'Language and Thought Online: Cognitive Consequences of Linguistic Relativity', in D. Gentner and S. Gocklin-Meadow (eds), *Language in the Mind: Advances in the Study of Language and Thought*. Cambridge, MA: MIT Press, pp. 157–92.

Smith, H. A. (trans.) (1975), *Gertrud Kolmar: Dark Soliloquy*. New York: Continuum.

Smith, M. S. (2010), *Treblinka Survivor: The Life and Death of Hershl Sperling*. Stroud: The History Press.

Solomon, P. (trans.) (1947), 'Tangoul Morţii', by Paul Celan. *Contemporanul*, 2 May 1947.

Sonesson, G. (2008), 'Prolegomena to a General Theory of Iconicity: Considerations on Language, Gesture and Pictures', in K. Willems and L. de Cuypere (eds), *Naturalness and Iconicity in Language*. Amsterdam: John Benjamins, pp. 47–71.

Sperber, D. (1996), *Exploring Culture: A Naturalistic Approach*. Oxford: Blackwell.

Sperber, D. and Wilson, D. (1995), *Relevance: Communication and Cognition* (2nd edn). Oxford: Blackwell.

Spiegelman, A. (2003), *The Complete Maus*. London: Penguin.

Steiner, G. (1985), *Language and Silence: Essays 1958-1966*. London: Faber and Faber.

Steiner, G. (1992), *After Babel: Aspects of Language and Translation*. Oxford: Oxford University Press.

Steiner, G. (2011), *The Poetry of Thought: From Hellenism to Celan*. New York: New Directions.

Stockwell, P. (2002), *Cognitive Poetics: An Introduction*. London: Routledge.

Stockwell, P. (2009), *Texture: A Cognitive Aesthetics of Reading*. Edinburgh: Edinburgh University Press.

Stockwell, P. (2013), 'The Positioned Reader'. *Language and Literature* 22(3): 263–77.

Stone, D. (2003), *Constructing the Holocaust: A Study in Historiography*. London: Vallentine Mitchell.

Stonebridge, L. (2011), *The Judicial Imagination: Writing after Nuremberg*. Edinburgh: Edinburgh University Press.

Sugihara, H. (trans.) (1995), *Yukiko Sugihara: Visas for Life*. Edu-Comm Plus.

Terrell, P., Schnorr, V., Morris, W. and Breitsprecher, R. (1991), *Collins German-English, English-German Dictionary*. London: Harper Collins.

Tiller, T. (1968), *Notes for a Myth and Other Poems*. London: Chatto and Windus.

Todorov, T. (1977), *The Poetics of Prose*, trans. R. Howard. New York: Cornell University Press.

Todorov, T. (1996), *Facing the Extreme: Moral Life in the Concentration Camps*. New York: Henry Holt.

Todorov, T. (2010), *The Fear of Barbarians*, trans. A. Brown. Cambridge: Polity.

Tompkins, J. P. (ed.) (1980), *Reader-Response Criticism From Formalism to Post-Structuralism*. Baltimore, MD: Johns Hopkins University Press.

Toolan, M. and Weber, J. J. (2007), 'Introduction'. *European Journal of English Studies* 9(2): 107–15.

Törne, V. von (1981), *Im Lande Vogelfrei*. Berlin: Wagenbach.

Toury, G. (1980), *In Search of a Theory of Translation*. Tel Aviv: Tel Aviv University.

Toury, G. (1995), *Descriptive Translation Studies and Beyond*. Amsterdam: John Benjamins.

Trautmann, M., Daldrup, C. and Marliani-Eyll, V. (eds) (2012), *'Endlich hat einer den Mut zu sprechen': Clemens August von Galen und die Predigten vom Sommer 1941*. Münster: Dialogverlag.

Tsur, R. (2003), *On the Shore of Nothingness: A Study in Cognitive Poetics*. Charlottesville, VA: Imprint Academic.

Tsur, R. (2008), *Toward a Theory of Cognitive Poetics* (2nd edn). Brighton: Sussex Academic Press.

Turner, M. (1996), *The Literary Mind: The Origins of Thought and Language*. Oxford: Oxford University Press.

Turner, M. (2003), 'Double-Scope Stories', in D. Herman (ed.), *Narrative Theory and the Cognitive Sciences*. Stanford, CA: CSLI Publications, pp. 117–42.

Tymoczko, M. (2007), *Enlarging Translation, Empowering Translators*. Manchester: St. Jerome Publishing.

Venuti, L. (ed.) (2004), *The Translation Studies Reader* (2nd edn). London: Routledge.

Venuti, L. (2008), *The Translator's Invisibility* (2nd edn). London: Routledge.

Verdonk, P. (2002), *Stylistics*. Oxford: Oxford University Press.

Verdonk, P. (2013), *The Stylistics of Poetry: Context, Cognition, Discourse, History*. London: Bloomsbury.

Vivis, A. and Boase-Beier, J. (trans.) (2014), *Rose Ausländer: Mother Tongue*. Todmorden: Arc Publications.

Wales, K. (2001), *A Dictionary of Stylistics* (2nd edn). London: Longman.

Watts, S., Cronyn, H. and McKane, R. (eds) (1995), *Voices of Conscience*. Manchester: Iron Press.

Waxman, Z. (2006), *Writing the Holocaust: Identity, Testimony, Representation*. Oxford: Oxford University Press.

Weinberg, F. (2013), *Boy 30529: A Memoir*. London: Verso.

Weinreich, M. (1999), *Hitler's Professors*. New Haven, CT: Yale University Press.

Weissbort, D. (ed.) (1989), *Translating Poetry: The Double Labyrinth*. London: Macmillan.

Weissbort, D. (ed.) (1991), *The Poetry of Survival: Post-War Poets of Central and Eastern Europe*. London: Penguin.

Weissman, G. (2004), *Fantasies of Witnessing: Postwar Efforts to Experience the Holocaust*. Ithaca, NY: Cornell University Press.

West, D. (2013), *I.A. Richards and the Rise of Cognitive Stylistics*. London: Bloomsbury.

Whiteley, S. (2011), 'Text World Theory, Real Readers and Emotional Responses to *The Remains of the Day*'. *Language and Literature* 20(1): 23–42.

Whittock, M. (2011), *A Brief History of the Third Reich*. London: Constable and Robinson.

Wiesel, E. (1990), *From the Kingdom of Memory: Reminiscences*. New York: Summit.

Wilson, D. and Sperber, D. (2012), *Meaning and Relevance*. Cambridge: Cambridge University Press.

Wind, B. (1996), *Jacob's Angels*. Newark, NJ: Emmet.

Winner, T. (1987), 'The Aesthetic Semiotics of Roman Jakobson', in K. Pomorska, E. Chodakowska, H. McLean and B. Vine (eds), *Language, Poetry and Poetics: The Generation of the 1890s - Jakobson, Trubetzkoy, Mayakovskij*. New York: Mouton de Gruyter, pp. 257–74.

Winstone, M. (2010), *The Holocaust Sites of Europe*. London: I.B. Tauris.

Witt, A. (trans.) (2006), *Lasjer Ajchenrand: Aus der Tiefe*. Zürich: Ammann.

The Yellow Spot: The Extermination of the Jews in Germany (1936). London: Victor Gollancz Ltd.

Young, G. (1993), 'The Poetry of the Holocaust', in S. S. Friedman (ed.), *Holocaust Literature: A Handbook of Critical, Historical and Literary Writings*. London: Greenwood Press, pp. 547–74.

Young, J. E. (1998), *Writing and Rewriting the Holocaust: Narrative and the Consequences of Interpretation*. Bloomington, IN: Indiana University Press.

Index

Titles of poems are given in English, with the name of the original poet.

Printed in the USA
CPSIA information can be obtained
at www.ICGtesting.com
LVHW010944140124
768964LV00041B/1522